Related Books of Int...

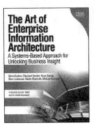

The Art of Enterprise Information Architecture
A Systems-Based Approach for Unlocking Business Insight

By Mario Godinez, Eberhard Hechler, Klaus Koenig, Steve Lockwood, Martin Oberhofer, and Michael Schroeck
ISBN: 0-13-703571-3

Architecture for the Intelligent Enterprise: Powerful New Ways to Maximize the Real-Time Value of Information

In this book, a team of IBM's leading information management experts guide you on a journey that will take you from where you are today toward becoming an "Intelligent Enterprise."

Drawing on their extensive experience working with enterprise clients, the authors present a new, information-centric approach to architecture and powerful new models that will benefit any organization. Using these strategies and models, companies can systematically unlock the business value of information by delivering actionable, real-time information in context to enable better decision-making throughout the enterprise—from the "shop floor" to the "top floor."

Enterprise Master Data Management
An SOA Approach to Managing Core Information

By Allen Dreibelbis, Eberhard Hechler, Ivan Milman, Martin Oberhofer, Paul Van Run, and Dan Wolfson
ISBN: 0-13-236625-8
The Only Complete Technical Primer for MDM Planners, Architects, and Implementers

Enterprise Master Data Management provides an authoritative, vendor-independent MDM technical reference for practitioners: architects, technical analysts, consultants, solution designers, and senior IT decision makers. Written by the IBM® data management innovators who are pioneering MDM, this book systematically introduces MDM's key concepts and technical themes, explains its business case, and illuminates how it interrelates with and enables SOA.

Drawing on their experience with cutting-edge projects, the authors introduce MDM patterns, blueprints, solutions, and best practices published nowhere else—everything you need to establish a consistent, manageable set of master data, and use it for competitive advantage.

 Listen to the author's podcast at:
ibmpressbooks.com/podcasts

Related Books of Interest

Data Integration Blueprint and Modeling
Techniques for a Scalable and Sustainable Architecture

By Anthony David Giordano
ISBN: 0-13-708493-5

A complete best-practice data integration blueprint for reducing data warehouse costs and improving results

Data integration now accounts for a major part of the expense and risk of typical data warehousing and business intelligence projects—and, as businesses increasingly rely on analytics, the need for a blueprint for data integration is increasing now more than ever. *Data Integration Blueprint and Modeling* presents the solution: a clear, consistent approach to defining, designing, and building data integration components to reduce cost, simplify management, enhance quality, and improve effectiveness. Leading IBM data management expert Anthony David Giordano brings together best practices for architecture, design, and methodology and shows how to do the disciplined work of getting data integration right.

The New Era of Enterprise Business Intelligence
Using Analytics to Achieve a Global Competitive Advantage

By Mike Biere
ISBN: 0-13-707542-1

A Complete Blueprint for Maximizing the Value of Business Intelligence in the Enterprise

The typical enterprise recognizes the immense potential of business intelligence (BI) and its impact upon many facets within the organization—but it's not easy to transform BI's potential into real business value. In *The New Era of Enterprise Business Intelligence*, top BI expert Mike Biere presents a complete blueprint for creating winning BI strategies and infrastructure, and systematically maximizing the value of information throughout the enterprise.

This product-independent guide brings together start-to-finish guidance and practical checklists for every senior IT executive, planner, strategist, implementer, and the actual business users themselves.

Listen to the author's podcast at:
ibmpressbooks.com/podcasts

Visit ibmpressbooks.com
for all product information

Related Books of Interest

Mining the Talk
Unlocking the Business Value in Unstructured Information

By Scott Spangler and Jeffrey Kreulen
ISBN: 0-13-233953-6

Leverage Unstructured Data to Become More Competitive, Responsive, and Innovative

In *Mining the Talk*, two leading-edge IBM researchers introduce a revolutionary new approach to unlocking the business value hidden in virtually any form of unstructured data–from word processing documents to websites, emails to instant messages.

The authors review the business drivers that have made unstructured data so important–and explain why conventional methods for working with it are inadequate. Then, writing for business professionals–not just data mining specialists–they walk step-by-step through exploring your unstructured data, understanding it, and analyzing it effectively.

Viral Data in SOA
An Enterprise Pandemic

Fishman
ISBN: 0-13-700180-0

DB2 9 for Linux, UNIX, and Windows
DBA Guide, Reference, and Exam Prep, 6th Edition

Baklarz, Zikopoulos
ISBN: 0-13-185514-X

DB2 pureXML Cookbook
Master the Power of the IBM Hybrid Data Server

Nicola, Kumar-Chatterjee
ISBN: 0-13-815047-8

Dynamic SOA and BPM
Best Practices for Business Process Management and SOA Agility

Fiammante
ISBN: 0-13-701891-6

Decision Management Systems
A Practicle Guide to Using Business Rules and Predictive Analytics

Taylor
ISBN: 0-13-288438-0

IBM® Cognos® 10 Report Studio

Practical Examples

IBM® Cognos® 10 Report Studio

Practical Examples

Filip Draskovic

Roger Johnson

IBM Press
Pearson plc
Upper Saddle River, NJ • Boston • Indianapolis • San Francisco
New York • Toronto • Montreal • London • Munich • Paris • Madrid
Cape Town • Sydney • Tokyo • Singapore • Mexico City

ibmpressbooks.com

IBM Press Program Managers: Steven M. Stansel, Ellice Uffer
Cover design: IBM Corporation

Associate Publisher: Dave Dusthimer
Marketing Manager: Stephane Nakib
Executive Editor: Mary Beth Ray
Publicist: Andrea Bledsoe
Senior Development Editor: Christopher Cleveland
Managing Editor: Kristy Hart
Designer: Alan Clements
Technical Editors: Sue Mitchell, Ronald Olenic
Senior Project Editor: Lori Lyons
Copy Editor: Cheri Clark
Indexer: Brad Herriman
Compositor: Nonie Ratcliff
Proofreader: Water Crest Publishing
Manufacturing Buyer: Dan Uhrig

Published by Pearson plc
Publishing as IBM Press

IBM Press offers excellent discounts on this book when ordered in quantity for bulk purchases or special sales, which may include electronic versions and/or custom covers and content particular to your business, training goals, marketing focus, and branding interests. For more information, please contact

U.S. Corporate and Government Sales
1-800-382-3419
corpsales@pearsontechgroup.com

For sales outside the U. S., please contact

International Sales
international@pearson.com

The following terms are trademarks or registered trademarks of International Business Machines Corporation in the United States, other countries, or both: IBM, the IBM Press logo, Cognos, and SPSS. Other company, product, or service names may be trademarks or service marks of others.

Library of Congress Cataloging-in-Publication Data

Johnson, Roger.

  IBM Cognos 10 Report Studio : practical examples / Roger Johnson, Filip Draskovic.

    p. cm.

  ISBN 978-0-13-265675-7 (pbk.)

  1. Business intelligence—Computer programs. 2. Business report writing—Computer programs. 3. Database management—Computer programs. 4. IBM software. I. Draskovic, Filip. II. Title.

  HD38.7.J63 2012

  651.7'4028553—dc23

                              2011032352

  Pearson Education, Inc
  Rights and Contracts Department
  501 Boylston Street, Suite 900
  Boston, MA 02116
  Fax (617) 671 3447

Text printed in the United States on recycled paper at R.R. Donnelley in Crawfordsville, Indiana.

First printing October 2011

ISBN-13: 978-0-13-265675-7
ISBN-10: 0-13-265675-2

I'd like to thank my wife, Danijela, for encouragement and support throughout the writing of this book and for letting me check one item off my bucket list. I also would like to thank my son Luka and daughter Mia for showing me what really is important in life and my parents for showing me that hard work and perseverance do pay off.
—Filip Draskovic

I'd like to thank my wife, Pearl, and daughters, Sylvie and Sapphire, for allowing me to make the work/life balance lean too heavily in one direction. The love you give means so much to me. I also want to thank my parents, Bill and Pat, for all of their love and support over the years.
—Roger Johnson

Contents

Acknowledgments

First, we would like to acknowledge all the Cognoids out there who have encouraged us to think beyond the course material and to look deeper into the functions of IBM Cognos Business Intelligence.

We would like to thank the crew at IBM Press for the opportunity to share this book with you. Our technical reviewers, Ronald Olenic and Sue Mitchell, provided some wonderful insights and even taught us a few more things that found their way into this book. Thanks go to Chris Cleveland for his help in bringing the best possible product to our readers.

Thank you to our Executive Editor, Mary Beth Ray, for allowing us the opportunity to create this book on a flexible schedule.

Being a part of a great team like the IBM North American Education Services Team, we would like to thank all of our peers on the team who shared tips with fellow educators and asked for new ways to answer student reporting questions.

We would also like to thank Jesus Salcedo for his assistance in reviewing the statistical analysis example. His understanding of statistics, matched with his passion, is an inspiration to us nonstatisticians.

Roger would like to thank Nathan Nyvall as the manager who interviewed him five years ago for the education specialist position and started him down the path of business analytics education. It has led to a continued effort toward "world domination."

Also, he would like to thank Filip for teaming together on our international efforts in this book. I think we did a pretty good job.

Filip would like to thank Roger for talking him into doing this book and teaching him patience.

About the Authors

Filip Draskovic has spent his professional career, which covers the past 11 years, living and breathing IBM Cognos. For the first 8 years of his career, he had been an IBM Cognos consultant and developed his skills applying IBM Cognos Business Intelligence and Planning solutions in multiple industries. Wanting to do something different, he spent the next 3 years as a Cognos trainer teaching public and private IBM Cognos courses in IBM's offices around North America. Following his desire to constantly gain new experiences and knowledge, he is currently filling the role of an IBM Cognos client technical professional. You can find him today in Toronto's financial district. At home, with his wife, he is enjoying raising their son and daughter.

Roger Johnson is a learning consultant on IBM Cognos technologies delivering a wide variety of courses focusing on the needs of his learners. His education experience has been honed over years of work in training software professionals, college students, and many types of technology users. After he started his career as a computer programmer, a co-worker said, "Hey, you do community theater productions. You would make a good trainer." With those words, his career took a different direction. Over the next 20 years, he never moved too far from either technology or education. As a learner, he has master's degrees in Systems Management and Education. Currently, he is researching the end-user adoption of technology as his doctoral dissertation at Capella University. He calls Orlando home, but is regularly seen around North America delivering any number of IBM Cognos courses. When he is home, he enjoys the time he gets to spend with family, and his dogs keep him busy jogging around the lake.

Foreword

When I was eight, I had a friend who could build absolutely anything out of those little bright-colored, plastic interlocking blocks. Spaceship with wings, solar-powered treehouse, prehistoric monster; you name it, he could build it. He had one giant pillowcase full of the blocks, and a stack of instructions by his bedside. I remember him looking at the step-by-step guides, picking and choosing among the patterns, and then combining them to provide me with the monster truck equipped with water skis that I had requested.

Mastering any creative process requires a thorough knowledge of available techniques and tools, as well as ongoing exposure to new ideas and ways to apply those techniques. I will not stretch my metaphor so much as to pretend that report authoring is as fun as building miniature skyscrapers. But if you are reading this book, you likely know that business analytics continue to be critical as available data increases in step with our need for information. Improving your skills in report authoring with IBM Cognos Report Studio allows you to deliver easily consumable information and business insights.

In the IBM Business Analytics curriculum development team, we develop courses that provide you with the skills you need to build effective reports. We write step-by-step instructions to help you practice report authoring techniques and build your competence with the variety of tools available to you. Self-paced courses offer flexible and quick ways to digest both the basics and the advanced techniques of IBM Cognos Report Studio. Online offerings enable you to attend class without incurring the added expense of travel. In-classroom courses deliver the skills practice combined with the expertise of experienced instructors.

This book does not replace training, nor does training replace the need for a book like this. They complement each other by giving you exposure to new techniques, new ideas. It is instructors like Roger and Filip who bring the classroom experience to life, who help you understand how report authoring techniques can be modified and adjusted to help you build the reports that impact your business. With this book, they are sharing with you the application of key concepts to a variety of problems. They have added a new stack of instructions to your bedside and some shiny new blocks for your pillowcase.

Erin Pyka
Business Analytics Curriculum Development

Preface

As instructors, we have seen many students who want to learn more about business analytics. They ask us questions about how to apply concepts in class to their reports back at the office. We are pushed to understand more about the product to be able to help them apply the technology. This book was inspired by the many questions that were asked and by our belief that IBM Cognos Report Studio's uses are limited only by your imagination.

Readers of this book should already have a good understanding of creating reports in IBM Cognos Report Studio. This book should not be considered as a replacement for more formal training classes, but as a method to enhance the concepts developed in the classroom. If you have purchased this book and have not attended training yet, we would encourage you to attend a class. Okay, we are being a little selfish here in saying that you should come attend our classes, but we feel that the interaction of an instructor and a learner can spark many more ideas about how to enhance the experience of learning new technology.

The promise of business analytics can transform the way organizations process information. This technology can close the gap between information technology and the business users who consume the information presented. Instead of presenting 500-page reports that force analysts to sift through them, report writers can create a series of reports that follow how those analysts look at the data. Reports can be generated that use both textual and graphical formats to allow complex relationships to become quickly evident.

IBM Cognos Business Intelligence (BI) 10 is a huge step toward the delivery of that promise. IBM Cognos Report Studio allows information technology specialists to create powerful tools for business analysis. Our goal for this book is to help report writers to think about report development in new ways and to help them think of report creation from a different perspective.

Approach

As an extension to your expertise in IBM Cognos Report Studio, this book looks to enhance your ability to create complex reports. While these reports are complete in their design, you may find that some of the examples could be further improved based on your skills. Our goal in this book is to introduce you to techniques that may not be evident. Hopefully you'll find a few tips in each example that you did not know already. Also, we would challenge you to look for ways to further enhance the design and interactivity within these examples. This is the method we used to create this book, and this is how you can improve your ability to deliver the reports that the users need in order to improve their decision-making processes.

While the focus of this book in on using IBM Cognos 10 for report development, the first five chapters can be completed in a similar manner in IBM Cognos 8 BI. Chapter 6 focuses on the features that are available only in the latest version of the software. We tested this book using the 8.4 and 10.1 releases of IBM Cognos BI. Other releases may not perform identically to what you see in the book.

The examples are based on the sample data sources that are available to IBM Cognos administrators as a part of the installation process. If you are not an administrator, find out where the samples are installed and see whether you can access them.

Some of the reports may require capabilities that are beyond your permissions (creating custom SQL) or that require extra software installed on your IBM Cognos BI server (statistics data containers). Again, talk to your administrator to see whether these features are available to you.

To help you complete the various examples, we have created a couple of resources. The first is that each of the examples has been completed and added to a deployment package. Working with your administrator, these packages can be imported into your IBM Cognos BI environment for review. Additionally, we have created a number of files to help you with some of the typing tasks. You will be able to copy and paste sections of code.

All of the files needed for creating reports are available from the accompanying book website at www.ibmpressbooks.com/title/9780132656757. In the Downloads section under **More Information**, you will find a supplements.zip file. This compressed file contains a readme file, text files with all the code, and any other external files that will make the process of creating these reports easier. We are both report writers at heart and we want to make the process of creating these examples as easy as possible for you.

How This Book Is Organized

Each example follows a similar format. The first section provides a scenario in which a customer needs a report. Here we show you how the completed report should look. Since you usually know what you want to design before beginning a report, we felt this would be helpful for you. As you go through the process to create the report, you will see that it is separated into different steps. We advocate a building-block approach to development in which you create a part of a report, test the smaller piece, and then continue to the next step. At the end of each chapter, you can see a recap of some of the concepts that were introduced.

- **Chapter 1, "Creating Consumer-Friendly Reports":** This chapter looks at creating reports that are designed to match how business users process information.

- **Chapter 2, "Matching the Report to the Analysis":** This chapter takes the ideas of Chapter 1 further by creating a series of reports that follow how managers would want to first see a dashboard of high-level metrics and then drill to reports focused on specific details.

- **Chapter 3, "Understanding the Report Hierarchy":** This chapter uses techniques to standardize report content and to manipulate the hierarchical relationships between objects in reports.

- **Chapter 4, "Overriding the Data Model":** This chapter looks at ways a report author can create complex queries that override the package information provided by the data modeler.

- **Chapter 5, "Additional Examples":** This chapter provides some "bonus content" that shows you how to create reports integrating HTML and to create a complex union.

- **Chapter 6, "New Techniques in Version 10":** This chapter provides examples that use the new graphing engine, active reports, and statistical analysis, which are all new features available only in IBM Cognos BI 10.

Report Snapshots

As programmers who have used books like this one to improve our skills, we have had to page through an entire book to look for one feature or example that will help us complete a task. We wanted to provide another way for you to find what you need. This section provides screenshots of the final products of each example. Hopefully you will find it valuable to see report styles and functions that will help you.

Chapter 1 Report Snapshots

Chapter 1 presents several reports that are designed to leverage features to create reports that focus on a specific task. The report functions and associated screen results are as follows:

- Highlight selected text (see Figure I.1)

Product number	Product	Product Description	Product color	Product size	Introduction date	Discontinued date
		Product Catalog records for keyword - rope				
42110	Husky Rope 50	11 mm diameter standard rope. Length: 50 m. Weight: 78 g per meter. Impact Force: 7.2 kN. Static Elongation: 7.8%. Number of UIAA Falls: 16.	Red	50 m	Jan 10, 2005 12:00:00 AM	
43110	Husky Rope 60	11 mm diameter standard rope. Length: 60 m. Weight: 78 g per meter. Impact Force: 7.2 kN. Static Elongation: 7.8%. Number of UIAA Falls: 16.	Red	60 m	Jan 10, 2005 12:00:00 AM	
44110	Husky Rope 100	11 mm diameter standard rope. Length: 100 m. Weight: 78 g per meter. Impact Force: 7.2 kN. Static Elongation: 7.8%. Number of UIAA Falls: 16.	Blue	100 m	Jan 10, 2005 12:00:00 AM	
45110	Husky Rope 200	11 mm diameter standard rope. Length: 200 m. Weight: 78 g per meter. Impact Force: 7.2 kN. Static Elongation: 7.8%. Number of UIAA Falls: 16.	Blue	200 m	Jan 10, 2005 12:00:00 AM	
51110	Granite Belay	The Granite Belay is an ingenious single rope belay device that uses carabiner movement to brake the rope.	Black	Unspecified	Jan 10, 2005 12:00:00 AM	
50110	Granite Carabiner	Made from 12 mm rod stock aluminum and a radius suitable for almost any rope size. Locks tight with almost any belay/rappel combination. Individually tested.	Silver	12 mm	Jan 10, 2005 12:00:00 AM	

Figure I.1   Completed enhanced product catalog

- Avoid query macros (see Figure I.2, Figure I.3, and Figure I.4)
- Create complex crosstab calculations (see Figure I.5)

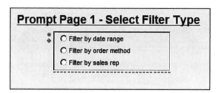

Figure I.2   Main prompt page for conditional filters

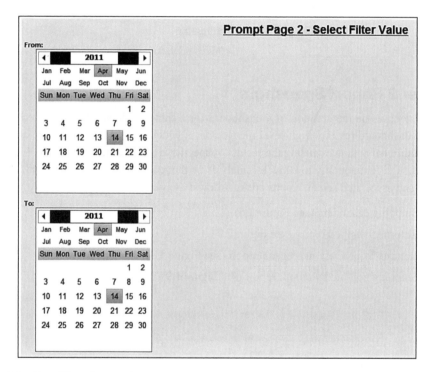

Figure I.3   Conditional prompt page

Product Line Summary for Filter by order method
Fax

Revenue	Quantity	Revenue	Gross profit
Camping Equipment	413,958	23,054,398.48	8,675,557.15
Golf Equipment	102,651	15,241,303.27	7,269,748.7
Mountaineering Equipment	292,408	11,848,370.08	4,743,720.54
Outdoor Protection	311,583	1,966,484.72	1,190,874.37
Personal Accessories	359,414	17,962,985.46	7,168,417.72

Figure I.4   Completed order method report

	2004			2005			2006			2007	
	Revenue	Planned revenue	% of Plan	Revenue	Planned revenue	% of Plan	Revenue	Planned revenue	% of Plan	Revenue	Planned re
Camping Equipment	332,986,338.06	361,495,088.97	92.11%	402,757,573.17	431,970,502.15	93.24%	500,382,422.83	531,010,839.07	94.23%	352,910,329.97	378,6
Golf Equipment	153,553,850.98	169,875,640.98	90.39%	168,006,427.07	182,227,978.19	92.20%	230,110,270.55	247,977,474.85	92.79%	174,740,819.29	190,17
Outdoor Protection	36,165,521.07	38,181,339.98	94.72%	25,008,574.08	26,157,261.77	95.61%	10,349,175.84	10,938,440.68	94.61%	4,471,025.26	4,72
Personal Accessories	391,647,093.61	398,923,067.59	98.18%	456,323,355.9	464,458,617.66	98.25%	594,009,408.42	602,227,218.07	98.64%	443,693,449.85	449,77
Mountaineering Equipment				107,099,659.94	113,363,106.75	94.47%	161,039,823.26	168,584,907.17	95.52%	141,520,649.7	148,62
Summary	914,352,803.72	968,475,137.52	94.41%	1,159,195,590.16	1,218,177,466.52	95.16%	1,495,891,100.9	1,560,738,879.84	95.85%	1,117,336,274.07	1,171,95

Figure I.5   Completed crosstab percentage calculation

Chapter 2 Report Snapshots

Chapter 2 focuses on the creation of a dashboard for a shipping department of a fictional company. The dashboard reviews high-level metrics, from which several reports can be created that provide additional details, focusing the results of specific areas. Additionally, each of the reports has drill-though functionality to allow for analysis by the report consumer. The dashboard/report functions and associated screen results are as follows:

- Shipping dashboard (see Figure I.6)
- Returned/shipped report (see Figure I.7)
- Returns by product and reason report (see Figure I.8)
- Shipping volume by month report (see Figure 1.9)

Figure I.6   Completed shipping dashboard

Volume Returned and Shipped for Americas

Americas Breakdown	Reason description	Return quantity	Quantity
United States -- Return/Ship Ratio: 1.564%		163,362	10,444,575
Returns by Reason for United States	Defective product	26,830	
	Incomplete product	17,712	
	Wrong product ordered	36,987	
	Wrong product shipped	16,068	
	Unsatisfactory product	65,765	
Canada -- Return/Ship Ratio: 1.476%		59,810	4,052,045
Returns by Reason for Canada	Defective product	10,942	
	Incomplete product	8,913	
	Wrong product ordered	16,062	
	Wrong product shipped	7,210	
	Unsatisfactory product	16,683	
Mexico -- Return/Ship Ratio: 1.088%		29,459	2,706,418
Returns by Reason for Mexico	Defective product	4,276	
	Incomplete product	2,189	
	Wrong product ordered	5,180	
	Wrong product shipped	6,357	
	Unsatisfactory product	11,457	
Brazil -- Return/Ship Ratio: 1.342%		22,926	1,708,632
Returns by Reason for Brazil	Defective product	4,124	
	Incomplete product	2,427	
	Wrong product ordered	10,291	

Figure I.7   Completed returned/shipped report

2005 Returns for Products Under Camping Equipment

Return quantity		Q1 2005	Q2 2005	Q3 2005	Q4 2005	2005
Camping Equipment	Unsatisfactory product	6,318	2,134	4,339	6,291	19,082
	Wrong product ordered	2,835	1,914	4,491	6,247	15,487
	Wrong product shipped	4,131	2,208	3,674	3,044	13,057
	Incomplete product	3,468	3,676	1,833	2,394	11,371
	Defective product	1,719	1,294	2,257	1,989	7,259
	Returns for Camping Equipment	18,471	11,226	16,594	19,965	66,256
Cooking Gear	Unsatisfactory product	4,713	398	1,403	3,367	9,881
	Wrong product shipped	904	1,460	2,373	1,817	6,554
	Incomplete product	2,193	2,044	769	1,318	6,324
	Defective product	593	173	521	1,180	2,467
	Wrong product ordered		135		1,806	1,941
	Returns for Cooking Gear	8,403	4,210	5,066	9,488	27,167
TrailChef Water Bag	Unsatisfactory product	1,462			2,661	4,123
	Defective product					
	Wrong product shipped					
	Incomplete product					
	Wrong product ordered					
	Returns for TrailChef Water Bag	1,462			2,661	4,123
TrailChef Water Bag 1110	Unsatisfactory product	1,462			2,661	4,123
	Defective product					

Figure I.8   Completed returns by product and reason report

Expected Volume vs. Actual Quantity Shipped for Amsterdam For April 2005

Retailer	Retailer site	Quantity
Expected Volume for: Amsterdam		48,880
Actual Quantity Shipped for: Amsterdam		59,285
Extra Sport	Wageningen	14,201
Extra Sport - Total		14,201
Sportworld	Deventer	7,455
Sportworld	Beets	2,937
Sportworld	Amstelveen	1,045
Sportworld - Total		11,437
Beter Buitenleven	Amsterdam	6,018
Beter Buitenleven	Marken	4,983
Beter Buitenleven - Total		11,001
Klimgek Bv.	Amsterdam	5,755
Klimgek Bv. - Total		5,755
Kampeer Top Shop	Dronten	5,182
Kampeer Top Shop - Total		5,182
Holland Zonzoekers	Laren	2,993
Holland Zonzoekers - Total		2,993
Topforma	Groningen	2,810
Topforma - Total		2,810
Get Out	Varsseveld	2,794

Figure I.9   Completed shipping volume by month report

Chapter 3 Report Snapshots

Chapter 3 focuses on the hierarchical nature of formatting, querying, and delivering report information. The chapter concludes with the design of a briefing book that incorporates elements of all the other reports into a single report that can be delivered on a scheduled basis. The report functions and associated screen results are as follows:

- Layout library (see Figure I.10 and Figure I.11)
- Layout library use (see Figure I.12)
- Formatting inheritance (see Figure I.13)
- Structure inheritance (see Figure 1.14)
- Briefing book creation (see Figure 1.15)

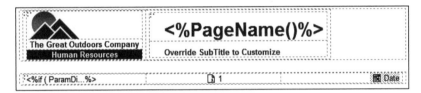

Figure I.10   Completed human resources header and footer

Figure I.11   Completed human resources footer with report ID populated

Figure I.12 Completed recruitment by organization report

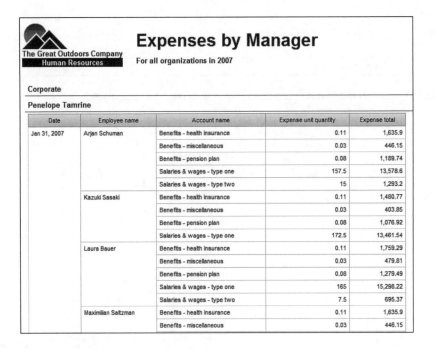

Figure I.13 Completed employee expense report

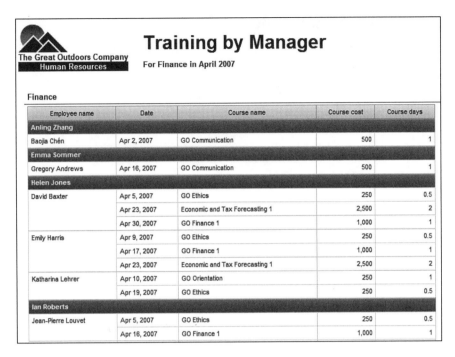

Figure I.14 Completed training by manager report

Figure I.15 Completed HR briefing book table of contents

Chapter 4 Report Snapshots

Chapter 4 focuses on creating a very functional, highly formatted, and easily maintained report. The report functions and associated screen results are as follows:

- Creating a union (see Figure I.16)

Boston
January 2004

Product type	Product	Closing inventory	Inventory on Hand
Binoculars	Seeker 35	2,443	
	Seeker 50	874	
	Seeker Extreme	631	
	Seeker Mini	805	
Climbing Accessories	Firefly Charger	0	
	Firefly Climbing Lamp	0	
	Firefly Rechargeable Battery	0	
	Granite Belay	0	
	Granite Carabiner	0	
	Granite Chalk Bag	0	
	Granite Pulley	0	
Cooking Gear	TrailChef Canteen	11,967	
	TrailChef Cook Set	7,049	
	TrailChef Cup	9,308	
	TrailChef Deluxe Cook Set	5,570	
	TrailChef Double Flame	3,201	
	TrailChef Kettle	11,736	
	TrailChef Kitchen Kit	8,990	
	TrailChef Single Flame	6,738	
	TrailChef Utensils	5,075	

Figure I.16   Completed inventory count report

- Joining SQL and model queries (see Figure I.17 and Figure I.18)

Forecast Audit Report

This report compares the results of the Revenue Forecast Report from the previous reporting tool to the results of the new data model for Report Studio. This page will display the summary results and the following pages will show the details of query results that are different and those that match in both queries.

Record status	Expected volume	New expected volume	Forecast revenue	New forecast revenue
1. Totals are different between the two queries	160,550,400	23,856,220	$9,951,864,926.05	$1,412,538,239.50
4. Volume and revenue match	51,640,790	51,640,790	$2,861,757,832.60	$2,861,757,832.60

Figure I.17   Completed query audit cover page

Forecast Audit Report

Year	Month	Country	Product	Expected volume	Forecast revenue	New expected volume	New forecast revenue
1. Totals are different between the two queries							
2004	April	Austria	Mountain Man Analog	120	$5,086.80	40	$1,695.60
			Mountain Man Deluxe	80	$6,969.60	40	$3,484.80
			Polar Ice	60	$5,805.00	30	$2,902.50
			Polar Sports	210	$25,907.70	30	$3,701.10
			Polar Sun	400	$23,104.00	50	$2,888.00
2004	April	Brazil	Mountain Man Analog	225	$9,537.75	75	$3,179.25
			Mountain Man Deluxe	160	$13,939.20	80	$6,969.60
			Polar Ice	100	$9,675.00	50	$4,837.50
			Polar Sports	350	$43,179.50	50	$6,168.50
			Polar Sun	360	$20,793.60	45	$2,599.20
2004	April	Canada	Mountain Man Analog	570	$24,162.30	190	$8,054.10
			Mountain Man Deluxe	310	$27,007.20	155	$13,503.60
			Polar Ice	160	$15,480.00	80	$7,740.00

Figure I.18 Completed query audit report

Chapter 5 Report Snapshots

Chapter 5 focuses on how to take advantage of HTML technology to enhance the presentation of your report in a web browser. Additionally, you will see how to perform a union of three queries at one time. The report functions and associated screen results are as follows:

- Using HTML to enhance functionality (see Figure I.19)
- Integrating multiple queries into a complex report (see Figure I.20)

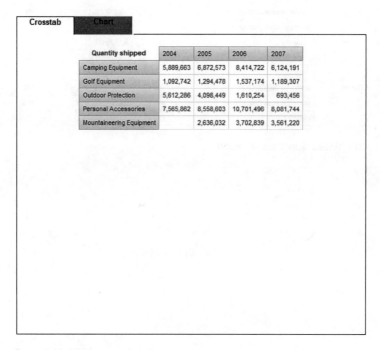

Figure I.19   Completed tab example

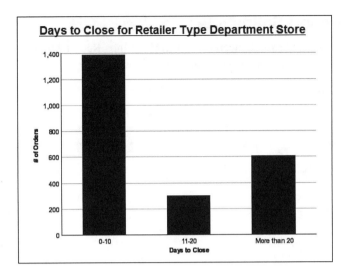

Figure I.20   Completed chart with a union of grouping

Chapter 6 Report Snapshots

Chapter 6 focuses on the key enhancements to IBM Cognos Report Studio in version 10. The report functions and associated screen results are as follows:

- Using active reports to replace HTML code (see Figure I.21)

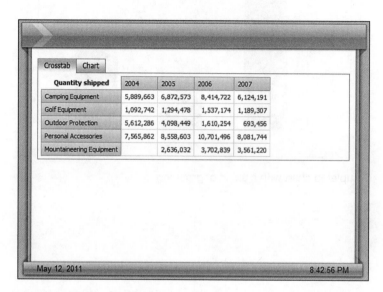

Figure I.21 Completed alternative tab example

- Adding local data sources to reports (see Figure I.22)
- New charting options and active reports (see Figure I.23)
- Statistical analysis (see Figure I.24 through Figure I.28)

Problem Orders Report

Order #:	100003
Retailer:	Universo Acampando
Retailer Contact:	PedroGomes
Retailer Phone:	55-11-32535232 ext. 121
Retailer E-mail:	Pedro.Gomes@Univ208.com

Ordered by Alexandre Pereira on Jan 12, 2004

Product number	Product	Quantity	Unit sale price	Revenue	Gross profit
72110	Polar Extreme	19	143.85	2,733.15	1,355.65
79110	Seeker 50	88	124.72	10,975.36	2,828.32
90110	BugShield Extreme	3,252	6.51	21,170.52	13,300.68
95110	Sun Shield	1,107	5.76	6,376.32	3,321
Overall - Total		4,466		41,255.35	20,805.65

Figure I.22   Completed problem orders report

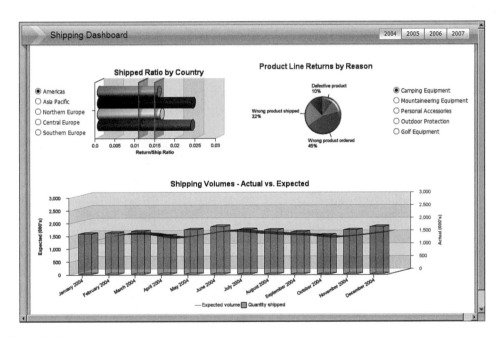

Figure I.23   Completed complex active report

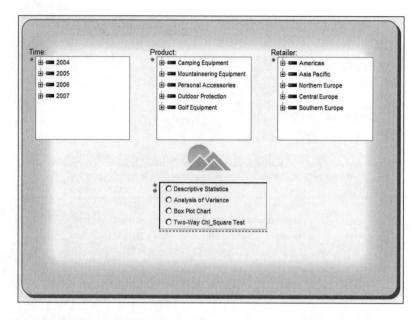

Figure I.24 Completed prompt page for statistical analyses

Analysis of Variance

Gross profit

ANOVA

	Sum of Squares	df	Mean Square	F	Sig.
Between Groups	4374614581.852	4	1093653645.463	15.605	.000
Within Groups	12474758372.164	178	70082912.203		
Total	16849372954.016	182			

Post Hoc Tests

Gross profit

Multiple Comparisons

	(I) Campaigns Only	(J) Campaigns Only	Mean Difference (I-J)	Std. Error	Sig.	95% Confidence Interval	
						Lower Bound	Upper Bound
Bonferroni	TrailChef Campaign	EverGlow Campaign	4,069.309	1,628.846	.134	-560.60	8,699.22
		Hibernator Campaign	-4,670.576	1,788.359	.098	-9,753.90	412.74
		Canyon Mule Campaign	-8,514.457[*]	2,433.860	.006	-15,432.58	-1,596.33
		Rising Star Campaign	-9,390.754[*]	1,986.700	.000	-15,037.85	-3,743.66
	EverGlow Campaign	TrailChef Campaign	-4,069.309	1,628.846	.134	-8,699.22	560.60

Figure I.25 Completed descriptive statistics report

Analysis of Variance

Gross profit

ANOVA

	Sum of Squares	df	Mean Square	F	Sig.
Between Groups	4374614581.852	4	1093653645.463	15.605	.000
Within Groups	12474758372.164	178	70082912.203		
Total	16849372954.016	182			

Post Hoc Tests

Gross profit

Multiple Comparisons

	(I) Campaigns Only	(J) Campaigns Only	Mean Difference (I-J)	Std. Error	Sig.	95% Confidence Interval	
						Lower Bound	Upper Bound
Bonferroni	TrailChef Campaign	EverGlow Campaign	4,069.309	1,628.846	.134	-560.60	8,699.22
		Hibernator Campaign	-4,670.576	1,788.359	.098	-9,753.90	412.74
		Canyon Mule Campaign	-8,514.457(*)	2,433.860	.006	-15,432.58	-1,596.33
		Rising Star Campaign	-9,390.754(*)	1,986.700	.000	-15,037.85	-3,743.66
	EverGlow Campaign	TrailChef Campaign	4,069.309	1,628.846	.134	8,699.22	560.60

Figure I.26 Completed analysis of variance report

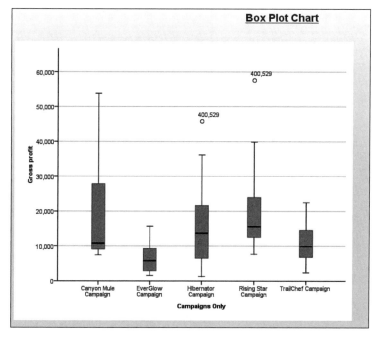

Figure I.27 Completed box plot report

% within Campaign

Campaign * Order method type Crosstabulation

		Order method type							Total
		Web	Special	Telephone	Sales visit	E-mail	Mail	Fax	
Campaign	Regular sale	35.0%	2.1%	23.9%	19.6%	13.5%	2.3%	3.5%	100.0%
	TrailChef Campaign	23.3%	6.7%	31.7%	18.3%	13.3%	3.3%	3.3%	100.0%
	EverGlow Campaign	33.3%		26.7%	20.0%	20.0%			100.0%
	Hibernator Campaign	38.0%		30.0%	18.0%	12.0%		2.0%	100.0%
	Canyon Mule Campaign	53.3%		6.7%	6.7%	20.0%		13.3%	100.0%
	Rising Star Campaign	26.9%		38.5%	23.1%	11.5%			100.0%
Total		34.7%	2.0%	24.5%	19.5%	13.7%	2.2%	3.4%	100.0%

Chi-Square Tests

	Value	df	Asymp. Sig. (2-sided)
Pearson Chi-Square	40.511[1]	30	.095
Likelihood Ratio	47.809	30	.021
Linear-by-Linear Association	.175	1	.676
N of Valid Cases	2512		

[1] 18 cells (42.9%) have expected count less than 5. The minimum expected count is .30.

Figure I.28   Completed chi-square test page

CHAPTER 1

Creating Consumer-Friendly Reports

One of the biggest advantages of creating reports in IBM® Cognos® Business Intelligence (BI) is that you can now create one (or more) reports that can be designed to match how business users process information. These consumers do not need to wade through waves of report pages. A series of small reports that independently focus on specific information can link to other reports. We will take a look at using drill-through in the next chapter, but you should look for ways to simplify the reports at every opportunity.

This means you, as the report author, should look for ways to present the data in a format that makes the exploration process easier for the consumers. This chapter provides examples of simple reports that present data.

In our training classes, we regularly hear from students who want to create very complex reports. We begin by asking what the users need to accomplish with the report and begin to build the report using an iterative building block process.

This chapter presents several reports that are designed to leverage features to create reports that focus on a specific task.

NOTE If you want some help with the files and typing involved in this chapter, go to www.ibmpressbooks.com/title/9780132656757 and download the supplements.zip file from the Downloads section under **More Information**.

Highlight Selected Text

You have been asked by the product marketing staff to create a product catalog. When you ask how it will be used, the market analyst wants to be able to find descriptions of products that use specific phrases to ensure that the proper messages are reaching the customer.

Search technology has become sophisticated enough that documents can be searched for text and the phrases can be highlighted to allow the searcher to focus on the text. The analyst would like to simulate that functionality in the report.

This report should be able to prompt the user for a search phrase and return a list of product descriptions that contain the phrase and highlight the selected text. The final result should look like Figure 1.1.

Product Catalog records for keyword - rope						
Product number	Product	Product Description	Product color	Product size	Introduction date	Discontinued date
42110	Husky Rope 50	11 mm diameter standard rope. Length: 50 m. Weight: 78 g per meter. Impact Force: 7.2 kN. Static Elongation: 7.8%. Number of UIAA Falls: 16.	Red	50 m	Jan 10, 2005 12:00:00 AM	
43110	Husky Rope 60	11 mm diameter standard rope. Length: 60 m. Weight: 78 g per meter. Impact Force: 7.2 kN. Static Elongation: 7.8%. Number of UIAA Falls: 16.	Red	60 m	Jan 10, 2005 12:00:00 AM	
44110	Husky Rope 100	11 mm diameter standard rope. Length: 100 m. Weight: 78 g per meter. Impact Force: 7.2 kN. Static Elongation: 7.8%. Number of UIAA Falls: 16.	Blue	100 m	Jan 10, 2005 12:00:00 AM	
45110	Husky Rope 200	11 mm diameter standard rope. Length: 200 m. Weight: 78 g per meter. Impact Force: 7.2 kN. Static Elongation: 7.8%. Number of UIAA Falls: 16.	Blue	200 m	Jan 10, 2005 12:00:00 AM	
51110	Granite Belay	The Granite Belay is an ingenious single rope belay device that uses carabiner movement to brake the rope.	Black	Unspecified	Jan 10, 2005 12:00:00 AM	
50110	Granite Carabiner	Made from 12 mm rod stock aluminum and a radius suitable for almost any rope size. Locks tight with almost any belay/rappel combination. Individually tested.	Silver	12 mm	Jan 10, 2005 12:00:00 AM	

Figure 1.1   Completed enhanced product catalog

Design

The trick to solving this problem is to utilize several string functions that are available in IBM Cognos Report Studio in order to find the requested part of the text and then cut the preceding and succeeding text. Once the searched text field has been separated into three parts, we can use the logic within our query items to put the strings back together within a single column and highlight only the searched text.

The list report should filter on only those products that contain the search text.

Step-by-Step

The key steps involve the creation of a query that parses the product description and removes any products that do not have the matching phrase. With the query built and tested, the list report is designed.

Step 1: Start the Report

1.   Launch **Report Studio** and select the **GO Data Warehouse (query)** package.
2.   Click on the **Create new** option.

COGNOS 8 NOTE   The option is **Create a new report or template**.

---

3. Select the **List** report template and click **OK**.

We will be using the **Sales (query)** namespace inside the **Sales and Marketing (query)** folder.

Step 2: Begin the Report Query

The key component of this report is the capability to parse the text of the report description for selected text. This step defines the two fields.

1. In the **Explorer Bar**, mouse over the **Query Explorer** tab and select the **Query1** object.

2. From the **Source** tab of the **Insertable Objects** pane, drag the **Product description** query item from the **Products** query subject into the **Data Items** pane of the query design window.

3. From the **Toolbox** tab of the **Insertable Objects** pane, drag a **Data Item** into the **Data Items** pane below **Product Description**.

The Data Item Expression window opens.

4. Type the following code in the **Expression** definition window:

```
?SearchText?
```

This creates a parameter called SearchText and assigns the value to the Data Item we just created. We will be searching for the text that will be typed into the server-generated prompt because we will not create a prompt page on our own in this example.

5. Validate the expression and click **OK** to close the dialog box.

6. In the **Properties** window for the **Data Item**, use the **Name** property to rename the **DataItem1** data item to **SearchText**.

Step 3: Include the Search Functionality

In this section, we will add the key functionality to the query. First, we will add a function to search for the matching text. If a match is found, we will break up the description into three fields. If a match is not found, we will leave the description in the first field.

1. From the **Toolbox** tab of the **Insertable Objects** pane, drag another **Data Item** into the **Data Items** pane below the **SearchText** data item.

The Data Item Expression window opens.

2. Create the following expression:

```
position([SearchText], [Product description])
```

HINT   Drag and drop the **SearchText** and **Product** description data items from the **Data Items** tab of the **Available Components** pane to avoid having to type in the whole expression. When referencing data item and query item names in IBM Cognos Report Studio, the names are case-sensitive.

The position function returns an integer value that represents where the first character of the searched text begins within the Product description string. If no match is found, the position function returns a zero.

3. Validate the expression and click **OK** to close the dialog box.

4. In the **Properties** window for the **Data Item**, use the **Name** property to rename the **DataItem1** data item to **Position**.

5. From the **Toolbox** tab of the **Insertable Objects** pane, drag another **Data Item** into the **Data Items** pane below the **Position** data item.

    The Data Item Expression window opens.

6. Create the following expression:
    ```
    IF ([Position]=0) THEN
        ([Product description])
    ELSE
        (substring([Product description], 1, [Position]-1))
    ```

    If the searched text does not exist in the Product description field, then we will set this first field to the full product description.

    In case the string is found, we want to cut off the text that precedes the string we are looking for, including the space before the string. This is why we use [Position] - 1 as the third argument in the substring function.

7. Validate the expression and click **OK**.

8. In the **Properties** window for the **Data Item**, use the **Name** property to rename the **DataItem1** data item to **PartOne**.

9. From the **Toolbox** tab of the **Insertable Objects** pane, drag another **Data Item** into the **Data Items** pane below the **PartOne** data item.

    The Data Item Expression window opens. This field contains the text to be highlighted only if the text is found.

10. Create the following expression:
    ```
    IF ([Position]=0) THEN
        ('')
    ELSE
        ([SearchText])
    ```

NOTE   The expression has two single quotes without spaces. If the searched text does not exist in the Product description field, we will just default to an empty string (two single quotes indicate an empty string).

---

11. Validate the expression and click **OK**.

12. In the **Properties** window for the **Data Item**, use the **Name** property to rename the **DataItem1** data item to **PartTwo**.

13. From the **Toolbox** tab of the **Insertable Objects** pane, drag another **Data Item** into the **Data Items** pane below the **PartTwo** data item.

    The Data Item Expression window opens.

14. Create the following expression:

```
IF ([Position]= 0) THEN
        ('')
ELSE
        (substring ([Product description], [Position] +
        char_length([SearchText]), char_length([Product
        description]) - char_length([SearchText]) -
        char_length([PartOne])))
```

NOTE The expression has two single quotes without spaces.

If the searched text does not exist in the Product description field, we will just default to an empty string.

If we do find the text, PartThree needs to contain text that is after the searched string, including the space after the searched string. This is why we need to use character length functions to figure out the positioning of the starting point for the substring function and the length of the remaining string.

15. Validate the expression and click **OK**.

16. In the **Properties** pane for the **Data Item**, change the **Name** property to **PartThree**.

    This completes our report query build.

17. Click on the **Run** menu item and choose the **View Tabular Data** option to test the Report query before starting the report design. The warning message pop-up can be dismissed by clicking the **OK** button.

    Sample text for a search that you could use is **rope**.

    Your results will be similar to Figure 1.2.

18. Close the **IBM Cognos Viewer** window to return to IBM Cognos Report Studio.

Product description	SearchText	Position	PartOne	PartTwo	PartThree
11 mm diameter standard rope. Length: 100 m. Weight: 78 g per meter. Impact Force: 7.2 kN. Static Elongation: 7.8%. Number of UIAA Falls: 16.	rope	25	11 mm diameter standard	rope	. Length: 100 m. Weight: 78 g per meter. Impact Force: 7.2 kN. Static Elongation: 7.8%. Number of UIAA Falls: 16.
11 mm diameter standard rope. Length: 200 m. Weight: 78 g per meter. Impact Force: 7.2 kN. Static Elongation: 7.8%. Number of UIAA Falls: 16.	rope	25	11 mm diameter standard	rope	. Length: 200 m. Weight: 78 g per meter. Impact Force: 7.2 kN. Static Elongation: 7.8%. Number of UIAA Falls: 16.
11 mm diameter standard rope. Length: 50 m. Weight: 78 g per meter. Impact Force: 7.2 kN. Static Elongation: 7.8%. Number of UIAA Falls: 16.	rope	25	11 mm diameter standard	rope	. Length: 50 m. Weight: 78 g per meter. Impact Force: 7.2 kN. Static Elongation: 7.8%. Number of UIAA Falls: 16.
11 mm diameter standard rope. Length: 60 m. Weight: 78 g per meter. Impact Force: 7.2 kN. Static Elongation: 7.8%. Number of UIAA Falls: 16.	rope	25	11 mm diameter standard	rope	. Length: 60 m. Weight: 78 g per meter. Impact Force: 7.2 kN. Static Elongation: 7.8%. Number of UIAA Falls: 16.
3.6x opera glasses maintain image and color fidelity in all lighting conditions. The brushed aluminum body fits snugly into any purse or pocket. Includes a soft leather case and carrying loop.	rope	0	3.6x opera glasses maintain image and color fidelity in all lighting conditions. The brushed aluminum body fits snugly into any purse or pocket. Includes a soft leather case and carrying loop.		
8x27x50 zoom binoculars include compass and range-finding reticle, multi-coated optics, and textured rubber armoring. Waterproof and lightweight.	rope	0	8x27x50 zoom binoculars include compass and range-finding reticle, multi-coated optics, and textured rubber armoring. Waterproof and lightweight.		
A compact tool that includes LED light, blade, tweezers, reamer, screwdriver, file, corkscrew and can opener.	rope	0	A compact tool that includes LED light, blade, tweezers, reamer, screwdriver, file, corkscrew and can opener.		
A complete medical kit suitable for families with children. Contains cough syrup, oral rehydration salts, advanced wound management, and more. Size: 22 x 12 x 7 cm. Weight: 0.6 kg.	rope	0	A complete medical kit suitable for families with children. Contains cough syrup, oral rehydration salts, advanced wound management, and more. Size: 22 x 12 x 7 cm. Weight: 0.6 kg.		

Figure 1.2   Tabular data view

Step 4: Create the Report Design

Now we will add the three parts to a list column named Product description.

1. Mouse over **Page Explorer** and click on **Page1**.

2. From the **Data Items** tab of the **Insertable Objects** pane, drag the following data items into the **List** object: **PartOne**, **PartTwo**, and **PartThree**.

3. Unlock the **List** object cells by clicking on the **Unlock (currently locked)** button on the toolbar.

4. Click on the **PartTwo** text item within the **PartTwo** list column body to select it. Drag it over into the list column body of the **PartOne** column to the right of the **PartOne** text item.

5. Click on the **PartThree** text item within the **PartThree** list column body to select it. Drag it over into the list column body of the **PartOne** column to the right of the **PartTwo** text item.

6. Click on the **PartTwo** text item and then click on the **Foreground Color** button on the toolbar and select the drop-down arrow. From the **Named Colors** menu, change the foreground color to **Red**. Click the **Bold** button on the toolbar to change the font effect to bold.

    Your design should look similar to Figure 1.3.

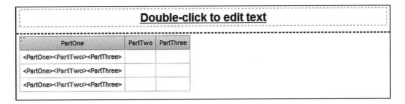

Figure 1.3   Start of the report design

7. Click on the **PartOne** text item within the **PartOne** list column title area.

8. In the **Properties** pane, change the **Source Type** property to **Text**.

9. Double-click the **Text** property and type **Product Description**.

10. Click **OK** to close the dialog box.

11. Lock the **List** object cells by clicking on the **Lock (currently unlocked)** button on the toolbar.

12. Ctrl-click the **PartTwo** and **PartThree** list column bodies and press **Delete** on the keyboard to remove them from the report design. Your design should now look similar to Figure 1.4.

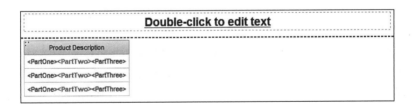

Figure 1.4   Key report design

13. From the **Run** menu, select **Run Report – HTML** to view the report.

    When prompted, click in the **Provide a value** prompt box and type **glasses**.

    Your results should look similar to Figure 1.5.

14. Close the **IBM Cognos Viewer** window to return to IBM Cognos Report Studio.

Product Description
3.6x opera glasses maintain image and color fidelity in all lighting conditions. The brushed aluminum body fits snugly into any purse or pocket. Includes a soft leather case and carrying loop.
8x27x50 zoom binoculars include compass and range-finding reticle, multi-coated optics, and textured rubber armoring. Waterproof and lightweight.
A compact tool that includes LED light, blade, tweezers, reamer, screwdriver, file, corkscrew and can opener.
A complete medical kit suitable for families with children. Contains cough syrup, oral rehydration salts, advanced wound management, and more. Size: 22 x 12 x 7 cm. Weight: 0.6 kg.
A durable plastic cooler with hinged top, perfect for storing small items. Size:100 x 50 x 50 cm.
A general purpose mountaineering axe for snow and glacier travel. Excellent mid-weight axe. Weight: 638 g
A high quality aluminum flashlight with Krypton bulb. Uses two D batteries, included.
A light-weight GPS receiver with a 56mm monochrome display and 24MB internal memory. Requires two AA batteries for 26 hours of service. Weighs only 156 grams.
A perfect tent for biking and hiking trips, compact and very light. Features three shock cord aluminum poles, and three large mesh windows. Packed size: 15 x 40 cm. Weight: 0.5 kg.
A personal first aid kit is recommended for every outdoor hiker or camper. Contains basic wound management, advanced infectious control, and more. Size: 17 x 10 x 7 cm. Weight: 0.3 kg.
A rubberized and water-resistant GPS receiver that includes a 70mm color screen, electronic compass and altimeter. Uses a 64MB memory card. Requires two AA batteries for 18 hours of service. Weighs 238 grams.
A single burner stove with integral tank. It features precise flame control so you will never have to settle for burnt camp food again. Weight 624 g, fuel is white gas.
A single tent peg made of heavy-duty plated steel. Long enough even for hard, rocky ground. Length: 25 cm
A solid hammer made with a solid hard wood handle and steel head. Weight: 800g.
A versatile pocket tool that includes LED light, 1GB memory stick, pen, serrated blade, corkscrew and serrated cutter. Comes with a life time warranty.
A weekend getaway requires this pack. It features a large front compression pocket, harness and waist belt, foam molded back panel, vinyl covered gear loops. 50,000 cu. cm.
Acrylex lenses in the Polar Wave sunglasses absorb up to 90% of visible light, 96% ultraviolet, and 82% infrared light. Unbreakable nylon frames.
Adjustable brightness control with auto ignition. Safely stores in its own protective case. Approximate burn time 5 hours on one 0.25 liter butane canister, included.
All you will ever need on the trail. Pot gripper and nylon carrying bag included. 1.5 and 2 liter pots with individual lids. Weight: 750 g.
All-purpose stainless steel pliers. Sheath included. Length (closed) 12cm, (open) 16 cm. Weight: 200 g.

Figure 1.5   Report view

Step 5: Finalize the Report Design

The core development of this report is finished; what is left are the finishing touches. We will add additional data elements for the product catalog and filter the report to show only the products whose descriptions contain the keyword that was entered at runtime.

1. In the **Explorer Bar,** mouse over the **Query Explorer** tab and select the **Query1** object.

2. From the **Data Items** pane, drag the **Position** data item into the **Detail Filters** pane.

    The Detail Filter Expression dialog box opens and shows [Position] in the Expression Definition box.

3. Add the following code in the **Expression Definition** window after the **[Position]** expression:

    ```
    <> 0
    ```

    Your expression should now be this:

    ```
    [Position] <> 0.
    ```

4. Click **OK** to close the Detail Filter Expression dialog box.

    This ensures that only product records with descriptions containing the keyword get retrieved from the database.

5. Mouse over **Page Explorer** and click on **Page1**.

6. Click on the **Report Title** text to select it.

7. Change the **Source Type** property to **Report Expression**.

8. Double-click the **Report Expression** property.

   The Report Expression dialog box window opens.

9. Create the following expression in the **Expression Definition** box:

   ```
   'Product Catalog records for keyword - ' +
   ParamDisplayValue('SearchText')
   ```

10. Validate the expression and click **OK** to close the Report Expression dialog box.

11. From the **Source** tab of the **Insertable Objects** pane, Ctrl-click and drag the **Product** query item from the **Products** query subject and the **Product Number** query item from the **Codes** folder as columns in front of the **Product Description** column in the report list.

COGNOS 8 NOTE   The **Product** query item is called **Product name**.

---

12. From the **Source** tab of the **Insertable Objects** pane, Ctrl-click and drag the **Product color**, **Product size**, **Introduction date**, and **Discontinued date** query items from the **Products** query subject as columns after the **Product Description** column in the report list.

    Your report design should now look similar to Figure 1.6.

<%'Product Cat...%>						
Product number	Product	Product Description	Product color	Product size	Introduction date	Discontinued date
<Product number>	<Product>	<PartOne><PartTwo><PartThree>	<Product color>	<Product size>	<Introduction date>	<Discontinued date>
<Product number>	<Product>	<PartOne><PartTwo><PartThree>	<Product color>	<Product size>	<Introduction date>	<Discontinued date>
<Product number>	<Product>	<PartOne><PartTwo><PartThree>	<Product color>	<Product size>	<Introduction date>	<Discontinued date>

Figure 1.6   Final report design

13. From the **Run** menu, select **Run Report – HTML** to view the report. When prompted, click in the **Provide a value** prompt box and type **rope**.

    Your results should look like Figure 1.7.

14. Close the **IBM Cognos Viewer** window to return to IBM Cognos Report Studio.

By using a combination of string functions, we were able to split the original text field into three text items that contained all text before the searched string, the actual search string, and all text after the searched string, respectively. Once the query was built, we were able to use a simple IBM Cognos Report Studio built-in feature to unlock the report list cells in order to be able to condense the report and combine all the row data in one defined column.

Product Catalog records for keyword - rope						
Product number	Product	Product Description	Product color	Product size	Introduction date	Discontinued date
42110	Husky Rope 50	11 mm diameter standard rope. Length: 50 m. Weight: 78 g per meter. Impact Force: 7.2 kN. Static Elongation: 7.8%. Number of UIAA Falls: 16.	Red	50 m	Jan 10, 2005 12:00:00 AM	
43110	Husky Rope 60	11 mm diameter standard rope. Length: 60 m. Weight: 78 g per meter. Impact Force: 7.2 kN. Static Elongation: 7.8%. Number of UIAA Falls: 16.	Red	60 m	Jan 10, 2005 12:00:00 AM	
44110	Husky Rope 100	11 mm diameter standard rope. Length: 100 m. Weight: 78 g per meter. Impact Force: 7.2 kN. Static Elongation: 7.8%. Number of UIAA Falls: 16.	Blue	100 m	Jan 10, 2005 12:00:00 AM	
45110	Husky Rope 200	11 mm diameter standard rope. Length: 200 m. Weight: 78 g per meter. Impact Force: 7.2 kN. Static Elongation: 7.8%. Number of UIAA Falls: 16.	Blue	200 m	Jan 10, 2005 12:00:00 AM	
51110	Granite Belay	The Granite Belay is an ingenious single rope belay device that uses carabiner movement to brake the rope.	Black	Unspecified	Jan 10, 2005 12:00:00 AM	
50110	Granite Carabiner	Made from 12 mm rod stock aluminum and a radius suitable for almost any rope size. Locks tight with almost any belay/rappel combination. Individually tested.	Silver	12 mm	Jan 10, 2005 12:00:00 AM	

Figure 1.7   Final enhanced product catalog

Our careful string manipulation and simple font-color change allowed us to create an illusion of word highlighting within a larger text field based on the word search entered by the user at runtime.

Avoiding Query Macros

In class, we teach students that query macros can be written to take advantage of the IBM Cognos BI capability to dynamically change the report queries at runtime. Query macros can be built to integrate information about the report consumer or to enhance the queries that are written. Unfortunately, the query macros are not easy to master because the documentation exists only in the IBM Cognos Framework Manager documentation. In our example, we will show how the solution to the common business problem can be resolved without resorting to the use of query macros.

The sales team wants to be able to quickly analyze how each retailer region is performing according to product quantities sold, revenue produced, and gross profit achieved. The sales team would like to be able to filter the results in one of three ways: by selected date, by selected order method, or by selected employee.

The team would like one report where they can select the type of filter and the value to include for the filter and see the results in a crosstab so that they can quickly compare the numbers between the products and the regions. The final prompt result we are trying to achieve should look similar to Figure 1.8.

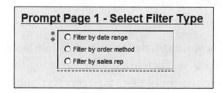

Figure 1.8   Main prompt page

After the prompt is selected, the report will run with a completely different filter option, and in case the prompt triggers another parameter, a new corresponding prompt will show up for the user to make the final selection.

Different second-page prompts are illustrated in Figures 1.9, 1.10, and 1.11.

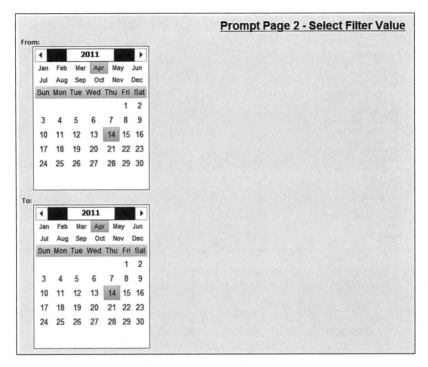

Figure 1.9   Second conditional prompt page: Date Range

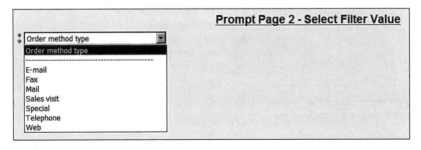

Figure 1.10   Second conditional prompt page: Order Method

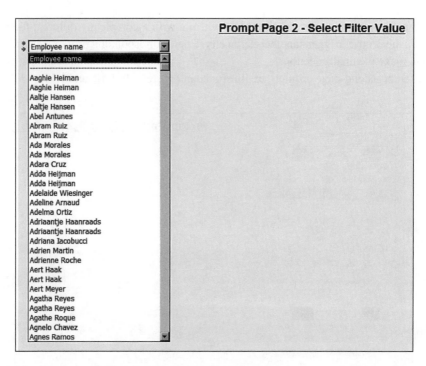

Figure 1.11   Second conditional prompt page: Employee

Figure 1.12 illustrates the final report that is desired (we are assuming an Order method prompt selection and a specific order method selection).

Figure 1.12   Final report

Design

We have discovered that macro code syntax help is not readily available for IBM Cognos Report Studio developers. It is covered extensively in IBM Cognos Framework Manager training and materials but not in IBM Cognos Report Studio user guides.

We have to change the syntax of the filter expression depending on what the user selects in the prompt at runtime.

The reason we cannot just pass the filter expression as a parameter value is that it will be treated by the report engine as a text value and not as "code" that has to be used as a filter expression.

For this reason, the expression is captured in a prompt macro function. However, writing the macro function or finding out what the correct syntax is may be difficult for novice report developers who may not have access to the IBM Cognos Framework Manager developers who can help them.

The solution we are proposing in this example will completely avoid the use of macros, and it will be easy for business users to understand and replicate.

Our sample report will be a crosstab report that will be filtered in one of the three ways that users select at runtime. The options will be by date range, by order method, or by sales rep.

Step-by-Step

We will start with a simple crosstab template.

Step 1: Start the Report

1. Launch **Report Studio** and select the **GO Data Warehouse (query)** package.

2. Click on **Create new** option.

COGNOS 8 NOTE   The option is **Create a new report or template**.

---

3. Select the **Crosstab** report template and click **OK**.

   We will be using the **Sales (query)** namespace inside the **Sales and Marketing (query)** folder (same as for the previous example).

Step 2: Set Up the Crosstab and the Query

When it comes to creating reports, there are two approaches. As in this example, you can build the query and the report layout at the same time. Our first example provides an approach where you can build the query first and then create the report layout.

1. From the **Source** tab of the **Insertable Objects** pane, drag the following query items into the **Crosstab**:

   • **Product Line** from the **Products** query subject to the **Rows** drop zone

   • **Quantity**, **Revenue**, and **Gross profit** from the **Sales fact** query subject to the **Columns** drop zone

---

COGNOS 8 NOTE   The **Products** query subject is called **Product**, and **Time** is called **Time Dimension**.

---

2. In the **Explorer** bar, mouse over the **Query Explorer** and select **Query1**.

3. From the **Toolbox** tab of the **Insertable Objects** pane, drag the **Filter** object into the **Detail Filters** pane.

    The Detail Filters Expression box pops up.

4. Create the following filter expression:
    ```
    CASE ?choice?
    WHEN 1 THEN ([Sales (query)].[Time].[Date] in_range ?Date?)
    WHEN 2 THEN ([Sales (query)].[Order method].[Order method code]
    = ?OrderMethod?)
    ELSE ([Sales (query)].[Employee by region].[Employee key] =
    ?Employee?)
    END
    ```

5. Validate the expression, choosing any prompt values, and click **OK** to close the dialog box.

NOTE   This is the filter expression we are using instead of the prompt macro expression, which would look like this:
```
#prompt('choice', 'token')#
```

---

6. To return to the page design, mouse over the **Page Explorer** tab and select **Page1**.

7. Click on any whitespace in the page body to select it and click on the **Center** button on the toolbar.

8. Click on the report title text to select it, and change the **Source Type** property from **Text** to **Report Expression**.

9. Double-click on the **Report Expression** property box.

    The Report Expression dialog box opens.

10. Create the following expression:
    ```
    'Product Line Summary for ' + ParamDisplayValue('choice')
    ```

11. Validate the expression, choosing any prompt values, and click **OK**.

    Our crosstab report setup is complete at this point.

Step 3: Set Up the First Prompt Page

1. Mouse over **Page Explorer** and select the **Prompt Pages** folder.

2. Drag a **Page** object from the **Insertable Objects** pane into the **Prompt Pages** pane.

    This will be Prompt Page1.

3. Double-click on **PromptPage1** to enter page design mode.

4. Change the page title text to this:

```
Prompt Page 1 - Select Filter Type
```

5. From the **Toolbox** tab of the **Insertable Objects** pane, drag a **Value Prompt** object into the page body of the prompt page.

   The Prompt Wizard dialog box opens.

6. Click on the **Use existing parameter** radio button, and from the drop-down menu, select the **choice** parameter.

7. Click on the **Finish** button to close the Prompt Wizard dialog box.

8. Click on the newly created value prompt to select it.

9. Double-click the **Static Choices** property in the **Properties** pane.

   The Static Choices dialog box is displayed.

10. Click on the **Add** button in the lower-left corner of the **Static Choices** dialog box.

    The Edit dialog box opens.

11. Type in the value **1** in the **Use** property text box and type **Filter by date range** in the **Display** property text box.

12. Repeat the preceding step to add two more static values:

    - Use: **2** and Display: **Filter by order method**
    - Use: **3** and Display: **Filter by sales rep**

    Your Static Choices dialog box should look similar to Figure 1.13.

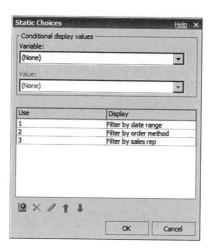

Figure 1.13   Static Choices dialog box

13. Click **OK** to close the Static Choices dialog box.

14. While you still have the value prompt selected, change the **Select UI** property to **Radio button group**.

15. Change the **Auto-Submit** property to **Yes**.

16. Click on any whitespace in the prompt page body to select it and click on the **Center** button on the **Toolbar**.

17. Click on the page footer (which has all the prompt buttons) and **Delete** it.

    We do not need the buttons because the prompt control we built on this page has the auto-submit property turned on, and it will submit the selections as soon as the user clicks on one of the radio buttons.

    We have completed the first prompt page.

Step 4: Set Up the Second Prompt Page

The prompt controls shown on the second prompt page will depend on the selections made in the first page.

1. Mouse over **Page Explorer** and select the

   Prompt Pages folder.

2. Drag a **Page** object from the **Insertable Objects** pane into the **Prompt Pages** pane below Prompt Page1.

   This will be Prompt Page2.

3. Double-click on **PromptPage2** to enter prompt page design mode.

4. Change the page title text to this:

   ```
   Prompt Page 2 - Select the Filter Value
   ```

5. From the **Toolbox** tab of the **Insertable Objects** pane, drag the **Conditional Blocks** object into the prompt page body.

NOTE   We will use the conditional blocks to display a different prompt based on selection from the previous prompt page.

---

6. Click on the **Conditional Blocks** object to select it.

7. Double-click on the **Block Variable** property in the **Properties** pane.

   The Block Variable dialog box opens.

8. From the **Variable** drop-down menu, select the **<New string variable>** option.

   The New Variable dialog box opens.

9. Make the **Name** of the new variable **choice**.

10. Click on the **Add** button in the lower-left corner of the dialog box.

    The Add dialog box opens.

11. Enter the value **1** and click **OK**.

    We will repeat the previous steps to add two more values: 2 and 3.

12. Click on the **Add** button again in the lower-left corner of the dialog box.

    The Add dialog box opens.

13. Enter the value **2** and click **OK**.

14. Click on the **Add** button one more time in the lower-left corner of the dialog box.

    The Add dialog box opens.

15. Enter the value **3** and click **OK**.

    Your New Variable dialog box will look similar to Figure 1.14.

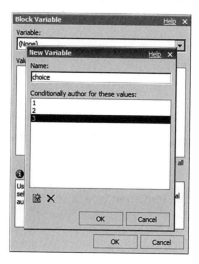

Figure 1.14   New Variable dialog box

16. Click **OK**.

    The Report Expression dialog box window opens.

17. Create the following expression:

    ```
    ParamValue('choice')
    ```

18. Validate the expression and click **OK** twice to close the Report Expression and Variable dialog boxes.

19. Change the **Current Block** property value from **(Other)** to **1**.

    We will now design the prompt for when the users select a date range filter type.

20. From the **Toolbox** tab of the **Insertable Objects** pane, drag a **Date** prompt into the conditional block.

    The Prompt Wizard dialog box is displayed.

21. Click on the **Use existing parameter** radio button, and from the drop-down menu, select the **Date** parameter.

22. Click the **Finish** button to close the Prompt Wizard dialog box.

23. Click on the newly inserted **Date prompt** control to select it.

24. Change the **Multi-Select** property to **No**.

25. Click on the background of the **Conditional Block** to select it.

26. Change the **Current Block** property to **2**.

    We will now design the prompt for when the users select an order method filter type.

27. From the **Toolbox** tab of the **Insertable Objects** pane, drag a **Value** prompt into the conditional block.

    The Prompt Wizard dialog box opens.

28. Select the **Use existing parameter** radio button and from the drop-down menu select the **OrderMethod** parameter.

29. Click the **Next** button.

30. Change the **Name** property from **Query2** to **OrderMethodPrompt**.

31. Set the **Values to display** value to **[Sales (query)].[Order method].[Order method type]**.

COGNOS 8 NOTE   The **Order method type** query item is called **Order method**.

---

32. Click on the **Finish** button to close the Prompt Wizard dialog box.

33. Click on the background of the **Conditional Block** to select it.

34. Change the **Current Block** property to **3**.

    We will now design the prompt for when the users select an employee filter type.

35. From the **Toolbox** tab of the **Insertable Objects** pane, drag a **Value** prompt into the conditional block.

    The Prompt Wizard dialog box opens.

36. Click on the **Use existing parameter** radio button, and from the drop-down menu, select **Employee** parameter.

37. Click on the **Next** button.

38. Change the **Name** property from **Query2** to **EmployeePrompt**.

39. Set the **Values to display** value to **[Sales (query)].[Employee by region].[Employee name]**.

40. Click on the **Finish** button to close the Prompt Wizard dialog box.

Our second prompt page design is finished at this point. It can be enhanced by the addition of text boxes for additional instructions to the users, or prompt controls can be modified to have a different UI.

You can now test the report prompt page flow.

Step 5: Adjust the Report Title to Show the Selected Prompt Value

The objective is to dynamically display the prompt selections that the user selected at runtime.

1. Mouse over **Page Explorer** and select the **Page1** object.

2. From the **Toolbox** tab of the **Insertable Objects** pane, drag the **Conditional Blocks** object into the page header area below the report title block.

We will reuse the variable we created for the purposes of the second prompt page.

3. Click on the **Conditional Block** object we have just inserted, and double-click on the **Block Variable** property in the **Properties** pane.

The Block Variable dialog box opens.

4. From the **Value** drop-down menu, select the **choice** variable that was created during the second prompt page design.

5. Click **OK** to close the Block Variable dialog box.

6. Change the **Conditional Block** property value from **(Other)** to **1**.

7. From the **Toolbox** tab of the **Insertable Objects** pane, drag a **Layout Calculation** object into the **Conditional Block**.

The Report Expression dialog box opens.

8. Click on the **Parameters** tab of the **Available Components** section of the dialog box.

9. Drag the **Date** parameter into the **Expression Definition** area.

10. Validate the expression and click **OK** to close the Report Expression dialog box.

11. From the **Toolbar**, click the **Center** button to center the parameter expression in the report title area.

12. Change the **Current Block** property value to **2**.

13. From the **Toolbox** tab of the **Insertable Objects** pane, drag a **Layout Calculation** object into the **Conditional Block**.

The Report Expression dialog box opens.

14. Click on the **Parameters** tab of the **Available Components** section of the dialog box.

15. Drag the **Order Method** parameter into the **Expression Definition** area.

16. Validate the expression and click **OK** to close the Report Expression dialog box.

17. From the **Toolbar**, click the **Center** button to center the parameter expression in the report title area.

18. Change the **Current Block** property value to **3**.

19. From the **Toolbox** tab of the **Insertable Objects** pane, drag a **Layout Calculation** object into the **Conditional Block**.

    The Report Expression dialog box opens.

20. Click on the **Parameters** tab of the **Available Components** section of the dialog box.

21. Drag the **Employee** parameter into the **Expression Definition** area.

22. Validate the expression and click **OK** to close the Report Expression dialog box.

23. From the toolbar, click the **Center** button to center the parameter expression in the report title area.

Our report design is completed for this example.

We have achieved the desired result by using a conditional block in a second prompt page, which will show different second prompt options depending on the selections made on the first prompt page.

Furthermore, we have integrated the dynamic filter logic without the use of macro functions in order to demonstrate that novice report developers can be quite capable of creating very complex dynamic prompts and filter reports without advanced macro programming knowledge.

Finally, we have shown you how to dynamically control what will be shown in the title of the report based on the user's selections during the prompt process.

Complex Crosstab Calculations

Sometimes, the easiest of report requests give report developers the hardest time. The solution is easy; however, it takes time to find the correct property or "discover" the correct button that does the trick.

The final result we are trying to achieve should look similar to Figure 1.15.

Design

The order of calculations in more complex data containers, such as crosstabs and charts, can sometimes cause report developers to get undesired results when summarizing data. In this example, we will explore the default behavior of summarizations in crosstabs and discover the alternatives and seldom-used properties.

	2004			2005			2006			2007	
	Revenue	Planned revenue	% of Plan	Revenue	Planned revenue	% of Plan	Revenue	Planned revenue	% of Plan	Revenue	Planned re
Camping Equipment	332,988,338.06	361,495,088.97	92.11%	402,757,573.17	431,970,502.15	93.24%	500,382,422.83	531,010,839.07	94.23%	352,910,329.97	378,6
Golf Equipment	153,553,850.98	169,875,640.98	90.39%	168,006,427.07	182,227,978.19	92.20%	230,110,270.55	247,977,474.85	92.79%	174,740,819.29	190,17!
Outdoor Protection	36,165,521.07	38,181,339.98	94.72%	25,008,574.08	26,157,261.77	95.61%	10,349,175.84	10,938,440.68	94.61%	4,471,025.26	4,72
Personal Accessories	391,647,093.61	398,923,067.59	98.18%	456,323,355.9	464,458,617.66	98.25%	594,009,408.42	602,227,218.07	98.64%	443,693,449.85	449,77
Mountaineering Equipment				107,099,659.94	113,363,106.75	94.47%	161,039,823.26	168,584,907.17	95.52%	141,520,849.7	148,62
Summary	914,362,803.72	968,475,137.52	94.41%	1,159,195,590.16	1,218,177,466.52	95.18%	1,495,891,100.9	1,560,738,879.84	95.85%	1,117,336,274.07	1,171,95

Figure 1.15 Completed crosstab percentage calculation example

Step-by-Step

We will start with a simple crosstab template.

Step 1: Start the Report

1. Launch **Report Studio** and select the **GO Data Warehouse (analysis)** package.
2. Click on the **Create new** option.

COGNOS 8 NOTE   The option is **Create a new report or template.**

---

3. Select the **Crosstab** report template and click **OK**.

   We will be using the **Sales (analysis)** namespace inside the **Sales and Marketing (analysis)** folder, same as we did for the previous examples in this chapter.

Step 2: Set Up the Crosstab

1. From the **Source** tab of the **Insertable Objects** pane, drag the following levels into the Crosstab:
   - **Product Line** from the **Products** dimension and **Products** hierarchy to the **Rows** drop zone
   - **Year** from the **Time** dimension and **Time** hierarchy to the **Columns** drop zone
2. Drag **Revenue** and **Planned revenue** from the **Sales fact** measures to the **Columns** drop zone and nest them under the **Year** data item.

COGNOS 8 NOTE   The **Products** and **Time** dimensions and hierarchies are called **Product** and **Time Dimension.**

---

3. Ctrl-click the **Revenue** and **Planned revenue** column headings in the **Crosstab**.

4. From the **Data** menu item, select **Calculate** and click on the **%(Revenue, Planned revenue)** option.

   This will create a calculation item under each Year column and next to the Revenue and Planned revenue data items. The calculation will represent the percentage of planned revenue achieved. In addition, you will notice when you run the report that the formatting of the data will already be in percentage format.

5. Right-click the newly created **%(Revenue, Planned revenue)** column title in the **Crosstab** and select the **Show Text...** option.

COGNOS 8 NOTE   The **Show Text...** option is called **Edit Text...**

   The Edit label dialog box opens.

6. Change the text to **% of Plan** and click **OK** to close the dialog box.

7. In the **Crosstab**, click on the **Product Line** row title to select it.

8. From the toolbar, click on the **Summarize** button and select the **Total** option.

COGNOS 8 NOTE   The **Summarize** toolbar button is the **Aggregate** button.

---

9. From the **Run** menu, select **Run Report – HTML** to view the report. Your results should be similar to Figure 1.16.

	2004			2005			2006			2007
	Revenue	Planned revenue	% of Plan	Revenue	Planned revenue	% of Plan	Revenue	Planned revenue	% of Plan	Revenue
Camping Equipment	332,986,338.06	361,495,088.97	92.11%	402,757,573.17	431,970,502.15	93.24%	500,382,422.83	531,010,839.07	94.23%	352,910
Golf Equipment	153,553,850.98	169,875,640.98	90.39%	168,006,427.07	182,227,978.19	92.20%	230,110,270.55	247,977,474.85	92.79%	174,740
Outdoor Protection	36,165,521.07	38,181,339.98	94.72%	25,008,574.08	26,157,261.77	95.61%	10,349,175.84	10,938,440.68	94.61%	4,471
Personal Accessories	391,647,093.61	398,923,067.59	98.18%	456,323,355.9	464,458,617.66	98.25%	594,009,408.42	602,227,218.07	98.64%	443,693
Mountaineering Equipment				107,099,659.94	113,363,106.75	94.47%	161,039,823.26	168,584,907.17	95.52%	141,52
Total	914,352,803.72	968,475,137.52	375.40%	1,159,195,590.16	1,218,177,466.52	473.76%	1,495,891,100.9	1,560,738,879.84	475.80%	1,117,336

Figure 1.16   Initial crosstab view

Notice how the Total line for the percentage calculations is actually adding the percentages. This is not the desired result. We are expecting to see the overall % of Plan for each year.

10. Close the **IBM Cognos Viewer** window to return to IBM Cognos Report Studio.

We will showcase two ways of correcting this problem in Steps 3a and 3b.

Step 3a: Fix the Crosstab Total Percentage Calculation

1. Click on the **% of Plan** column heading to select it.

2. In the **Properties** pane, change the **Solve Order** property from a blank value to **2**.

By default, all the data item properties do not have this property set.

Solve Order property indicates which values will be calculated first in crosstabs and charts. The items with the lowest sort order values are calculated first; otherwise, the calculations on the detail rows are performed first, and then all the summaries.

The percentage calculation column should be calculated last, and since the summaries of the Revenue and Projected Revenue will already exist, the report server will use them to calculate the overall Year percentage.

3. From the **Run** menu, select **Run Report – HTML** to view the report. The report results should look similar to Figure 1.17.

	2004			2005			2006			2007
	Revenue	Planned revenue	% of Plan	Revenue	Planned revenue	% of Plan	Revenue	Planned revenue	% of Plan	Revenu
Camping Equipment	332,986,338.06	361,495,088.97	92.11%	402,757,573.17	431,970,502.15	93.24%	500,382,422.83	531,010,839.07	94.23%	352,
Golf Equipment	153,553,850.98	169,875,640.98	90.39%	168,006,427.07	182,227,978.19	92.20%	230,110,270.55	247,977,474.85	92.79%	174,
Outdoor Protection	36,165,521.07	38,181,339.98	94.72%	25,008,574.08	26,157,261.77	95.61%	10,349,175.84	10,938,440.68	94.61%	4,
Personal Accessories	391,647,093.61	398,923,067.59	98.18%	456,323,355.9	464,458,617.66	98.25%	594,009,408.42	602,227,218.07	98.64%	443,
Mountaineering Equipment				107,099,659.94	113,363,106.75	94.47%	161,039,823.26	168,584,907.17	95.52%	141
Total	914,352,803.72	968,475,137.52	94.41%	1,159,195,590.16	1,218,177,466.52	95.16%	1,495,891,100.9	1,560,738,879.84	95.85%	1,117,

Figure 1.17   Final crosstab view

Notice how the Total line for the percentage calculations is now correct.

4. Close the **IBM Cognos Viewer** window to return to IBM Cognos Report Studio.

Step 3b: Try an Alternative Solution

There is actually an easier and quicker way to achieve the same result. Instead of task 8 in Step 2, do the following simple task:

1. From the **Toolbar**, click on the **Summarize** button and select the **Automatic Summary** option.

COGNOS 8 NOTE   The **Automatic Summary** option is called **Aggregate**.

---

2. From the **Run** menu, select **Run Report – HTML** to view the report. The results should resemble Figure 1.18.

	2004			2005			2006			2007
	Revenue	Planned revenue	% of Plan	Revenue	Planned revenue	% of Plan	Revenue	Planned revenue	% of Plan	Revenu
Camping Equipment	332,986,338.06	361,495,088.97	92.11%	402,757,573.17	431,970,502.15	93.24%	500,382,422.83	531,010,839.07	94.23%	352,9
Golf Equipment	153,553,850.98	169,875,640.98	90.39%	168,006,427.07	182,227,978.19	92.20%	230,110,270.55	247,977,474.85	92.79%	174,7
Outdoor Protection	36,165,521.07	38,181,339.98	94.72%	25,008,574.08	26,157,261.77	95.61%	10,349,175.84	10,938,440.68	94.61%	4,4
Personal Accessories	391,647,093.61	398,923,067.59	98.18%	456,323,355.9	464,458,617.66	98.25%	594,009,408.42	602,227,218.07	98.64%	443,6
Mountaineering Equipment				107,099,659.94	113,363,106.75	94.47%	161,039,823.26	168,584,907.17	95.52%	141
Summary	914,352,803.72	968,475,137.52	94.41%	1,159,195,590.16	1,218,177,466.52	95.16%	1,495,891,100.9	1,560,738,879.84	95.85%	1,117,3

Figure 1.18   Final crosstab view

Notice how the Total line for the percentage calculations is also correct using this alternative suggested step.

3. Close the **IBM Cognos Viewer** window to return to IBM Cognos Report Studio.

Sometimes the trick is just to find the correct property or a button. With the ever-changing list of features or options that are added to the new releases of IBM Cognos BI, you will keep discovering easier and better ways to solve the same report issues. Over time, you will notice that there are several ways to do the same thing, all correct, and it will come down to personal preference when you need to decide which approach to take.

Summary

In this chapter, we wanted to focus on some practical tips and hints to help report authors get some new ideas for their report requirement solutions that simplify the presentation of the reports.

In class, we cover most of the commonly used IBM Cognos Report Studio object properties; however, it takes some time and report-building experience to find out what the rest of the properties are useful for.

The first example builds on the exceptional highlighting techniques we cover in the IBM Cognos Report Studio Fundamentals and Advanced classes. For example, the classes teach the students how to highlight values in individual cells or the whole rows of data based on some kind of static or user-defined thresholds. Our example takes exceptional highlighting to the next level by combining the highlighting techniques with some complex report expression building to achieve the desired results.

The second example allows users to change the filter expression and avoid complex macro expressions that are not really expected from the majority of business report authors.

The third example showcases some of the less-used IBM Cognos Report Studio object properties and provides alternative approaches to solving the same report requirements.

Some techniques that you may want to integrate into other reports include these:

- Various string manipulation functions
- Unlocking of the list container cells to condense reports
- Multiple prompt pages to guide the user to narrow down the focus of the report
- Conditional blocks in the prompt pages and in the report pages
- Reuse of report parameters and conditional variables in different areas of the report
- Solve Order property adjustment for crosstab reports to resolve aggregation issues

Matching the Report to the Analysis

In the IBM Cognos Report Studio classes, we discuss that traditional report writing over the years was focused on delivering all the required data at one time, even if that meant building a report that consisted of hundreds of pages.

Report Studio allows report writers to build reports that focus on the specific aspects of the analysis of data. By using drill-up, drill-down, and drill-through tools, users can run reports that follow their analysis methods. The reports can be focused on the key data items at each point in the data review. Instead of creating one long-running report that forces the analyst to turn from page to page, you can create a series of reports to match how end users look for trends and anomalies.

This chapter looks at the creation of a dashboard for the shipping department of a fictitious organization called the Great Outdoors Company. Starting with a dashboard that reviews high-level metrics, several reports will be created that provide additional details, focusing on the results of specific areas.

After the reports have been created, each report will have drill-though functionality to allow for analysis by the report consumer. While each of the reports is important individually, a system linking them together allows real-time decision making based on the needs of the manager.

NOTE If you want some help with the files and typing involved in this chapter, go to www.ibmpressbooks.com/title/9780132656757 and download the supplements.zip file from the Downloads section under **More Information**.

If you chose to load the individual reports from the attached XML files, the drill-through functionality will be removed. You will need to complete the final section of this chapter to complete the interactive dashboard.

The Dashboard

Your customer is the manager of shipping for a fictitious global wholesaler. The key metrics for the organization are shipping volumes and returns. The manager is looking for any exceptional data to be able to quickly react to trends.

When looking at different warehouses at the country level, the manager wants to see whether any countries are not meeting service expectations by limiting returns to less than 1.1 percent of all items shipped. If a country exceeds 1.5 percent returns to shipped items, this is a cause for concern.

In reviewing the types of items that are shipped, the manager also wants to look for an exceptionally large percentage of return reasons that are a result of the warehouse.

Finally, the manager wants to look for trends between the expected and actual shipping volumes. Figure 2.1 shows the completed dashboard.

Figure 2.1   Completed shipping dashboard

Design

This dashboard will look at three measures that are important to the manager: returned item to items shipped ratio, number of returns, and shipping volumes.

The three data containers used in this report are a map, a pie chart, and a combination chart. After the items are added to the page, the queries will be developed.

After the queries are created, the data items will be added to the containers and formatted to match the expectations of the manager.

No drill capabilities will be added at this time. After the other reports are developed, the interactions will be added to improve the analytical aids.

Step-by-Step

The steps move from the creation of the report layout to the creation of the queries. After the queries are built, the layout will be formatted to match the manager's requirements.

Step 1: Start the Report

1. Launch **Report Studio** and select the **GO Data Warehouse (analysis)** package.
2. Click on the **Create New** option.

COGNOS 8 NOTE   The option is **Create a new report or template.**

---

3. Select the **Blank** report template and click **OK**.

   We will be using the **Inventory**, **Product Forecast**, **Returned items**, and **Sales** name-spaces inside the **Sales and Marketing (analysis)** folder.

Step 2: Create the Dashboard Header

The dashboard will have four components. The first will be a header that provides the time focus for the report. The data item attached to the header will take the last year from the data source. To display the results during the current year, three graphical data containers will be created: a map, a pie chart, and a combination chart.

1. From the **Toolbox** tab of the **Insertable Objects** pane, drag a **Singleton** object into the work area.

   In this example, the singleton will play the role of the canvas for the dashboard and will act as the master container for the year.
2. From the **Toolbox** tab, drag a **Block** object into the **Singleton** in the work area.
3. In the work area, click the **Block** to select it.
4. In the **Properties** pane, double-click the **Size & Overflow** property to open the dialog box.
5. Change the **Height** to **550** px and the **Width** to **950** px.
6. Click **OK** to close the dialog box.
7. From the **Toolbox** tab, drag a second **Block** object into the first **Block**.

   This block will act as the header for the dashboard. By working within the block, you have more control over the spacing on the page.
8. In the work area, click the header block to select it.
9. From the toolbar, click the **Center** button.
10. Click the drop-down list for **Size** to select **22 pt**.

Now, anything added into the block will be centered and any text will have the 22 pt font size.

11. From the **Toolbox** tab of the **Insertable Objects** pane, drag a **Text Item** into the header area.

The Text dialog box is displayed.

12. Type **Shipping Dashboard** (add a space before the text so we can add the current year before it) and click **OK** to close the dialog box.

We will now add the current year to the query for the singleton as a filter for the whole dashboard.

13. In the **Explorer Bar**, move over the **Query Explorer** tab and select the **Query1** query.

14. In the **Properties** pane, change the **Name** property of the query to **Current_Year**.

15. From the **Toolbox** tab of the **Insertable Objects** pane, drag a **Data Item** into the **Data Items** pane of the work area.

The **Data Item Expression** pane is displayed.

16. From the **Source** tab of the **Available Components** pane, expand the **Time** dimension and the **Time** hierarchy within the **Inventory** namespace.

COGNOS 8 NOTE   The **Time** dimension and hierarchy are both called **Time dimension**.

---

17. From the **Available Components** pane, drag the **Year** level into the **Expression Definition** pane.

18. To retrieve the current year, add the **closingPeriod** function around the **Year** level. The expression should look like this:

```
closingPeriod([Inventory].[Time].[Time].[Year])
```

19. Validate the expression and click **OK**.

20. In the **Properties** pane, change the **Name** property to **Current year**.

21. Change the **Aggregate Function** property to **None**.

22. In the **Explorer Bar**, mouse over the **Page Explorer** tab and select **Page1**.

23. From the **Data Items** tab of the **Insertable Objects** pane, drag the **Current year** data item into the header of the work area to the left of the static text title.

Because the singleton is a data container, Current year was added as a text item into the header, and any other objects added can have a master detail relationship to the current year.

This completes the header area.

Step 3: Create the Dashboard Content

The rest of this step focuses on adding the other three data containers onto the dashboard.

1. From the **Toolbox** tab in the **Insertable Objects** pane, drag a **Table** object into the work area below the header block.

   The Insert Table dialog box is displayed.

2. Set the **Number of Columns** and the **Number of Rows** to **2**.

3. Click **OK** to close the dialog box.

4. To convert the second row to have only one cell, Ctrl-click both table cells in the second row.

5. From the toolbar, click the **Merge Cells** button.

6. To change the alignment and add padding within each cell in the table, Ctrl-click on all three of the table cells.

7. On the toolbar, click the **Center** button to align the objects placed inside the table.

8. In the **Properties** pane, double-click the **Padding** property. In the Padding dialog box, add **25** to all the sides of the cell.

9. Click **OK** to close the dialog box.

10. From the **Toolbox** tab of the **Insertable Objects** pane, drag a **Map** object into the upper-left table cell.

    The Choose Map dialog box is displayed.

NOTE   Each map object consists of three layers: regions, points, and display. The Choose Map dialog box is displayed when the object is added to the report and can be reopened by right-clicking on the map and choosing **Edit Map Type**.

---

11. In the **Display Layer** pane, select **Oceans**. Verify that the **World** map is in the **Maps** pane, **Countries + Territories** in the **Regions Layer**, and (**None**) in the **Points Layer**.

12. Click **OK** to close the dialog box.

    Now that the map is added, the pie chart will be added. In IBM Cognos BI v10, you have the ability to use legacy styles for reports and charts. This dashboard will use the older styles for consistency between the two versions. Chapter 6 will use the new options to enhance the reports. You can go to the **Tools** menu and select the **Advanced** tab to see which options are currently selected.

13. From the **Toolbox** tab of the **Insertable Objects** pane, drag a **Chart** object into the upper-right table cell.

    The Insert Chart dialog box is displayed.

14. In the **Chart Group** pane, select **Pie, Donut**.

15. Click **OK** to select the default pie chart and close the dialog box.

Finally, in the bottom pane, the combination chart will be added.

16. From the **Toolbox** tab of the **Insertable Objects** pane, drag a **Chart** object into the bottom table cell.

17. In the **Chart Group** pane, select **Combination**.

18. Click **OK** to accept the default Column chart and close the dialog box.

Figure 2.2 shows the work area for the report.

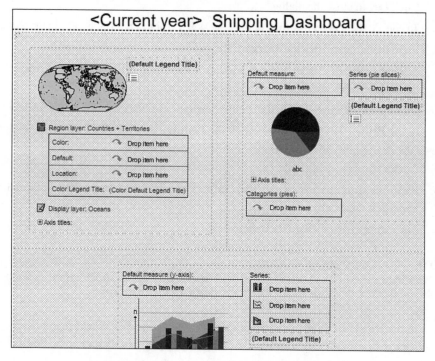

Figure 2.2   Initial dashboard design

Step 4: Set Up the Returned/Shipped Ratio Query

This query will retrieve the quantity sold and quantity returned for each country in order to calculate the ratio of items returned to items sold. This will be displayed on the dashboard's map.

After we added the three data containers to the dashboard, three new queries were created for each of them. In the next three steps, we will customize the queries that are associated with each object.

1. In the **Explorer Bar**, mouse over the **Query Explorer** tab and select the **Queries** folder.

2. Rename **Query1** to **Returned/Shipped_Ratio_by_Country**.

3. Double-click on the query to open the query definition.

4.   From the **Source** tab of the **Insertable Objects** pane, expand the **Employee by region** dimension and the **Employee by region** hierarchy within the **Sales** namespace.

COGNOS 8 NOTE   The **Employee by region** dimension is called **Employee (by region)**.

---

5.   Drag the **Country** level into the **Data Items** pane in the work area.

6.   Expand the **Time** dimension and the **Time** hierarchy.

7.   Drag the **Year** level into the **Data Items** pane in the work area.

8.   Expand the **Sales fact** measure dimension and drag **Quantity** to the **Data Items** pane.

9.   Expand the **Returned items** namespace and the **Returned items** measure dimension.

10. Drag **Return quantity** into the **Data Items** pane.

11. From the **Toolbox** tab of the **Insertable Objects** pane, drag a **Data Item** object into the **Data Items** pane.

     The Data Item Expression dialog box is displayed.

12. Using items from the **Data Items** tab on the **Available Components** pane, add the following expression in the **Expression Definition** pane:

     ```
     [Return quantity] / [Quantity]
     ```

13. Validate the expression and click **OK** to close the dialog box.

14. In the **Properties** pane, change the **Name** property to **Return/Ship Ratio**.

15. Change the **Aggregate Function** property to **Calculated**.

16. From the **Run** menu, select **View Tabular Data** to test your query.

     Your result should be similar to what's shown in Figure 2.3.

17. Close **IBM Cognos Viewer** to return to your report design.

Step 5: Set Up the Returns by Product Line Query

This query will count the number of items returned by both the product line and the reason that the customer returned the items. This will be displayed in the pie chart of the dashboard.

1.   In the **Explorer Bar**, mouse over the **Query Explorer** tab and select the **Queries** folder.

2.   Rename **Query2** to **Returns_by_Product_Line**.

3.   Double-click on the query to open the query definition.

4.   From the **Source** tab of the **Insertable Objects** pane, expand the **Products** dimension and the **Products** hierarchy within the **Returned items** namespace.

COGNOS 8 NOTE   The **Products** dimension and hierarchy are both called **Product**.

Country	Year	Quantity	Return quantity	Return/Ship Ratio
United States	2004	2,653,096	61,659	0.0232404
Canada	2004	979,581	15,364	0.01568426
Mexico	2004	522,235	12,245	0.0234473
Brazil	2004	415,979	6,221	0.01495508
Japan	2004	1,217,594	26,702	0.02193013
Singapore	2004	750,056	18,769	0.02502346
Korea	2004	840,150	15,053	0.01791704
China	2004	1,128,544	20,614	0.01826601
Australia	2004			
Netherlands	2004	582,440	8,431	0.01447531
Sweden	2004	403,987	11,245	0.02783505
Finland	2004	640,898	16,166	0.02522398
France	2004	1,229,528	26,126	0.0212488
Germany	2004	1,003,083	14,935	0.0148891
Switzerland	2004	5,450,263	42,085	0.00772165
United Kingdom	2004	1,012,612	24,386	0.02408227
Belgium	2004			
Austria	2004	324,921	9,411	0.02896396
Italy	2004	525,861	10,895	0.0207184
Spain	2004	493,902	12,716	0.025746

Figure 2.3   Returned/shipped ratio query results

5. Drag the **Product line** level into the **Data Items** pane in the work area.

6. Expand the **Time** dimension and the **Time** hierarchy.

7. Drag the **Year** level into the **Data Items** pane in the work area.

8. Expand the **Return reason** dimension and the **Return reason** hierarchy.

9. Drag the **Reason description** level into the **Data Items** pane.

COGNOS 8 NOTE   The **Reason description** level is called **Return reason**.

---

10. Expand the **Returned items** measure dimension.

11. Drag **Return quantity** into the **Data Items** pane.

12. From the **Run** menu, select **View Tabular Data** to test your query.

    Your results should resemble what's shown in Figure 2.4.

13. Close **IBM Cognos Viewer** to return to your report design.

Step 6: Set Up the Shipping Volume by Month Query

This query will retrieve all the months in the last year in the database and the expected and actual shipping volumes.

Product line	Year	Reason description	Return quantity
Camping Equipment	2004	Defective product	6,056
Personal Accessories	2004	Defective product	12,399
Outdoor Protection	2004	Defective product	53,932
Golf Equipment	2004	Defective product	891
Camping Equipment	2004	Incomplete product	6,802
Personal Accessories	2004	Incomplete product	5,420
Outdoor Protection	2004	Incomplete product	200
Golf Equipment	2004	Incomplete product	1,604
Camping Equipment	2004	Wrong product ordered	27,149
Personal Accessories	2004	Wrong product ordered	16,762
Outdoor Protection	2004	Wrong product ordered	4,989
Golf Equipment	2004	Wrong product ordered	2,563
Camping Equipment	2004	Wrong product shipped	13,602
Personal Accessories	2004	Wrong product shipped	19,244
Outdoor Protection	2004	Wrong product shipped	1,950
Golf Equipment	2004	Wrong product shipped	1,954
Camping Equipment	2004	Unsatisfactory product	7,357
Personal Accessories	2004	Unsatisfactory product	6,771
Outdoor Protection	2004	Unsatisfactory product	161,540
Golf Equipment	2004	Unsatisfactory product	1,838

Figure 2.4   Returns by product line query results

1. In the **Explorer Bar**, mouse over the **Query Explorer** tab and select the **Queries** folder.

2. Rename **Query3** to **Shipping_Volume_by_Month**.

3. Double-click on the query to open the query definition.

4. From the **Source** tab of the **Insertable Objects** pane, expand the **Time** dimension and the **Time** hierarchy in the **Inventory** namespace.

5. Drag the **Year** level into the **Data Items** pane in the work area.

6. From the **Source** tab of the **Insertable Objects** pane, expand the **Month** level.

COGNOS 8 NOTE   Drag the **Month** level into the **Data Items** pane and skip step 7. The caption of the Month level in version 10 contains both the month and the year, so you would need to explicitly define the month name attribute.

---

7. Drag the **Month** attribute into the **Data Items** pane.

8. In the **Insertable Objects** pane, expand the **Inventory fact** measure dimension.

9. Drag **Quantity shipped** into the **Data Items** pane.

10. From the **Source** tab, expand the **Product forecast** namespace and **Product forecast fact** measure dimension.

11. Drag **Expected volume** into the **Data Items** pane.

12. From the **Run** menu, select **View Tabular Data** to test your query.

Compare your results to those shown in Figure 2.5.

Year	Month	Quantity shipped	Expected volume
2004	April	1,507,285	1,294,250
2004	August	1,723,209	1,441,275
2004	December	1,844,284	1,534,885
2004	February	1,608,152	1,434,440
2004	January	1,575,400	1,224,340
2004	July	1,735,888	1,500,970
2004	June	1,860,657	1,562,440
2004	March	1,673,653	1,437,240
2004	May	1,736,204	1,430,725
2004	November	1,723,698	1,410,205
2004	October	1,529,071	1,314,295
2004	September	1,643,052	1,396,265
2005	April	1,893,842	1,632,720
2005	August	1,945,482	1,595,430
2005	December	2,160,019	1,806,500
2005	February	2,238,935	1,873,820
2005	January	2,016,119	1,508,210
2005	July	1,641,831	1,535,740
2005	June	1,866,577	1,632,885
2005	March	1,980,088	1,751,235

Figure 2.5   Shipping volume by month query results

13. Close **IBM Cognos Viewer** to return to your report design.

Step 7: Add Data Items to the Dashboard

With each query created, the data items can be added to the page layout, and master-detail relationships can be created between the graphic data containers and the report page with the current year.

1. In the **Explorer Bar**, mouse over the **Page Explorer** tab and select **Page1**.

2. From the **Data Items** tab of the **Insertable Objects** pane, drag **Country** from the **Returned/Shipped_Ratio_by_Country** query into the **Location** drop zone of the map.

3. Drag **Return/Ship Ratio** into the **Color** drop zone.

    Before setting the master-detail relationship, make sure that you have selected an object inside the map.

4. From the **Data** menu, select **Master Detail Relationships**.

    The dialog box to link the years together is displayed.

5. In the top center of the dialog box, click the **New Link** button.

    An arrow defining the link between the two queries is displayed.

6. In the **Detail** pane, click **Year** so that Current year and Year are linked.

7. Click **OK** to close the dialog box.

   Now we will build the pie chart.

8. From the **Data Items** tab, drag **Reason description** from the **Returns_by_Product_Line** query into the **Series (pie slices)** drop zone of the pie chart.

9. Drag **Return quantity** into the **Default measure** drop zone of the pie chart.

10. Drag **Product line** into the **Categories (pies)** drop zone.

11. Verify that an item inside the pie chart is selected in the work area, and from the **Data** menu, select **Master Detail Relationship**.

12. Click **New Link**.

13. Click **Year** to filter the year by Current year.

14. Click **OK** to close the Master Detail Relationship dialog box.

    Now we can build the third object on the dashboard, the combination chart.

15. From the **Data Items** tab, drag **Quantity shipped** from the **Shipping_Volume_by_Month** into the **Series** drop zone of the combination chart.

    This series will create a bar for the quantities shipped.

16. Drag **Expected volume** into the second **Series** drop zone.

    This series will create a line for the expected volumes.

17. Click the icon for the third series and press the **Delete** key on the keyboard to remove it since we do not need a series to show as an area chart.

18. Drag **Year** into the **Categories (x-axis)** drop zone.

19. Drag **Month** as a nested item under **Year**.

20. Verify that an item inside the combination chart is selected in the work area, and from the **Data** menu, select **Master Detail Relationship**.

21. Click **New Link**.

22. Click **Year** to filter the year by Current year.

23. Click **OK** to close the Master Detail Relationship dialog box.

24. From the **Run** menu, select **Run Report – HTML** to compare the dashboard to what's shown in Figure 2.6.

    Looking at the report, there are a number of changes to make for the formatting to display the information correctly.

    Also, the requestor wants to be able to display all of this on one screen of a monitor using a 1024x768 resolution.

25. Close **IBM Cognos Viewer** to return to your report design.

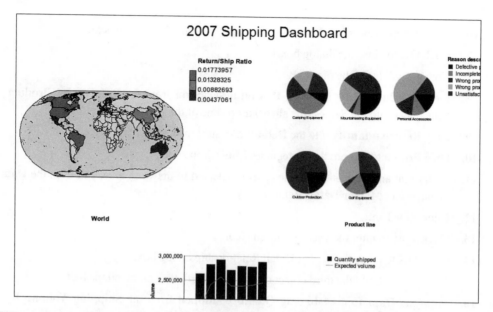

Figure 2.6   Dashboard with all objects added

Step 8: Fix the Size of the Objects

To fix the size of the objects, we have about 500 pixels to use for the height of the dashboard and 950 pixels in width. With the table having padding of 25 pixels on all sides, we can allocate 200 pixels for the height of each data container and 900 for the width.

1. In the work area, click in the lower-right corner of the **Map** object to select the entire map.

2. In the **Properties** pane, double-click the **Size & Overflow** property.

    The Size & Overflow dialog box is displayed.

3. Set the **Height** to **200 px** and the **Width** to **450 px**.

4. Click **OK** to close the dialog box.

5. Click in the lower-right corner of the **Pie Chart** object to select the chart.

6. In the **Properties** pane, double-click the **Size & Overflow** property.

    The Size & Overflow dialog box is displayed.

7. Set the **Height** to **200 px** and the **Width** to **450 px**.

8. Click **OK** to close the dialog box.

9. Click in the lower-right corner of the combination chart to select the chart.

10. In the **Properties** pane, double-click the **Size & Overflow** property.

    The Size & Overflow dialog box is displayed.

11. Set the **Height** to **200 px** and the **Width** to **900 px**.

12. Click **OK** to close the dialog box.

13. From the **Run** menu, select **Run Report – HTML** to view the dashboard and compare it to what's shown in Figure 2.7.

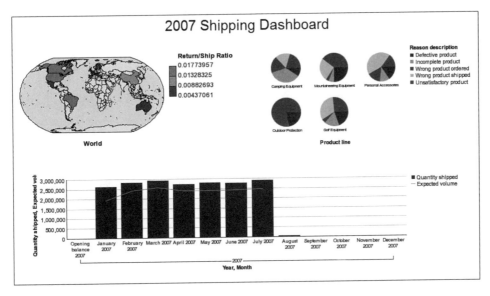

Figure 2.7   Resized dashboard

Now that the objects on the dashboard are the correct size, the formatting of each of the three objects needs to change too.

14. Close **IBM Cognos Viewer** to return to your report design.

Step 9: Format the Map

To begin, the palette needs to change to reflect the proper expectations for performance. The results should be displayed as a percentage. Also, the axis and the title need to reflect the requirements.

1. In the **Map** object in the work area, click **Region layer: Countries + Territories**.

2. Set the **Color Legend Title** property to **Hide**.

3. In the **Properties** pane, double-click the **Palette** property.

   The Palette dialog box is displayed.

   This is where the service commitment levels are added to the report to show how close the different countries are to meeting these numbers.

4. In the **Palette Type** area, remove the check mark next to **Percentage**.

   This will allow you to add specific target numbers for the commitment levels.

Any countries with returns less than or equal to 1.1 percent of items shipped is performing very well and within service commitments and should be displayed on the map as green.

5. In the **Palette** pane, click the first color (Red).

6. In the lower-right area of the dialog box, click **Color**.

   The Color dialog box is displayed.

7. Click the **Named Colors** tab.

8. Click **Green**.

9. Click **OK** to close the dialog box.

10. In the **Palette** pane, click the first boundary (33.33).

11. Change the numeric boundary to **0.011**.

12. Click the second boundary (66.66).

   Any countries with a returned to shipped ratio greater than 1.5 percent are not in compliance with the commitment levels and should be investigated further. These countries should be displayed as red.

13. Change the numeric boundary to **0.015**.

14. In the **Palette** pane, click the last Color (pale green).

15. Click **Color** to open the Color dialog box.

16. Click the **Named Colors** tab.

17. Click **Red**.

   The Palette dialog box should look like Figure 2.8.

   Even though the boundary numbers have been rounded, they will still work appropriately in the map.

18. Click **OK** to close the Palette dialog box.

   Now that the colors have been set, the ratio numbers should be formatted as a percentage.

19. Select the **Return/Ship Ratio** in the work area.

20. In the **Properties** pane, double-click the **Data Format** property.

   The Data Format dialog box is displayed.

21. Change the **Format Type** option to **Percent**.

22. In the **Properties** pane of the dialog box, change the **No. of decimal places** property to **3**.

23. Click **OK** to close the dialog box.

   Finally, the other map attributes should be changed to match the requirements.

24. In the **Properties** pane, click **Select Ancestor**.

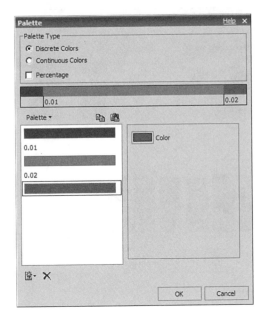

Figure 2.8 Redesigned map palette

25. Select the **Map** object from the list.

26. Set the **Title** property to **Show**.

27. Set the **Axis Title** property to **Hide**.

28. Verify that the **Tooltips** property is set to **Show**.

29. In the work area, double-click on the newly created text item at the top of the map object. The Text dialog box is displayed.

30. Type **Returned to Shipped Ratio by Country** and click **OK** to close the dialog box.

31. In the work area, click the **Legend** object.

32. On the toolbar, change the font size for the legend to **8 pt**.

33. In the **Properties** pane, change the **Legend Title** property to **Hide**.

34. From the **Run** menu, select **Run Report – HTML** to view the dashboard. Figure 2.9 shows the completed map.

35. Close **IBM Cognos Viewer** to return to your report design.

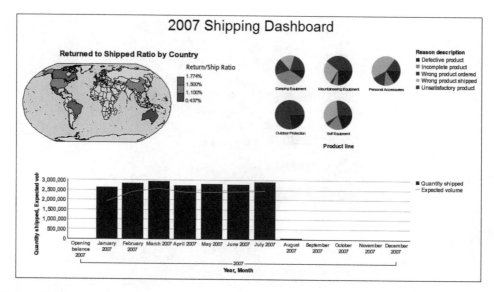

Figure 2.9   Completed map

Step 10: Format the Pie Chart

The pie chart should have the legend in a different position to take advantage of the whitespace in the region, and the text in the chart needs to change to make it easier to read.

1. In the work area, click the **Legend** object in the pie chart to select it.

    With five different product lines, the legend can be displayed explicitly in the place of a sixth pie chart.

2. In the **Properties** pane, change the **Absolute Position** property to **Yes**.

3. Change the **Right Position (px)** property to **450**.

NOTE   The right position needs to change before the left position or you will receive an error stating that the left position needs to be less than the right position.

---

4. Change the **Left Position (px)** property to **300**.

5. Change the **Top Position (px)** property to **100**.

6. In the **Properties** pane, click **Select Ancestor**.

7. Choose **Pie Chart** to select the object.

8. Set the **Title** property to **Show**.

9. Set the **Axis title** property to **Hide**.

10. In the work area, double-click on the newly created text item at the top of the pie chart object.

    The Text dialog box is displayed.

11. Type **Product Line Returns by Reason** and click **OK** to close the dialog box.

12. In the work area, click the **Pie Labels** in the pie chart object.

13. On the toolbar, change the **Font Size** to **10 pt**.

14. From the **Run** menu, select **Run Report – HTML** to view the dashboard.

    Your result should look similar to Figure 2.10.

15. Close **IBM Cognos Viewer** to return to your report design.

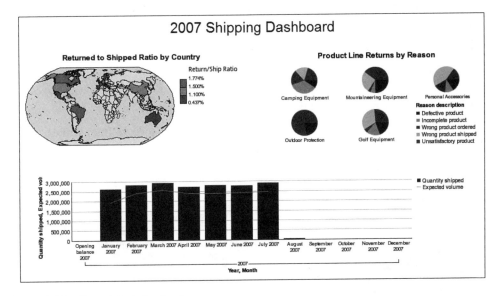

Figure 2.10   Completed pie chart

Step 11: Format the Combination Chart

To improve the chart, the text items need to change. Along with that, the shipping volumes do not slip below 1.5 million units over any one month, so the chart should reflect that to better display the results.

1. In the work area, expand the **Axis Titles** in the combination chart object.

2. From the **Toolbox** tab of the **Insertable Objects** pane, drag a **Text Item** into the first **Axis** drop zone.

    The Text dialog box is displayed.

3. Type **Current Year** and click **OK** to close the dialog box.

4. Drag another **Text Item** object from the **Insertable Objects** pane into the second **Axis** drop zone.

5. Type **Expected vs. Actual** and click **OK** to close the dialog box.

6. In the work area, click in the lower-right corner of the combination chart object to select it.

7. In the **Properties** pane, change the **Title** property to **Show**.

8. In the work area, double-click on the newly created text item at the top of the combination chart object.

    The Text dialog box is displayed.

9. Type **Shipping Volumes Actual vs. Expected** and click **OK** to close the dialog box.

10. In the work area, select the **Y1 Axis** object of the combination chart.

11. In the **Properties** pane, change the **Minimum Value** property to **1500000**.

    Even though we added the Month attribute into the Categories, the caption (which includes the year) is displayed in the chart. We need to change how the members are displayed.

12. In **Categories (x-axis)**, click **Month** to select it.

13. In the **Properties** pane, change the **Source Type** property to **Data Item Value**.

14. From the **Run** menu, select **Run Report – HTML** to view the dashboard. Figure 2.11 shows the completed column chart.

Figure 2.11   Completed column chart

15. Close **IBM Cognos Viewer** to return to your report design.

16. Save this report as **Shipping Dashboard**.

The dashboard now graphically displays the key metrics that drive the shipping organization. Now that the dashboard has been built, you can create the reports that provide supporting information for the data on the dashboard. The manager has three reports in mind. These reports should be designed to work independently and then drill-through links can be added to the dashboard.

The next three sections will build the detail reports and the last section will link all of them together.

Prompting from an Entire Hierarchy

To analyze the efficiency of a shipping location, a manager may look at the ratio of items returned to items shipped. An advantage of working with a multidimensional data source is that you can drill from higher- to lower-level details easily. At a corporate level, a manager may want to see ratios on a global, regional, or local basis, depending on the situation. Instead of creating multiple reports, you can create a single report that will allow a user to respond to a prompt at any level of detail.

In addition to being a nice analysis tool, this same report can provide additional details from our dashboard. Figure 2.12 shows how the completed returned/shipped report should look after prompting a user for a location.

Design

We will prompt the user to pick a member from the Employee by region hierarchy. You want to allow users to pick from any level (any time period) and not just a single one, like Year. Another set will list the members that exist one level below the selected one. This set will allow users to see the numbers for a region and all the countries in it. Another user could run the report to look at the employees in a selected city.

The manager would like to see totals of the reasons products were returned, along with the returned/shipped ratio. Since the orders shipped are not directly linked to how they were returned, we will provide totals in list headers along with the ratio.

The list will show details for the sub-location, and totals for the selected location will be displayed at the bottom of the report.

Step-by-Step

After creating the query, the list report will provide more details regarding the returned to shipped ratio by the prompted locations.

Step 1: Start the Report

1. Launch **Report Studio** and select the **GO Data Warehouse (analysis)** package.

2. Click on the **Create New** option.

Volume Returned and Shipped for Americas

Americas Breakdown	Reason description	Return quantity	Quantity
United States -- Return/Ship Ratio: 1.564%		163,362	10,444,575
Returns by Reason for United States	Defective product	26,830	
	Incomplete product	17,712	
	Wrong product ordered	36,987	
	Wrong product shipped	16,068	
	Unsatisfactory product	65,765	
Canada -- Return/Ship Ratio: 1.476%		59,810	4,052,045
Returns by Reason for Canada	Defective product	10,942	
	Incomplete product	8,913	
	Wrong product ordered	16,062	
	Wrong product shipped	7,210	
	Unsatisfactory product	16,683	
Mexico -- Return/Ship Ratio: 1.088%		29,459	2,706,418
Returns by Reason for Mexico	Defective product	4,276	
	Incomplete product	2,189	
	Wrong product ordered	5,180	
	Wrong product shipped	6,357	
	Unsatisfactory product	11,457	
Brazil -- Return/Ship Ratio: 1.342%		22,926	1,708,632
Returns by Reason for Brazil	Defective product	4,124	
	Incomplete product	2,427	
	Wrong product ordered	10,291	

Figure 2.12   Completed returned/shipped report

COGNOS 8 NOTE   The option is **Create a new report or template**.

---

3.   Select the **List** report template and click **OK**.

We will be using the **Sales** and **Returned Items** namespaces inside the **Sales and Marketing (analysis)** folder.

Step 2: Set Up the Returned/Shipped Ratio Query

The query we will use for this report will list a member from the Employee by region dimension selected by the report consumer. Thus, a sub-location query item can display the child members.

1.   In the **Explorer Bar**, mouse over the **Query Explorer** tab and select the **Queries** folder.

2.   Rename **Query1** to **Returned/Shipped_Ratio_by_Location**.

3.   Double-click on the query to open the query definition.

4.   From the **Toolbox** tab of the **Insertable Objects** pane, drag a **Data Item** object into the **Data Items** pane of the work area.

The Data Item Expression dialog box is displayed.

5. In the **Available Components** pane, expand the **Employee by region** dimension within the **Returned items** namespace.

COGNOS 8 NOTE The **Employee by region** dimension is called **Employee (by region)**.

6. Drag the **Employee by region** hierarchy into the **Expression Definition** pane.

7. In the **Expression Definition** pane, add **->?Selected Location?** after the hierarchy.

8. Add **item(** before the expression and **, 0)** after it.

The Expression should look like the following:

```
item (
[Returned items].[Employee by region].[Employee by region]
->?Selected Location?, 0)
```

9. Click the **Validate** button and then **OK** if there are no errors.

10. In the **Properties** pane for the Data Item, change the **Name** property to **Location**.

11. Change the **Aggregate Function** property to **None**.

12. In the **Toolbox** tab of the **Available Components** pane, drag another **Data Item** object into the **Data Items** pane.

13. In the **Expression Definition** pane, create the following expression:

```
children( [Location] )
```

14. Click the **Validate** button and then **OK** if the validation returned no errors.

15. In the **Properties** pane for the Data Item, change the **Name** property to **Sub-location**.

16. Change the **Aggregate Function** property to **None**.

17. In the **Source** tab of the **Insertable Objects** pane, drag the **Reason description** level from the **Returned reason** dimension and the **Returned reason** hierarchy into the **Data Items** pane in the work area.

COGNOS 8 NOTE The **Reason description** level is called **Return reason** in IBM Cognos 8 BI.

18. Expand the **Returned items** measure dimension.

19. Drag **Return quantity** into the **Data Items** pane.

20. Expand the **Sales** namespace and the **Sales fact** measure dimension.

21. Drag **Quantity** to the **Data Items** pane.

22. From the **Toolbox** tab of the **Insertable Objects** pane, drag a **Data Item** object into the **Data Items** pane.

    The Data Item Expression dialog box is displayed.

23. Using items from the **Data Items** tab of the **Available Components** pane, add the following expression in the **Expression Definition** pane:

    ```
    [Return quantity] / [Quantity]
    ```

24. Validate the expression and click **OK** to close the dialog box.

25. In the **Properties** pane, change the **Name** property to **Return/Ship Ratio** and change the **Aggregate Function** property to **Calculated**.

26. From the **Run** menu, select **View Tabular Data** to test your query.

27. Click **OK** to dismiss the warning message and, when prompted, expand **Employee by region** and select **Americas**.

    Match your results to those shown in Figure 2.13.

28. Close **IBM Cognos Viewer** to return to your report design.

Location	Sub-location	Reason description	Return quantity	Quantity	Return/Ship Ratio
Americas	United States	Defective product	26,830	10,444,575	0.0025688
Americas	United States	Incomplete product	17,712		
Americas	United States	Wrong product ordered	36,987		
Americas	United States	Wrong product shipped	16,068		
Americas	United States	Unsatisfactory product	65,765		
Americas	Canada	Defective product	10,942	3,672,987	0.00297905
Americas	Canada	Incomplete product	8,913		
Americas	Canada	Wrong product ordered	16,062	241,497	0.06651014
Americas	Canada	Wrong product shipped	7,210	114,897	0.06275186
Americas	Canada	Unsatisfactory product	16,683	22,664	0.73610131
Americas	Mexico	Defective product	4,276	2,663,519	0.00160539
Americas	Mexico	Incomplete product	2,189		
Americas	Mexico	Wrong product ordered	5,180		
Americas	Mexico	Wrong product shipped	6,357	42,899	0.14818527
Americas	Mexico	Unsatisfactory product	11,457		
Americas	Brazil	Defective product	4,124	1,633,374	0.00252484
Americas	Brazil	Incomplete product	2,427		
Americas	Brazil	Wrong product ordered	10,291	75,258	0.13674294
Americas	Brazil	Wrong product shipped	2,204		
Americas	Brazil	Unsatisfactory product	3,880		

Figure 2.13   Returned/shipped ratio query results

Step 3: Build the List Report

This step creates a standard list report where the list is grouped by both location and sub-location and summarizes the numbers.

1. In the **Explorer Bar**, mouse over the **Page Explorer** tab and select **Page1**.
2. From the **Data Items** tab of the **Insertable Objects** pane, select all the data items in the query and drag them onto the list object in the work area.
3. In the work area, select the **List Column Body** object for both the **Location** and the **Sub-location** data items.
4. From the toolbar, click the **Group/Ungroup** button.
5. Select the **List Column Body** for **Return quantity**, **Quantity**, and **Return/Ship Ratio**.
6. From the toolbar, click the **Summarize** button to display the list of aggregate options and select **Automatic Summary**.

   This will allow you to aggregate the data according to the method defined by the data modeler.

COGNOS 8 NOTE   The **Summarize** toolbar button is the **Aggregate** button and the **Automatic Summary** option is also **Aggregate** in IBM Cognos 8 Report Studio.

---

7. From the **Run** menu, select **Run Report – HTML** to test your report. If prompted, expand **Employee by region** and select **Americas**. Compare the results to what's shown in Figure 2.14.
8. Close **IBM Cognos Viewer** to return to your report design.

Step 4: Format the List Report

We will enhance the list report to emphasize the numbers by moving some to the headers and removing them from the footers.

1. In the work area, select the **List Column Body** for **Location**.
2. On the toolbar, click the **Cut** button to remove Location from the list.

   It will be added as a title for the report.
3. Click the **List Column Body** for **Return quantity** to select it.
4. On the toolbar, click the **Right** button to align the numbers to the right side of the column.
5. From the **Structure** menu, select **Headers & Footers** and then click **List Headers & Footers**.

   The List Headers & Footers dialog box is displayed.

Location	Sub-location	Reason description	Return quantity	Quantity	Return/Ship Ratio
Americas	United States	Defective product	26,830	10,444,575	0.0025688
		Incomplete product	17,712		
		Wrong product ordered	36,987		
		Wrong product shipped	16,068		
		Unsatisfactory product	65,765		
	United States - Summary		163,362	10,444,575	0.01564085
	Canada	Defective product	10,942	3,672,987	0.00297905
		Incomplete product	8,913		
		Wrong product ordered	16,062	241,497	0.06651014
		Wrong product shipped	7,210	114,897	0.06275186
		Unsatisfactory product	16,683	22,664	0.73610131
	Canada - Summary		59,810	4,052,045	0.01476045
	Mexico	Defective product	4,276	2,663,519	0.00160539
		Incomplete product	2,189		
		Wrong product ordered	5,180		
		Wrong product shipped	6,357	42,899	0.14818527
		Unsatisfactory product	11,457		
	Mexico - Summary		29,459	2,706,418	0.01088487
	Brazil	Defective product	4,124	1,633,374	0.00252484
		Incomplete product	2,427		
		Wrong product ordered	10,291	75,258	0.13674294
		Wrong product shipped	2,204		
		Unsatisfactory product	3,880		

Figure 2.14   Initial list report results

6. From the dialog box, select **Sub-location (header)**.

   This will be the area to add the sales information and the ratio.

7. Click **OK** to close the dialog box.

   The totals for the location will now be moved to the top of the report.

8. In the work area, select the **List Header** for **Sub-location**.

9. From the **Structure** menu, select **Headers & Footers** and then click **Split List Row Cell**. The entire row has cells for each column.

   For the header, you want to merge the header for both sub-location and return reason.

10. In the work area, Ctrl-click the first two cells in the **List Header** for the sub-location.

11. From the **Structure** menu, select **Headers & Footers** and then click **Merge List Row Cells**.

    Now you want to move the totals from the footer into the header.

12. From the toolbar, click the **Unlock (currently locked)** button.

13. In the work area, drag the text item **Summary(Return quantity)** from the footer to the matching cell in the header.

NOTE   Be sure to drag the text item and not the cell in which the text item exists. You will not be able to drag and drop the cell.

---

14. Drag **Summary(Quantity)** from the footer to the matching cell in the header.

    Because the quantity sold is not related to returned description details, we will remove it from the detail lines of the report.

15. In the **List Column Body** for **Quantity**, select the **Text Item** named **Quantity**.

16. From the **Properties** pane, change the **Visible** property to **No**.

NOTE   In order to properly calculate the ratio, the quantity cannot be deleted from the list.

---

17. From the **Toolbox** tab of the **Insertable Objects** pane, drag a **Text Item** object to the immediate right of the **Sub-location** data item in the group header.

    The Text Item dialog box is displayed.

18. Type the following text and click **OK**:

    ```
    -- Return/Ship Ratio:
    ```

    Place spaces at the beginning of the text and after the colon for padding.

19. In the work area, select the **Text Item** for **Summary(Return/Ship Ratio)**.

20. From the toolbar, click **Data Format**.

    The Data Format dialog box is displayed.

21. Select the **Percent** format type.

22. In the **Properties** pane, change the **No. of Decimal Places** to **3**.

23. Click **OK** to close the dialog box.

24. Drag **Summary(Return/Ship Ratio)** from the footer into the header to the right of the text item you just added.

    The list report design should look as shown in Figure 2.15.

    Now the column for Return/Ship Ratio can be removed along with the footer.

25. From the toolbar, click the **Lock (currently unlocked)** button.

26. In the work area, select the **List Column Body** for **Return/Ship Ratio**.

27. From the toolbar, click the **Delete** button.

    Now we will remove the sub-location and overall footers from the report. The location footer will display at the bottom of the report if only one location is selected.

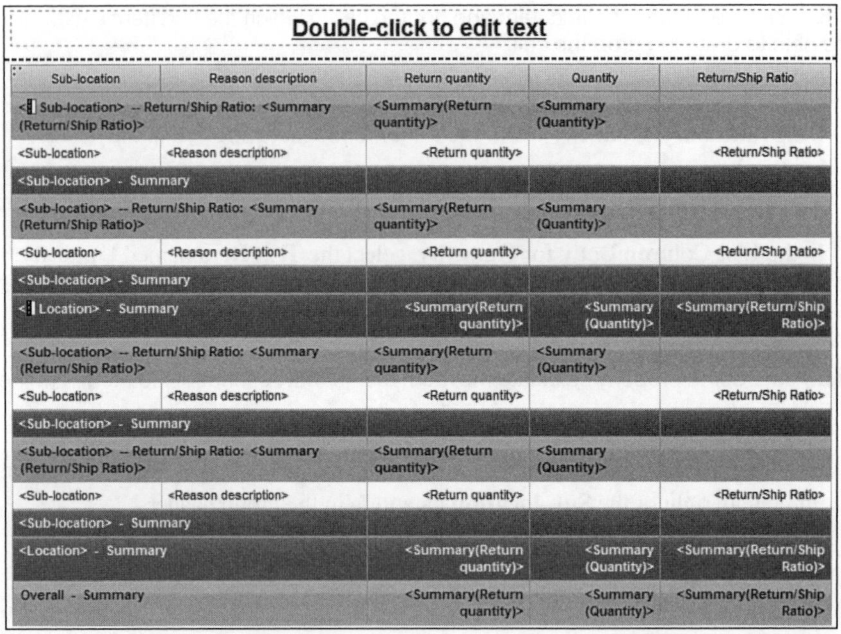

Figure 2.15   New report headings

28. From the **Structure** menu, select **Headers & Footers** and then click **List Headers & Footers**.

    The List Headers & Footers dialog box is displayed.

29. Deselect **Sub-location (footer)** and **Overall footer**.

30. Click **OK** to close the dialog box.

31. From the **Run** menu, select **Run Report – HTML** to test your report. If prompted, expand **Employee by region** and select **Americas**. The results should look like Figure 2.16.

32. Close **IBM Cognos Viewer** to return to your report design.

Step 5: Customize the First Column

To enhance the presentation, the first column of the list will have some additional text.

1. In the work area, select the **List Column Title** for **Sub-location**.

2. In the **Properties** pane, change the **Source Type** from **Data Item Label** to **Report Expression**.

3. Double-click the **Report Expression** property.

    The Report Expression dialog box is displayed.

4. From the **Queries** tab in the **Available Components** pane, drag **Location** to the **Expression Definition** pane.

Sub-location	Reason description	Return quantity	Quantity
United States -- Return/Ship Ratio: 1.564%		163,362	10,444,575
United States	Defective product	26,830	
	Incomplete product	17,712	
	Wrong product ordered	36,987	
	Wrong product shipped	16,068	
	Unsatisfactory product	65,765	
Canada -- Return/Ship Ratio: 1.476%		59,810	4,052,045
Canada	Defective product	10,942	
	Incomplete product	8,913	
	Wrong product ordered	16,062	
	Wrong product shipped	7,210	
	Unsatisfactory product	16,683	
Mexico -- Return/Ship Ratio: 1.088%		29,459	2,706,418
Mexico	Defective product	4,276	
	Incomplete product	2,189	
	Wrong product ordered	5,180	
	Wrong product shipped	6,357	
	Unsatisfactory product	11,457	
Brazil -- Return/Ship Ratio: 1.342%		22,926	1,708,632
Brazil	Defective product	4,124	
	Incomplete product	2,427	
	Wrong product ordered	10,291	
	Wrong product shipped	2,204	

Figure 2.16 Completed return/ship ratio list

5. Add the following text at the end of the expression:

```
+ ' Breakdown'
```

The expression should look like this:

```
[Returned/Shipped_Ratio_by_Location].[Location] + ' Breakdown'
```

6. Validate the expression and click **OK** to close the dialog box. If prompted, expand **Employee by region** and select **Americas**.

7. In the work area, select the **List Column Body** for **Sub-location**.

8. In the **Properties** pane, change the **Source Type** from **Data Item Value** to **Report Expression**.

9. Double-click the **Report Expression** property.

The Report Expression dialog box is displayed.

10. In the **Expression Definition** pane, add the following text:

```
'Returns by Reason for ' +
```

11. From the **Queries** tab of the **Available components** pane, drag **Sub-location** to the **Expression Definition** pane after the text.

The expression should look like this:

```
'Returns by Reason for ' +
[Returned/Shipped_Ratio_by_Location].[Sub-location]
```

12. Validate the expression and click **OK** to close the dialog box.

13. From the **Run** menu, select **Run Report – HTML** to test your report. If prompted, expand **Employee by region** and select **Americas**.

The report should resemble what's shown in Figure 2.17.

Americas Breakdown	Reason description	Return quantity	Quantity
United States -- Return/Ship Ratio: 1.564%		163,362	10,444,575
Returns by Reason for United States	Defective product	26,830	
	Incomplete product	17,712	
	Wrong product ordered	36,987	
	Wrong product shipped	16,068	
	Unsatisfactory product	65,765	
Canada -- Return/Ship Ratio: 1.476%		59,810	4,052,045
Returns by Reason for Canada	Defective product	10,942	
	Incomplete product	8,913	
	Wrong product ordered	16,062	
	Wrong product shipped	7,210	
	Unsatisfactory product	16,683	
Mexico -- Return/Ship Ratio: 1.088%		29,459	2,706,418
Returns by Reason for Mexico	Defective product	4,276	
	Incomplete product	2,189	
	Wrong product ordered	5,180	
	Wrong product shipped	6,357	
	Unsatisfactory product	11,457	
Brazil -- Return/Ship Ratio: 1.342%		22,926	1,708,632
Returns by Reason for Brazil	Defective product	4,124	
	Incomplete product	2,427	
	Wrong product ordered	10,291	
	Wrong product shipped	2,204	

Figure 2.17   List with enhanced details

14. Close **IBM Cognos Viewer** to return to your report design.

Step 6: Build the Header

1. In the work area, double-click the **Text Item** in the header.

The Text dialog box is displayed.

2. Type the following text and click **OK**:

```
Volume Returned and Shipped for
```

Place a space after the phrase for padding.

3. From the **Toolbox** tab of the **Insertable Objects** pane, drag a **Singleton** object to the right of the header text.

4. In the work area, click the **Singleton** object to select it.

5. In the **Properties** pane, change the **Query** property to **Returned/Shipped_Ratio_by_Location**.

6. From the **Data Items** tab of the **Insertable Objects** pane, drag the **Location** data item into the **Singleton** object.

7. To match the style of the rest of the title, click the **Text Item** object for the title to select it.

8. On the toolbar, click the **Pick up Style** button.

9. In the work area, click the **Location** text item in the **Singleton** object.

10. On the toolbar, click the **Apply Style** button.

11. From the **Run** menu, select **Run Report – HTML** to test your report. If prompted, expand **Employee by region** and select **Americas**.

    Compare the results to those shown in Figure 2.18.

12. Close **IBM Cognos Viewer** to return to your report design.

Volume Returned and Shipped for Americas			
Americas Breakdown	Reason description	Return quantity	Quantity
United States -- Return/Ship Ratio: 1.564%		163,362	10,444,575
Returns by Reason for United States	Defective product	26,830	
	Incomplete product	17,712	
	Wrong product ordered	36,987	
	Wrong product shipped	16,068	
	Unsatisfactory product	65,765	
Canada -- Return/Ship Ratio: 1.476%		59,810	4,052,045
Returns by Reason for Canada	Defective product	10,942	
	Incomplete product	8,913	
	Wrong product ordered	16,062	
	Wrong product shipped	7,210	
	Unsatisfactory product	16,683	
Mexico -- Return/Ship Ratio: 1.088%		29,459	2,706,418
Returns by Reason for Mexico	Defective product	4,276	
	Incomplete product	2,189	
	Wrong product ordered	5,180	
	Wrong product shipped	6,357	
	Unsatisfactory product	11,457	
Brazil -- Return/Ship Ratio: 1.342%		22,926	1,708,632
Returns by Reason for Brazil	Defective product	4,124	
	Incomplete product	2,427	
	Wrong product ordered	10,291	

Figure 2.18   Report with header

Step 7: Add the Summary Singleton in the Report Body

This step will create a data container for the location-specific totals. A singleton object will return a single row of data. Since the entire report is focused on one location, the singleton will display the location totals if we only add the numbers.

1. In the work area, click below the **List** object to select the **Page Body** object.

2. In the **Properties** pane, change the **Horizontal Alignment** property to **Center**.

3. From the **Toolbox** tab of the **Insertable Objects** pane, drag a **Singleton** object below the **List** object in the work area.

NOTE   Be careful not to drop the Singleton inside the List.

---

4. In the work area, click the **Singleton** in the page body to select it.

5. In the **Properties** pane, change the **Query** property to **Returned/Shipped_Ratio_ by_Location**.

6. From the **Toolbox** tab of the **Insertable Objects** pane, drag a **Table** object into the new **Singleton** object.

   The Insert Table dialog box is displayed.

7. Change the **Number of columns** to **1**.

8. Change the **Number of rows** to **3**.

9. In the **Table style** section, deselect the **Maximize width** check box.

10. Click **OK** to close the dialog box.

11. From the **Data Items** tab of the **Insertable Objects** pane, drag **Return quantity** into the top row of the table.

12. Drag **Quantity** into the middle row.

13. Drag **Return/Ship Ratio** in the bottom row.

14. Select the **Return/Ship Ratio** data item in the table.

15. From the toolbar, click **Data Format**.

   The Data Format dialog box is displayed.

16. Select the **Percent** format type.

17. In the **Properties** pane, change the **No. of Decimal Places** to **3**.

18. From the **Toolbox** tab of the **Insertable Objects** pane, drag a **Text Item** to the left of the **Return quantity** data item in the table.

   The Text dialog box is displayed.

19. Type **Total items returned:** and add a space after the colon.

20. Click **OK**.

21. Drag another **Text Item** object from the **Insertable Objects** pane to the left of the **Quantity** data item in the table.

22. Type **Total items sold:** and add a space after the colon.

23. Click **OK**.

24. Drag a third **Text Item** from the **Insertable Objects** pane to the left of the **Return/Ship Ratio** data item in the table.

25. Type **Return/Ship Ratio:** and add a space after the colon.

26. Click **OK**.

27. To format the table, click an item inside the table object to select it.

28. In the **Properties** pane, click the **Select Ancestor** button.

29. Click the **Table** object in the list.

30. Double-click the **Margin** property.

    The Margin dialog box is displayed.

31. Set all margins to **25** pixels.

32. Click **OK** to close the dialog box.

33. Change the **Horizontal Alignment** property to **Center**.

34. Double-click the **Table Properties** property.

    The Table Properties dialog box is displayed.

35. Deselect the **Collapse Borders** check box.

    The Cell Spacing options are now available.

36. Set the **Cell Spacing** to **10** pixels.

    This adds spacing between the cells within the table itself to make it look as though there are three different singleton items.

37. Click **OK** to close the dialog box.

38. On the toolbar, click the **Bold** button to change all the text in the table to bold weight.

39. From the **Run** menu, select **Run Report – HTML** to test your report. If prompted, expand **Employee by region** and select **Americas**.

    The completed report should look as shown in Figure 2.19.

40. Close **IBM Cognos Viewer** to return to your report design.

41. Save the report as **Return/Ship Ratio by Location**.

Returns by Reason for Canada	Defective product	10,942	
	Incomplete product	8,913	
	Wrong product ordered	16,062	
	Wrong product shipped	7,210	
	Unsatisfactory product	16,683	
Mexico -- Return/Ship Ratio: 1.088%		29,459	2,706,418
Returns by Reason for Mexico	Defective product	4,276	
	Incomplete product	2,189	
	Wrong product ordered	5,180	
	Wrong product shipped	6,357	
	Unsatisfactory product	11,457	
Brazil -- Return/Ship Ratio: 1.342%		22,926	1,708,632
Returns by Reason for Brazil	Defective product	4,124	
	Incomplete product	2,427	
	Wrong product ordered	10,291	
	Wrong product shipped	2,204	
	Unsatisfactory product	3,880	
Americas - Summary		275,557	18,911,670

Total items returned: 275,557

Total items sold: 18,944,382

Return/Ship Ratio: 1.455%

Figure 2.19   Completed returned/shipped report

The Return/Ship Ratio by Location report allows users to analyze this key performance indicator at different levels of detail based on the member selected by the users. The other feature of note in here is that the ability to nest items allowed us to use a table in a singleton object to focus the results to one single query row.

Additional Dimensional Functions

Also, shipping managers are interested in learning more about which specific products are being returned by customers. They would like to see a report in which they can pick a product line, product type, or individual product and see detailed return reasons for a selected time period (year, quarter, or month). Figure 2.20 shows the completed design of this report.

Design

Using a dimensional source, prompting should allow users to select items from both the Time and the Product dimensions. As in the previous example, we will also display the time periods that are one level below the selected item.

In the previous example, we used data items in our query definition to provide customized calculations. These data items are created and used in the same manner if our data model is relational or dimensional. IBM Cognos Report Studio allows you to create calculations that are uniquely dimensional. This will help us create calculations that will create data items that work on sets or tuples.

2005 Returns for Products Under Camping Equipment						
Return quantity		Q1 2005	Q2 2005	Q3 2005	Q4 2005	2005
Camping Equipment	Unsatisfactory product	6,318	2,134	4,339	6,291	19,082
	Wrong product ordered	2,835	1,914	4,491	6,247	15,487
	Wrong product shipped	4,131	2,208	3,674	3,044	13,057
	Incomplete product	3,468	3,676	1,833	2,394	11,371
	Defective product	1,719	1,294	2,257	1,989	7,259
	Returns for Camping Equipment	**18,471**	**11,226**	**16,594**	**19,965**	**66,256**
Cooking Gear	Unsatisfactory product	4,713	398	1,403	3,367	9,881
	Wrong product shipped	904	1,460	2,373	1,817	6,554
	Incomplete product	2,193	2,044	769	1,318	6,324
	Defective product	593	173	521	1,180	2,467
	Wrong product ordered		135		1,806	1,941
	Returns for Cooking Gear	**8,403**	**4,210**	**5,066**	**9,488**	**27,167**
TrailChef Water Bag	Unsatisfactory product	1,462			2,661	4,123
	Defective product					
	Wrong product shipped					
	Incomplete product					
	Wrong product ordered					
	Returns for TrailChef Water Bag	**1,462**			**2,661**	**4,123**
TrailChef Water Bag 1110	Unsatisfactory product	1,462			2,661	4,123
	Defective product					

Figure 2.20   Completed returns by product and reason report

The query will show the time period and product information selected by the report consumer. The children of the time period will be added along with all the descendants of the selected product information. The query results will be displayed in a crosstab to allow a quick analysis and comparison of the numbers.

Step-by-Step

Step 1: Start the Report

1. Launch **Report Studio** and select the **GO Data Warehouse (analysis)** package.
2. Click on the **Create New** option.

COGNOS 8 NOTE   The option is **Create a new report or template**.

---

3. Select the **Crosstab** report template and click **OK**.

   We will be using the **Returned Items** namespace inside the **Sales and Marketing (analysis)** folder.

Step 2: Set Up the Returns by Product Query

The report will start with a query that works with the three regular dimensions: Time, Products, and Return Reason. After the dimensions are built, the measure is added to the query.

1. In the **Explorer Bar**, mouse over the **Query Explorer** tab and select the **Queries** folder.

2. Rename **Query1** to **Product_Returns_by_Product**.

3. In the work area, double-click the query to open the query definition.

4. From the **Toolbox** tab of the **Insertable Objects** pane, drag a **Data Item** object into the **Data Items** pane of the work area.

   The Data Item Expression dialog box is displayed.

5. In the **Available Components** pane, expand the **Time** dimension within the **Returned items** namespace.

6. Drag the **Time** hierarchy from the **Available Components** pane into the **Expression Definition** pane.

7. In the **Expression Definition** pane, add **->?Selected Time?** after the hierarchy.

   The Expression should be this:

   ```
   [Returned items].[Time].[Time]->?Selected Time?
   ```

8. Click **Validate** and then **OK** if there are no errors.

9. In the **Properties** pane, change the **Name** property to **Time** and change the **Aggregate Function** property to **None**.

10. In the **Toolbox** tab of the **Available Components** pane, drag a **Data Item** object into the **Data Items** pane.

    The Data Item Expression dialog box is displayed.

11. In the **Expression Definition** pane, type the following function:

    ```
    descendants ( [Time], 1 )
    ```

    This function shows all the members that are one level below the select Time dimension member.

12. Click **Validate** and **OK** if the validation returned no errors.

13. In the **Properties** pane, change the **Name** property to **Time Group**, and change the **Aggregate Function** property to **None**.

    With the time periods selected, you will add the product details below the selected product information.

14. In the **Toolbox** tab of the **Available Components** pane, drag a **Data Item** object into the **Data Items** pane.

    The Data Item Expression dialog box is displayed.

15. In the **Available Components** pane, expand the **Products** dimension.

16. Drag the **Products** hierarchy from the **Available Components** pane into the **Expression Definition** pane.

COGNOS 8 NOTE   The **Products** dimension and hierarchy are called **Product**.

---

17. In the **Expression Definition** pane, add **->?Selected Product?** after the hierarchy. The Expression should be this:

    ```
    [Returned items].[Products].[Products]->?Selected Product?
    ```

18. Click **Validate** and then **OK** if there are no errors.

19. In the **Properties** pane, change the **Name** property to **Product** and change the **Aggregate Function** property to **None**.

    Now we will show all the product information below the selected item, as well as the selected item.

20. In the **Toolbox** tab of the **Available Components** pane, drag a **Data Item** object into the **Data Items** pane.

    The Data Item Expression dialog box is displayed.

21. In the **Expression Definition** pane, type the following function:

    ```
    descendants ( [Product], 1, self after )
    ```

22. Click **Validate** and **OK** if the validation returned no errors.

23. In the **Properties** pane, change the **Name** property to **Product Details** and change the **Aggregate Function** property to **None**.

24. In the **Source** tab of the **Insertable Objects** pane, expand the **Return reason** dimension and the **Return reason** hierarchy.

25. Drag the **Reason description** level into the **Data Items** pane in the work area.

COGNOS 8 NOTE   The **Reason description** level is named **Return reason** in IBM Cognos 8 BI.

If you click on the **Return reason** data item, you will see in the properties that you created a level set that displays all Return reason members.

26. In the **Source** tab of the **Insertable Objects** pane, expand the **Returned items** measure dimension.

27. Drag **Return quantity** into the **Data Items** pane.

28. From the **Run** menu, select **View Tabular Data** to test your query. When prompted, expand **Products** and select **Camping Equipment**. Also, select **Time** and click **OK**.

COGNOS 8 NOTE   The **Products** member is **Products (all)**, and the **Time** member is **Time dimension (all)** in IBM Cognos 8 BI.

The results of the query should resemble what's shown in Figure 2.21.

29. Close **IBM Cognos Viewer** to return to your report design.

Time	Time Group	Product	Product Details	Reason description	Return quantity
Time	2004	Camping Equipment	Lanterns	Wrong product shipped	4,133
Time	2004	Camping Equipment	Lanterns	Defective product	1,667
Time	2004	Camping Equipment	Lanterns	Unsatisfactory product	896
Time	2004	Camping Equipment	Lanterns	Wrong product ordered	4,204
Time	2004	Camping Equipment	Lanterns	Incomplete product	1,397
Time	2004	Camping Equipment	Flicker Lantern	Wrong product shipped	380
Time	2004	Camping Equipment	Flicker Lantern	Defective product	58
Time	2004	Camping Equipment	Flicker Lantern	Unsatisfactory product	137
Time	2004	Camping Equipment	Flicker Lantern	Wrong product ordered	254
Time	2004	Camping Equipment	Flicker Lantern	Incomplete product	107
Time	2004	Camping Equipment	Flicker Lantern 41110	Wrong product shipped	380
Time	2004	Camping Equipment	Flicker Lantern 41110	Defective product	58
Time	2004	Camping Equipment	Flicker Lantern 41110	Unsatisfactory product	137
Time	2004	Camping Equipment	Flicker Lantern 41110	Wrong product ordered	254
Time	2004	Camping Equipment	Flicker Lantern 41110	Incomplete product	107
Time	2004	Camping Equipment	EverGlow Double	Wrong product shipped	
Time	2004	Camping Equipment	EverGlow Double	Defective product	
Time	2004	Camping Equipment	EverGlow Double	Unsatisfactory product	8
Time	2004	Camping Equipment	EverGlow Double	Wrong product ordered	102
Time	2004	Camping Equipment	EverGlow Double	Incomplete product	

Figure 2.21   Product_Returns_by_Product query results

Step 3: Build the Crosstab Report

1. In the **Explorer Bar**, mouse over the **Page Explorer** tab and select **Page1**.
2. From the **Data Items** tab of the **Insertable Objects** pane, drag **Time Group** into the **Columns** area in the crosstab.
3. Drag **Return quantity** into the **Measures** area of the crosstab.
4. Drag **Product** into the **Rows** area of the crosstab.
5. Drag **Product Details** into the **Rows** area below **Product**.

This is known as making **Product Details** a peer of **Product**. This will list the product you selected in the row first followed by all the child members.

6. In the work area, click **Product Details** in the rows to select it.

7. In the **Properties** pane, double-click the **Level Indentation** property.

    A dialog box is displayed.

8. Change the **Indentation type** property to **Based on the level in the hierarchy**.

9. Click **OK** to close the dialog box.

    Since **Product** and **Product Details** are treated as separate sets, we will need to nest **Return reason** under both sets.

10. From the **Data Items** tab of the **Insertable Object** pane, drag **Reason description** to the right of **Product** in the rows.

    This is known as nesting the **Return** description within **Product**.

11. Drag **Reason description** to the right of **Product Details** in the rows.

    The crosstab should look like Figure 2.22.

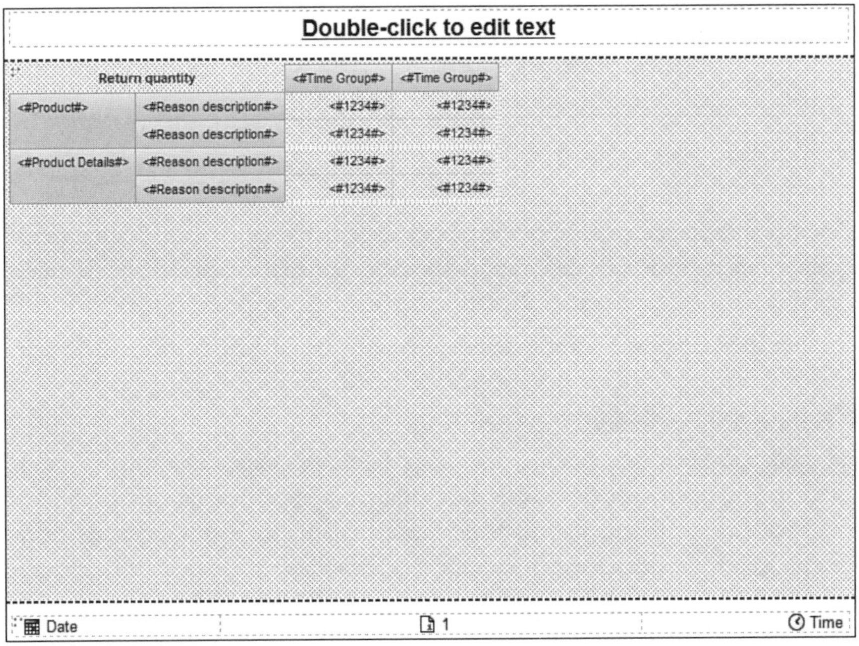

Double-click to edit text			

Return quantity		<#Time Group#>	<#Time Group#>
<#Product#>	<#Reason description#>	<#1234#>	<#1234#>
	<#Reason description#>	<#1234#>	<#1234#>
<#Product Details#>	<#Reason description#>	<#1234#>	<#1234#>
	<#Reason description#>	<#1234#>	<#1234#>

Date   1   Time

Figure 2.22   Initial crosstab design

12. From the **Run** menu, select **Run Report – HTML** to test your report. If prompted, expand **Products** and select **Camping Equipment**. Also, expand **Time** and select **2005**. The report output should have values similar to those shown in Figure 2.23.

Return quantity		Unspecified 2005	Q1 2005	Q2 2005	Q3 2005	Q4 2005
Camping Equipment	Unsatisfactory product		6,318	2,134	4,339	6,291
	Defective product		1,719	1,294	2,257	1,989
	Wrong product shipped		4,131	2,208	3,674	3,044
	Incomplete product		3,468	3,676	1,833	2,394
	Wrong product ordered		2,835	1,914	4,491	6,247
Cooking Gear	Unsatisfactory product		4,713	398	1,403	3,367
	Defective product		593	173	521	1,180
	Wrong product shipped		904	1,460	2,373	1,817
	Incomplete product		2,193	2,044	769	1,318
	Wrong product ordered			135		1,806
TrailChef Water Bag	Unsatisfactory product		1,462			2,661
	Defective product					
	Wrong product shipped					
	Incomplete product					
	Wrong product ordered					
TrailChef Water Bag 1110	Unsatisfactory product		1,462			2,661
	Defective product					
	Wrong product shipped					
	Incomplete product					
	Wrong product ordered					

Figure 2.23   Initial report results

Notice that the return descriptions are all listed in the same order. To improve the value of the report, the Return descriptions should be sorted for each row and the selected time period.

13. Close **IBM Cognos Viewer** to return to your report design.

Step 4: Refine the Sorting on the Row Data

In the preceding query, we created three group sets that work independently of one another. Now you want to arrange the Return reasons in descending order based on the product information in the row and the selected time period. To do this, we will define the set sorting to be a tuple (intersection) of the return reason, selected time, and quantity returned.

1. In the **Explorer Bar**, mouse over the **Query Explorer** tab and select **Product_ Returns_by_Product**.

A tuple represents the intersection of members, so the **Time** set in the query needs to be cast as a member before the set can be sorted by the selected time period.

2.   From the **Toolbox** tab of the **Insertable Objects** pane, drag a **Query Calculation** object into the **Data Items** pane of the work area.

A dialog box is displayed.

COGNOS 8 NOTE   In the prior version, IBM Cognos Report Studio has a Toolbox object called **Calculated Member**, which would reduce the number of steps required to create the **Selected Time** data item. In this case, drag a **Calculated Member** object into the **Data Items** pane. Skip the next step and continue with step 4.

---

3.   Verify that the **Calculated member** radio button is selected.

4.   In the **Name** field, type **Selected Time**.

5.   In the **Hierarchy** drop-down list, select the **Time** hierarchy from the **Returned Items** namespace.

6.   Click **OK** and the Calculated Member Expression dialog box is displayed.

7.   In the **Expression Definition** pane, type the following function:

```
item ( [Time], 0 )
```

This function returns the first member of a set. Since **Time** is selected as a single item, there will be only one item in the set.

8.   Click **Validate** and **OK** if the validation returned no errors. If prompted, expand **Products** and select **Camping Equipment**. Also, expand **Time** and select **2005**.

9.   In the work area, click **Reason description** to select it.

10. In the **Properties** pane, double-click the **Set Sorting** property to open the dialog box.

11. In the Set Sorting dialog box, change the **Sort type** to **Descending**.

12. In the **Sort by** section, select the **Intersection (tuple)** radio button and click the ellipsis for the selection.

The Members dialog box is displayed.

We will select the newly created **Selected Time** member and **Returned items** measure for the intersection values.

13. From the **Available members and measures** pane, expand **Sales and Marketing (analysis)** and **Returned Items** namespaces.

14. Drag **Return quantity** from the **Returned items** measure dimension to the **Intersection members and measures** pane.

15. From the **Calculated members and measures** tab in the **Available members and measures** pane, drag **Selected Time** to the pane on the right.

16. Click **OK** to close the dialog box.

Because the returned reasons are nested inside the product sets, they are considered in the overall context of the sorting for the items returned and we will not create a member for the sorting.

17. Click **OK** to close the Set Sorting dialog box.

18. From the **Run** menu, select **Run Report – HTML** to test your report. If prompted, expand **Products** and select **Camping Equipment**. Also, expand **Time** and select **2005**. The report output should have values similar to Figure 2.24.

Return quantity		Unspecified 2005	Q1 2005	Q2 2005	Q3 2005	Q4 2005
Camping Equipment	Unsatisfactory product		6,318	2,134	4,339	6,291
	Wrong product ordered		2,835	1,914	4,491	6,247
	Wrong product shipped		4,131	2,208	3,674	3,044
	Incomplete product		3,468	3,676	1,833	2,394
	Defective product		1,719	1,294	2,257	1,989
Cooking Gear	Unsatisfactory product		4,713	398	1,403	3,367
	Wrong product shipped		904	1,460	2,373	1,817
	Incomplete product		2,193	2,044	769	1,318
	Defective product		593	173	521	1,180
	Wrong product ordered			135		1,806
TrailChef Water Bag	Unsatisfactory product		1,462			2,661
	Defective product					
	Wrong product shipped					
	Incomplete product					
	Wrong product ordered					
TrailChef Water Bag 1110	Unsatisfactory product		1,462			2,661
	Defective product					
	Wrong product shipped					
	Incomplete product					
	Wrong product ordered					

Figure 2.24   Sorted crosstab report

Notice that the return reasons are sorted in a different order within each product. Now we will add aggregations to summarize the results.

19. Close **IBM Cognos Viewer** to return to your report design.

Step 5: Aggregate the Results

1. In the **Explorer Bar**, mouse over the **Page Explorer** tab and select **Page1**.

Before aggregating the numbers, we want to remove the Unspecified member from the columns.

2. From the toolbar, click the **Suppress** button and the **Suppress Columns Only** option. We still will display all return reasons for each product.

3. In the work area, Ctrl-click each of the **Return reason** sets in the rows of the crosstab.

4. From the toolbar, click the **Summarize** button to display the list of aggregate options and select **Automatic Summary**.

   Two subtotals are created that are nested under **Product** and **Product Details**. The aggregate function allows the dimensional data to be aggregated according to the data model.

COGNOS 8 NOTE   The **Summarize** toolbar button is the **Aggregate** button and the **Automatic Summary** option is also **Aggregate** in IBM Cognos 8 Report Studio.

---

5. Click the first summarized item to select it.

6. In the **Properties** pane, change the **Source Type** to **Report Expression**.

7. Double-click the **Report Expression** property to open the dialog box.

8. In the **Report Expression** pane, type the following function:

   ```
   'Returns for ' + [Product_Returns_by_Product].[Product]
   ```

   This function returns the first member of a set. Since **Product** is selected as a single item, there will be only one item in the set.

9. Click **Validate** and **OK** if the validation returned no errors.

10. Click the second aggregated item to select it.

11. In the **Properties** pane, change the **Source Type** to **Report Expression**.

12. Double-click the **Report Expression** property to open the dialog box.

13. In the **Report Expression** pane, type the following function:

    ```
    'Returns for ' + [Product_Returns_by_Product].[Product Details]
    ```

14. Click **Validate** and **OK** if the validation returned no errors.

15. From the **Data Items** tab of the **Insertable Objects** pane, drag **Time** to the right of **Time Group** in the crosstab columns.

    This creates a peer relationship between **Time** and **Time Group** in the columns.

16. To change the format of the new column to match the aggregations, click one of the blue summarized crosstab node members to select it.

COGNOS 8 NOTE   In the prior version, IBM Cognos Report Studio has different style sheets for formatting of data containers. The summarized crosstab node members are going to have a grey background.

---

17.   On the toolbar, select **Pick Up Style**.

18.   In the columns, click **Time** to select it.

19.   On the toolbar, select **Apply Style**.

20.   In the columns, right-click **Time** to open the shortcut menu.

21.   Choose **Select Member Fact Cells** to choose all the measures associated with Time.

22.   On the toolbar, select **Apply Style**.

23.   From the **Run** menu, select **Run Report – HTML** to test your report. If prompted, expand **Products** and select **Camping Equipment**. Also, expand **Time** and select **2005**. The report output should have values similar to those shown in Figure 2.25.

Return quantity		Q1 2005	Q2 2005	Q3 2005	Q4 2005	2005
Camping Equipment	Unsatisfactory product	6,318	2,134	4,339	6,291	19,082
	Wrong product ordered	2,835	1,914	4,491	6,247	15,487
	Wrong product shipped	4,131	2,208	3,674	3,044	13,057
	Incomplete product	3,468	3,676	1,833	2,394	11,371
	Defective product	1,719	1,294	2,257	1,989	7,259
	Returns for Camping Equipment	**18,471**	**11,226**	**16,594**	**19,965**	**66,256**
Cooking Gear	Unsatisfactory product	4,713	398	1,403	3,367	9,881
	Wrong product shipped	904	1,460	2,373	1,817	6,554
	Incomplete product	2,193	2,044	769	1,318	6,324
	Defective product	593	173	521	1,180	2,467
	Wrong product ordered		135		1,806	1,941
	Returns for Cooking Gear	**8,403**	**4,210**	**5,066**	**9,488**	**27,167**
TrailChef Water Bag	Unsatisfactory product	1,462			2,661	4,123
	Defective product					
	Wrong product shipped					
	Incomplete product					
	Wrong product ordered					
	Returns for TrailChef Water Bag	**1,462**			**2,661**	**4,123**
TrailChef Water Bag 1110	Unsatisfactory product	1,462			2,661	4,123
	Defective product					

Figure 2.25   Completed crosstab example

24.   Close **IBM Cognos Viewer** to return to your report design.

Step 6: Complete the Formatting

1. In the work area, click the title text to select it.

2. In the **Properties** pane, change the **Source Type** to **Report Expression**.

3. Double-click the **Report Expression** property to open the dialog box.

4. In the **Report Expression** pane, type the following function:

```
ParamDisplayValue('Selected Time') +
' Returns for Products Under ' +
ParamDisplayValue('Selected Product')
```

   This function returns the first member of a set. Since **Time** is selected as a single item, there will be only one item in the set.

5. Click **Validate** and **OK** if the validation returned no errors.

6. In the work area, click **Time Group** and Ctrl-click **Time** to select both columns of the crosstab.

7. In the **Properties** pane, change the **Horizontal Alignment** to **Center**.

8. Double-click the **Size & Overflow** property to open the dialog box.

9. Change the **Width** to **70** pixels.

   This will allow for more spacing on the screen and make the crosstab look less cluttered.

10. Click **OK** to close the dialog box.

11. In the work area, click in the center whitespace to select the **Page Body**.

12. In the **Properties** pane, double-click the **Padding** property to open the dialog box.

13. Type **40** pixels in the top padding field to ensure spacing between the title and the details.

14. Click **OK** to close the dialog box.

15. From the toolbar, click **Center**.

16. From the **Run** menu, select **Run Report – HTML** to test your report. If prompted, expand **Products** and select **Camping Equipment**. Also, expand **Time** and select **2005**. The report output should have numbers similar to Figure 2.26.

17. Close **IBM Cognos Viewer** to return to your report design.

18. Save the report as **Product Returns by Time Period**.

Product Returns by Time Period provides an example of using dimensional query calculations to create complex queries that take advantage of sets (edges) and tuples (intersections) to perform complex behaviors when building queries.

2005 Returns for Products Under Camping Equipment

Return quantity		Q1 2005	Q2 2005	Q3 2005	Q4 2005	2005
Camping Equipment	Unsatisfactory product	6,318	2,134	4,339	6,291	19,082
	Wrong product ordered	2,835	1,914	4,491	6,247	15,487
	Wrong product shipped	4,131	2,208	3,674	3,044	13,057
	Incomplete product	3,468	3,676	1,833	2,394	11,371
	Defective product	1,719	1,294	2,257	1,989	7,259
	Returns for Camping Equipment	18,471	11,226	16,594	19,965	66,256
Cooking Gear	Unsatisfactory product	4,713	398	1,403	3,367	9,881
	Wrong product shipped	904	1,460	2,373	1,817	6,554
	Incomplete product	2,193	2,044	769	1,318	6,324
	Defective product	593	173	521	1,180	2,467
	Wrong product ordered		135		1,806	1,941
	Returns for Cooking Gear	8,403	4,210	5,066	9,488	27,167
TrailChef Water Bag	Unsatisfactory product	1,462			2,661	4,123
	Defective product					
	Wrong product shipped					
	Incomplete product					
	Wrong product ordered					
	Returns for TrailChef Water Bag	1,462			2,661	4,123
TrailChef Water Bag 1110	Unsatisfactory product	1,462			2,661	4,123
	Defective product					

Figure 2.26   Final report

Master-Detail Report from Two Separate Lists

Shipping managers are interested in learning more about shipping patterns against expectations. While product forecasts are tracked by sales branch, the manager would like to see the retailers (and their locations) that are receiving the shipments.

The manager would like to be able to see the results for one specific sales branch or all sales branches for a selected time period. Figure 2.27 shows an example of the final report design.

Design

Since the levels of detail are fixed for this report, a relational data model will be queried. Two different queries will be created to retrieve the expected and actual numbers. To simplify the development, two list reports will be created and tested.

After they have been tested and reformatted, one list will be moved into the header of another list and a master-detail relationship will be defined.

Step-by-Step

Step 1: Start the Report

1.   Launch **Report Studio** and select the **GO Data Warehouse (query)** package.

Expected Volume vs. Actual Quantity Shipped for Amsterdam For April 2005		
Retailer	Retailer site	Quantity
Expected Volume for: Amsterdam		48,880
Actual Quantity Shipped for: Amsterdam		59,285
Extra Sport	Wageningen	14,201
Extra Sport - Total		14,201
Sportworld	Deventer	7,455
Sportworld	Beets	2,937
Sportworld	Amstelveen	1,045
Sportworld - Total		11,437
Beter Buitenleven	Amsterdam	6,018
Beter Buitenleven	Marken	4,983
Beter Buitenleven - Total		11,001
Klimgek Bv.	Amsterdam	5,755
Klimgek Bv. - Total		5,755
Kampeer Top Shop	Dronten	5,182
Kampeer Top Shop - Total		5,182
Holland Zonzoekers	Laren	2,993
Holland Zonzoekers - Total		2,993
Topforma	Groningen	2,810
Topforma - Total		2,810
Get Out	Varsseveld	2,794

Figure 2.27   Completed shipping volume by month report

2. Click on **Create New** option.

COGNOS 8 NOTE   The option is **Create a new report or template**.

---

3. Select **List** report template and click **OK**.

   We will be using both the **Product Forecast (query)** and the **Sales (query)** namespaces inside the **Sales and Marketing (query)** folder.

Step 2: Set Up the Expected Volumes by Branch Query

This query will be used by the list which will be the detail in the master-detail relationship, so any filtering will be handled by the second query.

1. In the **Explorer Bar**, mouse over the **Query Explorer** tab and select the **Queries** folder.

2. Rename **Query1** to **Expected_Volume_by_Branch**.

3. Double-click on the query to open the query definition.

4. From the **Source** tab in the **Insertable Objects** pane, drag the following query items from the **Product forecast (query)** namespace into the **Data Items** pane in the work area:

    • **Year** from **Time**

    • **Month** from **Time**

    • **City** from **Branch**

    • **Expected volume** from **Product forecast fact**

COGNOS 8 NOTE   The **Time** query subject is called **Time dimension**.

---

5. In the **Data Items** pane, click **City** to select it.

6. In the **Properties** pane, change the **Name** to **Branch**.

7. Change the **Pre-Sort** property to **Sort ascending**.

8. From the **Run** menu, select **View Tabular Data** to test your query. The query results should match what's shown in Figure 2.28.

9. Close **IBM Cognos Viewer** to return to your report design.

Year	Month	City	Expected volume
2004	April	Amsterdam	40,605
2004	August	Amsterdam	38,480
2004	December	Amsterdam	41,855
2004	February	Amsterdam	42,445
2004	January	Amsterdam	36,125
2004	July	Amsterdam	35,475
2004	June	Amsterdam	35,650
2004	March	Amsterdam	43,720
2004	May	Amsterdam	36,570
2004	November	Amsterdam	44,755
2004	October	Amsterdam	41,880
2004	September	Amsterdam	39,250
2005	April	Amsterdam	48,880
2005	August	Amsterdam	51,105
2005	December	Amsterdam	41,875
2005	February	Amsterdam	55,490
2005	January	Amsterdam	37,220
2005	July	Amsterdam	49,485
2005	June	Amsterdam	55,275
2005	March	Amsterdam	27,885

Figure 2.28   Expected_Volume_by_Branch query results

Step 3: Set Up the Actual Shipped by Branch Query

With the expected volume query providing high-level details about shipping, the actual sales volumes will provide additional details and then become the master query in the report. This query will have static filters for testing purposes that will have parameters added later.

1. In the **Explorer Bar**, mouse over the **Query Explorer** tab and select the **Queries** folder.

2. From the **Insertable Objects** pane, drag a **Query** object to the work area below the other query.

3. Rename **Query1** to **Actual_Shipped_by_Branch**.

4. Double-click on the query to open the query definition.

5. From the **Source** tab of the **Insertable Objects** pane, drag the following query items from the **Sales (query)** namespace into the **Data Items** pane in the work area:

   - **Year (ship date)** from **Time (ship date)**
   - **Month (ship date)** from **Time (ship date)**
   - **City** from **Employee by region**
   - **Retailer** from **Retailers**
   - **Retailer site** from **Retailers**
   - **Quantity** from **Sales fact**

COGNOS 8 NOTE The **Retailers** query subject is called **Retailer site**. Inside the **Retailer site** query subject, **Retailer** is called **Retailer name** and the **Retailer site** query item is called **City** inside the query subject.

---

6. From **Data Items** in the work area, drag **Year (ship date)** to the **Detail Filters** pane.

   The Detail Filter Expression dialog box is displayed.

7. In the **Expression Definition** pane, add **=2007** after the data item.

   The Expression should be as follows:

   ```
   [Year (ship date)] = 2007
   ```

8. Click **Validate** and then **OK** if there are no errors.

9. Drag **Month (ship date)** to the **Detail Filters** pane.

   The Detail Filter Expression dialog box is displayed.

10. In the **Expression Definition** pane, add **= 'May'** after the data item.

    The Expression should be this:

    ```
    [Month (ship date)] = 'May'
    ```

11. Click **Validate** and then **OK** if there are no errors.

12. In the **Data Items** pane, click **City** to select it.

13. In the **Properties** pane, change the **Name** to **Branch**.

14. Drag **Branch** to the **Detail Filters** pane.

     The Detail Filter Expression dialog box is displayed.

15. In the **Expression Definition** pane, add **= 'Bilbao'** after the data item name.
     The Expression should be this:

     ```
     [Branch] = 'Bilbao'
     ```

16. Click **Validate** and then **OK** if there are no errors.

17. In the **Properties** pane for the Branch detail filter, change the **Usage** to **Optional**.

     This will allow you to run the report for all branches or a single one.

18. In the **Data Items** pane, click **Retailer site** to select it.

19. In the **Properties** pane, change the **Name** to **City**.

20. From the **Run** menu, select **View Tabular Data** to test your query. The query results
     should match what's shown in Figure 2.29.

Year (ship date)	Month (ship date)	City	Retailer	Retailer site	Quantity
2007	May	Bilbao	Bazar Sport	Bilbao	931
2007	May	Bilbao	Equipo del deporte	Bilbao	3,178
2007	May	Bilbao	Golf España	Logroño	8,666
2007	May	Bilbao	Mundo del deporte	Bilbao	1,291
2007	May	Bilbao	Naranco de Bulnes	Barcelona	21,460
2007	May	Bilbao	Naranco de Bulnes	Bilbao	2,053
2007	May	Bilbao	Naranco de Bulnes	Logroño	3,811
2007	May	Bilbao	Objetivo Sport	Bilbao	7,271
2007	May	Bilbao	Ocio y Aventura	Barcelona	9,571
2007	May	Bilbao	Ocio y Aventura	Madrid	2,020
2007	May	Bilbao	Ocio y Aventura	Zaragoza	4,847
2007	May	Bilbao	Sport Gestion	Bilbao	6,609
2007	May	Bilbao	Supremas Montañas	Zaragoza	684
2007	May	Bilbao	Universo del deporte	Bilbao	4,127

Figure 2.29   Actual_Shipped_by_Branch query results

21. Close **IBM Cognos Viewer** to return to your report design.

Step 4: Build the First List Report

Because this list will be embedded inside another, we want this list to look like a table entry.

1. In the **Explorer Bar**, mouse over the **Page Explorer** tab and select **Page1**.

2. From the **Data Items** tab in the **Insertable Objects** pane, double-click the following items in the **Expected_Volume_by_Branch** query to add them to the list:

- **Branch**
- **Expected volume**

3. In the work area, click inside the list object to select an item.

4. In the **Properties** pane, click **Select Ancestor** and select the **List** object.

   This list will be converted into a nested header, so the headers will be removed and text will be added to describe the data in the list.

5. On the toolbar, click the **Bold** button.

6. On the toolbar, click the **Right** button.

7. In the **Properties** pane, change the **Column Titles** property to **Hide**.

8. From the toolbar, click the **Unlock (currently locked)** button.

9. From the **Toolbox** tab of the **Insertable Objects** pane, drag a **Text Item** object into the first column to the left of **Branch**.

   The Text dialog box is displayed.

10. Type **Expected Volume for:** and click **OK**.

11. From the toolbar, click the **Lock (currently unlocked)** button.

12. To remove any padding and make the list look like another detail row, click the first column and Ctrl-click the second column to select both list column bodies.

13. In the **Properties** pane, double-click the **Classes** property to open the dialog box.

14. Click the class (**List column body cell**) in the **Selected classes** pane.

15. Click the **Remove** button in the middle of the dialog box.

16. Click **OK** to close the dialog box.

    With the padding removed, no spacing exists between columns.

17. In the work area, click the **List Column Body** for **Expected Volume** to select it.

18. In the **Properties** pane, double-click the **Size & Overflow** property to open the dialog box.

19. Change the **Width** item to **60** pixels and click **OK** to close the dialog.

    The list data container should resemble what's shown in Figure 2.30.

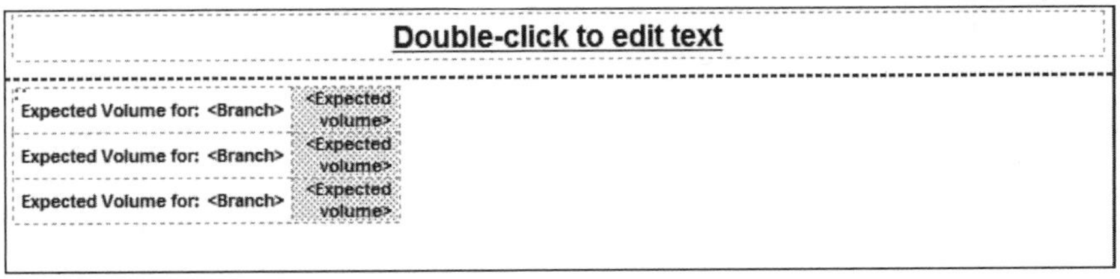

Figure 2.30   Initial list report design

Step 5: Build the Main List Report

Now we will create the select list report that will be used as the main list in the report.

1. From the **Data Items** tab in the **Insertable Objects** pane, drag the **Actual_Shipped_ by_Branch** query into the **Page Body** of the work area.

   You noticed that if you drag a query onto the page without specifying a data container, it will create a list report for that query.

2. In the new list, cut the **Year (ship date)** and **Month (ship date)** columns from the list.

3. Click the **Branch** column to select it.

4. From the toolbar, click the **Group/Ungroup** button.

   Now we want to sort the retailers within the branch based on the quantity sold to that retailer.

5. From the toolbar, click the **Sort** button and select **Edit Layout Sorting** to open the Grouping & Sorting dialog box.

COGNOS 8 NOTE   The toolbar option in IBM Cognos 8 Report Studio is **Sort**, and the item in the list is **Advanced Sorting** instead of **Edit Layout Sorting**.

---

6. In the dialog box, drag **Retailer** from the **Data Items** pane into the **Groups** folder in the **Groups** pane.

NOTE   This is another way of creating grouping in a report, but it will not change the **Group Span** property, so the retailer names will repeat for every city.

---

7. From the **Data items** pane, drag **Quantity** into the **Sort List** folder for **Retailer**.

8. Click the **Sort Order** button to change the order from **Ascending** to **Descending**.

   Now the Retailers are sorted from highest to lowest for each branch in the report. We also want to sort the retailer sites in descending order based on quantity.

9. From the **Data items** pane, drag **Quantity** into the **Detail Sort List** folder.

10. Change the **Sort Order** from **Ascending** to **Descending**.

11. Click **OK** to close the dialog box.

12. In the list, click **Quantity**.

13. From the toolbar, click the **Summarize** button and select **Total** to create the footer data that will be moved to the header.

COGNOS 8 NOTE   The **Summarize** button is called **Aggregate**.

---

14. From the toolbar, click **Headers & Footers** and select **List Headers & Footers**. The dialog box is displayed.

15. Select the **Branch (header)** option from the list and click **OK**.

16. Click the **List Column Body** for **Branch** to select it.

17. From the toolbar, click the **Cut** button to remove it from the list.

18. To create a cell for **Total(Quantity)** in the header, click the header to select it.

19. From the toolbar, click the **Split Cell** button.

Now the first two cells in the header should be merged to allow for additional text.

20. Click the **Retailer** header cell and Ctrl-click the **City** header cell.

21. From the toolbar, click the **Merge Cells** button.

Now the header can be customized.

22. From the toolbar, click the **Right** button.

This will right-justify any content for this cell.

23. From the toolbar, click the **Unlock (currently locked)** button.

24. From the **Overall – Total** footer cell, drag **Total(Quantity)** into the header cell. Be careful to select the **Text Item** and not the **List Cell** object.

25. To remove the footers, make sure you select any part of the list and click the **Headers & Footers** button from the toolbar and select **List Header & Footers** option.

26. Deselect the **Branch (footer)** and the **Overall footer** selections.

27. Click **OK** to close the dialog box.

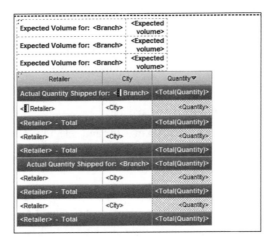

Figure 2.31   Master list design

28. From the **Toolbox** tab of the **Insertable Objects** pane, drag a **Text Item** object into the first column to the left of **Branch**.

    The Text dialog box is displayed.

29. Type **Actual Quantity Shipped for:** and click **OK**.

30. From the toolbar, click the **Lock (currently unlocked)** button.

    The second list should match what's shown in Figure 2.31.

Step 6: Merge the Lists

Now that two lists have the expected and actual volumes, we will merge the two together. This is done by dragging one list inside of the other and then defining the master-detail relationship between the two queries.

1. Click on the text **Actual Quantity Shipped** to select the header of the second list.

2. From the **Structure** menu above the toolbar, select **Headers & Footers** and the **Insert List Row Cells Above** option.

    A dialog box appears to insert a single row above the header.

3. Click **OK** to accept this.

4. In the new row that was added, click the first cell and Shift-click the last cell to select all the cells.

5. From the toolbar, click the **Merge Cells** button.

    Now the style should match that of the other header.

6. In the **Properties** pane, double-click the **Classes** property to open the **Classes** dialog box.

7. In the **Global classes** pane of the dialog box, double-click **List outer header cell** to add it to the **Selected classes** pane on the right.

8. Click **OK** to apply the changes and close the dialog box.

    The new header line is now ready to accept the other list.

9. From the toolbar, click **Unlock (currently locked)**.

10. Click in the **Expected volume** list to select it.

11. In the **Properties** pane, click **Select Ancestor** and select the **List** object.

    Before moving the first list into the master list, change the class of the list to match the header.

12. In the **Properties** pane, double-click the **Classes** property to open the **Classes** dialog box.

13. In the **Global classes** pane of the dialog box, double-click **List outer header cell** to add it to the **Selected classes** pane on the right along with the **List Table** class.

14. Click **OK** to apply the changes and close the dialog box.

15. Drag the selected list into the top header of the master list.

16. Click an item in the inner list to allow us to create a master-detail relationship between the lists.

17. From the **Data** menu, select **Master-Detail Relationships** to open the dialog box.

18. Click the **New Link** button.

19. In the **Master** pane, click **Branch**.

20. In the **Detail** pane, click **Branch**.

    The inner report will now be filtered by the branch of the outer report. The filtering should happen for the month and year also.

21. Click **New Link** again and match **Month (ship date)** to **Month**.

22. Click **New Link** again to match **Year (ship date)** to **Year**.

23. Click **OK** to close the dialog box.

24. From the toolbar, click **Lock (currently unlocked)**.

    The report layout should look like Figure 2.32.

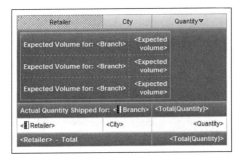

Figure 2.32   All_Products query results

Step 7: Add Prompts and Titles to the Report

1. In the **Explorer Bar**, mouse over the **Query Explorer** tab and select **Actual_Shipped_ by_Branch**.

2. In the **Detail Filters** pane of the work area, double-click the filter for **Year (ship date)**.

3. Replace 2007 with **?Selected Year?**. The expression should look like the following:

   ```
   [Year (ship date)] = ?Selected Year?
   ```

4. Click **OK** to close the Detail Filter Expression dialog box.

5. Double-click the filter for **Month (ship date)**.

6. Replace **'May'** with **?Selected Month?** The expression should look like this:

    ```
    [Month (ship date)] = ?Selected Month?
    ```

7. Click **OK** to close the Detail Filter Expression dialog box.

8. Double-click the filter for **Branch**.

9. Replace **'Bilbao'** with **?Selected Branch?**. The expression should look like this:

    ```
    [Branch] = ?Selected Branch?
    ```

10. Click **OK** to close the Detail Filter Expression dialog box.

    Now that the prompting has been added, we can add a title that shows the selected values.

11. In the **Explorer Bar**, mouse over the **Page Explorer** tab and select **Page1**.

12. Double-click the text item in the page header to change the title to the following:

    ```
    Expected Volume vs. Actual Quantity Shipped for
    ```

13. From the **Toolbox** tab of the **Insertable Objects** pane, drag a **Layout Calculation** object to the right of the text in the title.

    The Report Expression dialog box is displayed.

14. In the Report Expression dialog box, type the following:

    ```
    if( ParamDisplayValue('Selected Branch') <> '' )
    then ( ParamDisplayValue('Selected Branch') )
    else ( 'All Branches' )
    ```

NOTE   Be sure to place two single quotes without a space in the opening condition. This
will check to see whether an optional branch was selected by the user.

---

15. Validate the expression and click **OK** to close the dialog box. If prompted, select **April** for the **Month** and **2005** for the **Year**.

16. With the title text highlighted, click the **Pick up Style** button in the toolbar.

17. Click the **Layout Calculation** object next to the text in the title area.

18. From the toolbar, click the **Apply Style** button.

19. To add the parameter values for the date, drag a **Block** from the **Toolbox** tab to the right of the **Layout Calculation** in the title area.

20. Drag a **Layout Calculation** object from the toolbox and drop it in the newly added block.

21. In the Report Expression dialog box, type the following:

    ```
    'For ' + ParamDisplayValue('Selected Month') +
    ' ' + ParamDisplayValue('Selected Year')
    ```

22. Validate the expression and click **OK** to close the dialog box.

23. In the work area, click in the whitespace of the page body to select it.

24. From the toolbar, click the **Center** button.

25. In the **Properties** pane, double-click the **Padding** property to open the dialog box.

26. Change the top padding to **20** pixels.

27. Click **OK** to close the dialog box.

28. From the **Run** menu, select **Run Report – HTML** to test your report. When prompted, select **Amsterdam**, **April**, and **2005**. The report output should have numbers similar to Figure 2.33.

Expected Volume vs. Actual Quantity Shipped for Amsterdam For April 2005		
Retailer	Retailer site	Quantity
Expected Volume for: Amsterdam		48,880
Actual Quantity Shipped for: Amsterdam		59,285
Extra Sport	Wageningen	14,201
Extra Sport - Total		14,201
Sportworld	Deventer	7,455
Sportworld	Beets	2,937
Sportworld	Amstelveen	1,045
Sportworld - Total		11,437
Beter Buitenleven	Amsterdam	6,018
Beter Buitenleven	Marken	4,983
Beter Buitenleven - Total		11,001
Klimgek Bv.	Amsterdam	5,755
Klimgek Bv. - Total		5,755
Kampeer Top Shop	Dronten	5,182
Kampeer Top Shop - Total		5,182
Holland Zonzoekers	Laren	2,993
Holland Zonzoekers - Total		2,993
Topforma	Groningen	2,810
Topforma - Total		2,810
Get Out	Varsseveld	2,794

Figure 2.33 Completed expected versus actual report

29. Close **IBM Cognos Viewer** to return to your report design.

30. Save the report as **Expected to Actual Shipping Volumes**.

This report showcased the capability to nest data containers after they were created independently. The relational data model was designed for reporting without any complex analysis capability. Also, this example will help us show more complex drill behaviors in the next section.

Configuring the Interactive Dashboard

This last section shows the power of IBM Cognos Report Studio to create a series of reports that match the analysis techniques of the report consumer. Instead of forcing analysts to create very large reports or to generate multiple reports individually, report drill-throughs can create an interactive process that matches the steps analysts will follow to look for exceptional data.

Scenario

We created four reports in this section that each provide information needed by a shipping manager to understand sales and returns trends in the organization. Each of these can be executed, scheduled, and distributed independently, but the power of IBM Cognos Report Studio lies in the ability to link the different reports together, allowing managers to review dashboard data and look for anomalies. By linking the reports, the manager can quickly focus the reports to lower levels of details, providing for complex analysis.

Design

From the dashboard, we will define drill-through definitions to the other three reports created in this chapter.

The Cognos BI environment does allow for more dynamic package-based drill-through, but this section focuses specifically on report-based drill-through in which the report author has control over navigation in the report.

Step-by-Step

Step 1: Add Drill from the Dashboard to the Ratio by Location Report

1. From **IBM Cognos Connection**, open the **Shipping Dashboard** report in IBM Cognos Report Studio.

    If you were to rerun the report, it should look like what's shown in Figure 2.34.

    The goal of this step is to enable a user to click a country and run the report Return/Ship Ratio by Location filtering on the country selected.

2. In the work area, click in the lower-right corner of the **Returned to Shipped Ratio by Country** map to select the whole map.

3. In the **Properties** pane, double-click the **Drill-Through Definitions** property to open the dialog box.

4. To create a new definition, click the **New Drill-Through Definition** button in the lower-left corner of the dialog box.

    Drill-Through Definition1 is created and the options for the drill are displayed on the right side of the dialog box.

5. Click the ellipsis for the report to display the Open dialog box.

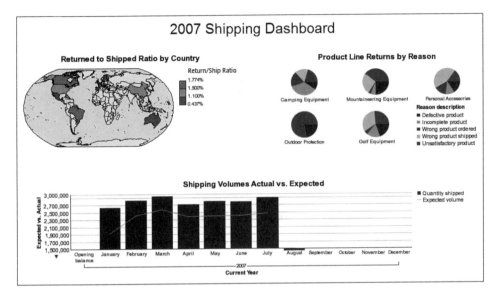

Figure 2.34   Completed shipping dashboard report

6. Select **Return/Ship Ratio by Location**.

This was created in the second section of this chapter.

7. Click **Open** to close the dialog box and to add the report to the definition.

8. Click the **Edit** button below the **Parameters** pane to open the dialog box.

It should show **Selected Location** as the parameter requested by the report and show that the type of the parameter is **memberUniqueName**. We will pass a member as a parameter.

9. Click the drop-down list for **Method** and select **Pass data item value**.

10. Click the drop-down list for **Value** and select **Country**.

Since **Country** is a member, we do not need to change the **Property to Pass**.

11. Click **OK** to close the Parameter dialog box.

12. In the lower-right corner of the **Drill-Through Definitions** dialog box, click the **Rename** button.

A dialog box is displayed showing the name of the definition.

13. Change the **Name** to **Drill to Ratio by Location**.

This will allow report consumers to see multiple reports and to understand the details that will be displayed.

14. Click **OK** to close the dialog box.

15. From the **Run** menu, select **Run Report – HTML** to view the dashboard.

The dashboard will look as shown in Figure 2.35.

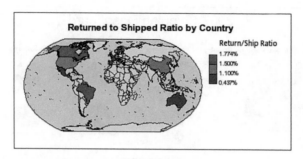

Figure 2.35   Shipping dashboard with exceptional data

Notice that Brazil has an exceptionally high ratio of returned to shipped items.

16. To see how the sales staff in Brazil performed according to this metric, click on the **Brazil** area of the world map.

The drill report is displayed and should look as shown in Figure 2.36.

Now you can look for any trends by employee who may have excessive returns and the reasons customers are returning products. The problem with this report is that the target is not filtered by year so the country totals are across all years.

Volume Returned and Shipped for Brazil

Brazil Breakdown	Reason description	Return quantity	Quantity
Alexandre Pereira -- Return/Ship Ratio: 0.284%		**111**	**39,120**
Returns by Reason for Alexandre Pereira	Defective product		
	Incomplete product		
	Wrong product ordered	19	
	Wrong product shipped	92	
	Unsatisfactory product		
Alexandre Pereira -- Return/Ship Ratio: 1.406%		**9,354**	**665,344**
Returns by Reason for Alexandre Pereira	Defective product	1,259	
	Incomplete product	682	
	Wrong product ordered	5,327	
	Wrong product shipped	247	
	Unsatisfactory product	1,839	
Morela Castro -- Return/Ship Ratio: 7.496%		**2,709**	**36,138**
Returns by Reason for Morela Castro	Defective product		
	Incomplete product		
	Wrong product ordered	2,709	
	Wrong product shipped		
	Unsatisfactory product		
Beatriz Couto -- Return/Ship Ratio: 1.419%		**1,012**	**71,304**
Returns by Reason for Beatriz Couto	Defective product	513	
	Incomplete product		
...		...	

Figure 2.36   Return to ship ratio report for Brazil

17. Close **IBM Cognos Viewer** to return to your report design.

Step 2: Add Drill from the Dashboard to the Product Returns by Reason Report

1. In the work area, click in the lower-right corner of the **Product Line Returns by Reason** pie chart to select the whole chart.

2. In the **Properties** pane, double-click the **Drill-Through Definitions** property to open the dialog box.

3. To create a new definition, click the **New Drill-Through Definition** button in the lower-left corner of the dialog box.

   Drill-Through Definition1 is created and the options for the drill are displayed on the right side of the dialog box.

4. Click the ellipsis for the report to display the Open dialog box.

5. Select **Product Returns by Time Period**.

   This was created in the third section of this chapter.

6. Click **Open** to close the dialog box and to add the report to the definition.

7. Click the **Edit** button below the **Parameters** pane to open the dialog box.

   It should show **Selected Product** and **Selected Time** as the parameters requested by the report.

8. In the line for the **Selected Product** parameter, click the drop-down list for **Method** and select **Pass data item value**.

9. Click the drop-down list for **Value** and select **Product Line**.

10. In the line for the **Selected Time** parameter, click the drop-down list for **Method** and select **Pass data item value**.

11. Click the drop-down list for **Value** and select **Year**.

12. Click **OK** to close the Parameters dialog box.

13. In the **Drill-Through Definitions** dialog box, rename the definition to **Drill to Product Returns**.

14. Click **OK** to close the dialog box.

15. From the **Run** menu, select **Run Report – HTML** to view the dashboard. The dashboard will look like what's shown in Figure 2.37. Notice that the Outdoor Protection has an exceptionally high percentage of Unsatisfactory product returns as compared to other product lines.

16. To see specific counts for returns for Outdoor Protection products, click on the **Outdoor Protection** pie. You will be prompted for a **Time** period with a standard tree prompt. Even though we explicitly said in step 11 to include the Year item from the query, it is not accepted as a parameter by the target report.

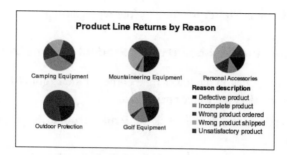

Figure 2.37   Shipping dashboard with exceptional data

17.   Expand **Year** and select **2007**. Click **OK** to open the target report. The drill report is displayed and should look like what's shown in Figure 2.38.

Return quantity		Q1 2007	Q2 2007	Q3 2007	2007
Outdoor Protection	Unsatisfactory product	3,601	1,446	165	5,212
	Defective product	1,336	167	24	1,527
	Incomplete product		32		32
	Wrong product shipped	4			4
	Returns for Outdoor Protection	**4,941**	**1,645**	**189**	**6,775**
Insect Repellents	Unsatisfactory product	530	801	150	1,481
	Defective product		108		108
	Wrong product shipped				
	Incomplete product				
	Returns for Insect Repellents	**530**	**909**	**150**	**1,589**
BugShield Natural	Unsatisfactory product	199			199
	Wrong product shipped				
	Defective product				
	Incomplete product				
	Returns for BugShield Natural	**199**			**199**
BugShield Natural 86110	Unsatisfactory product	199			199
	Wrong product shipped				
	Defective product				
	Incomplete product				
	Returns for BugShield Natural 86110	**199**			**199**

Figure 2.38   Shipping dashboard with exceptional data

Now you can look for any trends by product lines that may have excessive returns.

18.   Close **IBM Cognos Viewer** to return to your report design.

If you would like to drill-through and send the year, you can add the **Year** data item of
the query as a nested item in the Series (pie slices) region of the report.

Step 3: Add Drill from the Dashboard to the Branch Shipping Volumes Report

1. In the work area, click in the lower-right corner of the **Shipping Volumes Actual vs. Expected** combination chart to select the whole chart.

2. In the **Properties** pane, double-click the **Drill-Through Definitions** property to open the dialog box.

3. To create a new definition, click the **New Drill-Through Definition** button in the lower-left corner of the dialog box. **Drill-Through Definition1** is created and the options for the drill are displayed on the right side of the dialog box.

4. Click the ellipsis for the report to display the Open dialog box.

5. Select **Expected to Actual Shipping Volumes**. This was created in the fourth section of this chapter.

6. Click **Open** to close the dialog box and to add the report to the definition.

7. Click the **Edit** button below the **Parameters** pane to open the dialog box.

   It should show Selected Branch, Selected Month and Selected Year as the parameters requested by the report. The first two parameter types are string and Selected Year is expecting a number. Since the dashboard is a dimensional source and the target report is based on a relational source, we will explicitly define the member properties to pass to the target.

   The combination chart on the dashboard does not run the query on the branch so we will not be passing the branch as a parameter.

8. In the line for the **Selected Branch** parameter, click the drop-down list for **Method** and select **Do not use parameter**.

9. In the line for the **Selected Month** parameter, click the drop-down list for **Method** and select **Pass data item value**.

10. Click the drop-down list for **Value** and select **Month**.

11. In the line for the **Selected Year** parameter, change the **Method** to **Pass data item value**.

12. Change the **Value** to **Year**.

13. Click **OK** to close the Parameters dialog box.

14. In the **Drill-Through Definitions** dialog box, rename the definition to **Drill to Shipping Volumes**.

15. Click **OK** to close the dialog box.

16. From the **Run** menu, select **Run Report – HTML** to view the dashboard. The dashboard will look like what's shown in Figure 2.39. Notice the difference between the actual and expected volumes for January. It seems to be significantly greater than the differences in other months.

Figure 2.39   Shipping dashboard with exceptional data

17. To see branch-specific counts for shipped items for January 2007, click on the column
     for **January 2007**. The drill report is displayed and should look as shown in Figure 2.40.

Expected Volume vs. Actual Quantity Shipped for All Branches For January 2007

Retailer	Retailer site	Quantity
Expected Volume for: Amsterdam		55,785
Actual Quantity Shipped for: Amsterdam		78,408
Kampeer Top Shop	Dronten	22,147
Kampeer Top Shop - Total		22,147
Beter Buitenleven	Laren	18,133
Beter Buitenleven - Total		18,133
Sportworld	Beets	8,912
Sportworld	Den Haag	2,027
Sportworld	Deventer	617
Sportworld - Total		11,556
Extra Sport	Wageningen	9,311
Extra Sport	Rotterdam	1,064
Extra Sport	Nieuweschans	393
Extra Sport - Total		10,768
Holland Zonzoekers	Amsterdam	3,655
Holland Zonzoekers - Total		3,655
Eurobal	Amsterdam	3,312
Eurobal - Total		3,312
Get Out	Varsseveld	2,906

Figure 2.40   Shipping dashboard with exceptional data

Now you rerun the report and you will be prompted to select another time period or
branch.

18. Close **IBM Cognos Viewer** to return to your report design.

Now you can manage relationships between reports to provide analysis capabilities so that the report consumer can have reports that match how they analyze data, instead of providing a 500-page report and asking consumers to change how they analyze data to match the report.

Summary

In this chapter, we wanted to focus on your role as a report author to understand how report consumers will use the data presented in reports. With this understanding, you can create a series of reports that are linked together using drill-through technology to allow the users to look for exceptional data and run focused reports that isolate the numbers they seek. Although each of these reports can run independently, the analytic power comes from the relationship that you defined as a report developer.

The first example in the chapter creates a dashboard that presents the high-level overview of the key numbers for a manager.

The second example allows a report consumer to pick a location (region, country, or branch) and see the ratio of returned to shipped items organized by country.

The third example allows users to pick a time period and product and see a breakdown for the time period and all the product information within a specific group.

The fourth report shows a breakdown of branch sales by its retailers, as well as a summary of the expected volumes to be shipped.

Some techniques that you may want to integrate into other reports include the following:

- Prompting users to pick from a hierarchy
- Using dimensional functions to enhance the query
- Using dimensional query items to easily add functionality in your query
- Manipulating the headers and footers to highlight the numbers
- Nesting objects after you tested them independently

CHAPTER 3

Understanding the Report Hierarchy

One of the keys to understanding how the IBM Cognos BI solution functions is to apply a hierarchical perspective on everything you do: setting up folders, applying security, formatting reports, and so on.

IBM Cognos Report Studio is no exception to the rule. The IBM Cognos Framework Manager model is created for use hierarchically. The report specification is stored in XML format, which is hierarchical. This chapter looks at how we can take advantage of this nature in designing reports.

This chapter shows the hierarchical nature of formatting, querying, and delivering report information. Our perspective is that of a human resources department and the reports that we can derive from the data warehouse. We will create several reports that will take advantage of the hierarchical nature of report creation.

After creating individual reports, we will design a briefing book that will incorporate elements of all the other reports into a single report that can be delivered on a scheduled basis.

> **NOTE** If you want some help with the files and typing involved in this chapter, go to www.ibmpressbooks.com/title/9780132656757 and download the supplements.zip file from the Downloads section under **More Information**.

Layout Library

The human resources department of our fictitious Great Outdoors Company has a number of reports that are generated and distributed to a number of offices throughout the company. The personnel would like to have the headers and footers have a consistent design that is separate from the other units. In this standard layout, they would like to be able to customize the report title, modify the subtitle, and assign a report ID number.

As time progresses, they would like the option to change the styles without having to update all the reports individually. They would like their initial header to resemble what's shown in Figure 3.1 and their footer to look like what's shown in Figure 3.2.

Figure 3.1   Completed human resources header

| Report ID: HRYEARLY | 1 | Apr 15, 2011 |

Figure 3.2   Completed human resources footer

Design

The layout library is a report specification that will be used only to store components that will be used in other reports as layout component references. Like objects in the Toolbox, layout component references are objects nested inside a report. These objects can contain only elements that are not associated with a query. Additional pieces can be customized by creating names objects.

A later section of the chapter shows how we can integrate the components of the layout library into a template.

Step-by-Step

The steps involve creating a report without any data containers. The standard header and footer will be created. The key aspect of this exercise is to design as many predefined features as possible while allowing report writers to override key aspects, like the title of the report.

Every layout component and any items to be overridden need to be defined by name in order for this process to work correctly. To simplify the design, a named block will contain the formatting for the header, and another named block will hold the footer details.

Step 1: Start the Report

1. Launch **Report Studio** and select the **GO Data Warehouse (query)** package.

NOTE   Although we are working on layout-only components, we still need to choose a package to build the report.

---

2. Click on the **Create New** option.

COGNOS 8 NOTE   The option is **Create a new report or template**.

---

3. Select the **Blank** report template and click **OK**.

Step 2: Create the Header

The header will have two columns. In the first column, a logo will be added with the name of the company and department directly below it. The second column will have the title of the report and a subtitle. This will take three tables to create: one table for the left and right side of the header, along with two nested tables to allow for stacking of text in each half.

Because most of the work in this step has to do with organizing and customizing embedded objects, we will use the Page Structure view to organize the header.

1. From the **View** menu, select **Page Structure**.

   The objects in the report hierarchy will be displayed in the work area.

2. In the work area, expand **Page—Page1**.

   Because the report template we chose was blank, the only object on Page1 is the Page Body.

3. From the **Toolbox** tab of the **Insertable Objects** pane, drag a **Block** object into **Page Body**.

   The block should be nested as a child to the page body.

4. In the work area, click the **Block** object to select it.

5. In the **Properties** pane, change the **Name** property to **ReportHeader**.

6. From the **Toolbox** tab, drag a **Table** object into the block.

   The Insert Table dialog box is displayed.

7. Verify that the **Number of Columns** is **2** and the **Number of Rows** is **1**.

8. Click the **Maximize Width** check box to remove the selection.

9. Click **OK** to close the dialog box.

    The table object is nested in the block.

10. In the work area, expand the **Block**, **Table**, and **Table Row** objects.

    The two table cells in that row are displayed.

11. From the **Toolbox**, drag a second **Table** object into the first cell of the header table.

12. Change the **Number of Columns** to **1** and the **Number of Rows** to **3**.

13. Click **OK** to close the dialog box.

14. Drag a third **Table** object into the second cell of the header table.

15. Change the **Number of Columns** to **1** and the **Number of Rows** to **2**.

16. Click **OK** to close the dialog box.

17. Expand all the objects in the work area to display all the objects in the header. Your page structure should look like what's shown in Figure 3.3.

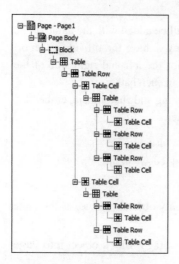

Figure 3.3   Initial header structure

With the layout of a table and two nested tables created, we can add the presentation objects into the work area. All the objects will be added at the lowest level of our hierarchy. There are five **Table Cell** objects at the lowest level and they extend the farthest toward the right side of the work area.

18. From the **Toolbox**, drag an **Image** object into the first cell.

19. Drag a **Text Item** into the second cell.

    The Text dialog box is displayed.

20. Type **The Great Outdoors Company** in the text box.

21. Click **OK** to close the dialog box.

22. In the work area, expand the **Table Cell** object to show the newly added text item.

23. Drag a **Text Item** into the third cell.

    The Text dialog box is displayed.

24. Type **Human Resources** in the Text dialog box.

25. Click **OK** to close the dialog box.

26. Expand the **Table Cell** object to show the last text item.

27. Drag a **Layout Calculation** into the fourth cell.

    The Report Expression dialog box is displayed.

28. Type **PageName()** in the **Expression Definition** pane.

    This function displays the name of the report page.

29. Validate the expression and click **OK** to close the dialog box.

30. Expand the **Table Cell** object to show the title layout calculation.

31. Click the **Layout Calculation** to select it.

32. In the **Properties** pane, change the **Name** property to **ReportTitle**.

    This will allow report writers to override the default behavior and create a customized title.

33. Drag a **Text Item** into the fifth cell.

    The Text dialog box is displayed.

34. Type **Override SubTitle to Customize** in the Text dialog box.

35. Click **OK** to close the dialog box.

36. Expand the **Table Cell** object to show the title text item.

37. Click the **Text Item** to select it.

38. In the **Properties** pane, change the **Name** property to **SubTitle**.

    We will be overriding this text item with a layout calculation in our later reports.

Figure 3.4 shows the work area for the report.

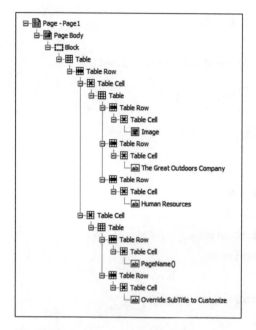

Figure 3.4   Updated header design

Step 3: Format Header Objects

With the objects added for the header, we will now add the image and format the header.

Layout Component References allow you to override a named object with any other object. Even though we added a layout calculation and a text box, any object can be added to replace the items. To maintain the appropriate formatting, we will format the parent objects and allow the nested objects to inherit the properties.

1. In the work area, click the **Block** object to select it.

2. Double-click the **Margin** property to open the Margin dialog box.

3. Change the bottom margin to **20 px** to allow for spacing after the header in the report.

4. Click **OK** to close the dialog box.

5. In the work area, double-click on the **Image** object to open the Image URL dialog box.

   You can use any logo you prefer; we will be using one from the samples that are installed as part of a standard IBM Cognos BI installation. You might need to ask your IBM Cognos administrator for information on how to access these images.

6. Click **Browse** to open the Image Browser dialog box.

7. Select **logo_great_outdoors.gif** from the list.

8. Click **OK** to close the dialog box.

9. Click **OK** to close the Image URL dialog box.

    With the image added, the first of the four table cells has been formatted. We will now format the four table cells that have the embedded text items.

10. Click the second **Table Cell**, which has The Great Outdoors Company text item.

    When you choose the table cell, all formatting will automatically apply to objects added into the cell.

11. From the toolbar, click the drop-down arrow next to **Foreground Color** to show the **Named Colors** palette.

12. Select **Blue**.

13. From the toolbar, click the **Bold** button.

14. Click the third **Table Cell**, which has the Human Resources text item.

15. From the toolbar, click the drop-down arrow next to **Foreground Color**.

16. Select **White**.

17. From the toolbar, click the **Center** button.

18. From the toolbar, click the drop-down arrow next to **Background Color**.

19. Select **Blue**.

20. From the toolbar, click the **Bold** button.

21. Click the fourth **Table Cell**, which has the report title layout calculation.

    Even though a report author may later override the title, the default formatting of the cell will pass to any new objects added into the cell.

22. In the **Properties** pane, double-click the **Padding** property to open the Padding dialog box.

23. Change the top padding to **10 px** and the left padding to **25 px**.

24. Click **OK** to close the dialog box.

25. From the toolbar, change the **Size** to **24 pt**.

26. From the toolbar, click the drop-down arrow next to **Foreground Color** to show the **Named Colors** palette.

27. Select **Blue**.

28. From the toolbar, click the **Bold** button.

29. Click the fifth **Table Cell**, which has the report subtitle text item.

30. In the **Properties** pane, double-click the **Padding** property to open the Padding dialog box.

31. Change the top padding to **10 px** and the left padding to **25 px**.

32. Click **OK** to close the dialog box.

33. From the toolbar, click the drop-down arrow next to **Foreground Color** to show the **Named Colors** palette.

34. Select **Blue**.

35. From the toolbar, click the **Bold** button.

36. From the **Run** menu, select **Run Report – HTML** to compare the header to what you see in Figure 3.5.

Figure 3.5   Completed header

37. Close **IBM Cognos Viewer** to return to your report design.

38. In the work area, collapse the block hierarchy as we are finished with the header.

Step 4: Create the Footer

The footer will have three columns. In the first column, the report ID will be added. This will be a prompted value that can be set in the report using the layout component reference. The middle column will have the page number centered in it. The last column will have the date of the report run.

1. From the **Toolbox** tab of the **Insertable Objects** pane, drag a **Block** object into **Page Body**.

The block should be nested at the same level as the header block created in Step 2.

2. In the work area, click the **Block** object to select it.

3. Double-click the **Margin** property to open the Margin dialog box.

4. Change the top margin to **20 px** to allow for spacing between the bottom of the report body and the footer.

5. Click **OK** to close the dialog box.

6. In the **Properties** pane, change the **Name** property to **ReportFooter**.

7. From the **Toolbox** tab, drag a **Table** object into the block.

The Insert Table dialog box is displayed.

8. Set the **Number of Columns** to **3** and the **Number of Rows** to **1**.

9. Click **OK** to close the dialog box.

The table object is nested in the block.

10. In the work area, expand the **Block**, **Table**, and **Table Row** objects.

    The three table cells in that row are displayed.

11. Click the first **Table Cell** object to select it.

12. Double-click the **Size & Overflow** property.

    The Size & Overflow dialog box is displayed.

13. Change the **Width** to **200 px**.

14. Click **OK** to close the dialog box.

15. From the **Toolbox** tab, drag a **Layout Calculation** object into the first table cell.

    The Report Expression dialog box is displayed.

16. Enter the following into the Expression Definition pane:

    ```
    if ( ParamDisplayValue ('ReportID') is null ) then
        ( 'No ReportID parameter exists in the report.' )
    else
        ( 'Report ID: ' + ParamDisplayValue ('ReportID') )
    ```

    This will check the report for a parameter named ReportID. If it doesn't exist, the report will display a message to set the value. This will not prompt the user for ReportID in any report using the layout component reference, but just check to see whether the parameter exists.

17. Validate the expression and click **OK** to close the dialog box.

18. In the work area, click the second **Table Cell** object.

19. From the toolbar, click the **Center** button.

20. From the **Toolbox** tab of the **Insertable Objects** pane, drag a **Page Number** object into the second table cell.

21. In the work area, click the third **Table Cell** object.

22. From the toolbar, click the **Right** button.

23. Double-click the **Size & Overflow** property.

    A dialog box is displayed.

24. Change the **Width** to **200 px**.

    By setting the width of the first and third columns, we are fixing the left and right sides of the footer and allowing the size of the middle column to be dynamic.

25. Click **OK** to close the dialog box.

26. From the **Toolbox** tab, drag a **Date** object into the third table cell.

27. From the **Run** menu, select **Run Report – HTML** to compare the footer to what's shown in Figure 3.6.

Figure 3.6   Completed footer

28.   Close **IBM Cognos Viewer** to return to your report design.

29.   From the **View** menu, select **Page Design** to return to the traditional work area view.

30.   Save the report as **HR Layout Library**.

This layout library has completed header and footer objects that can be added to additional reports and templates. By using Layout Component References to these objects, report writers can reuse these pieces of code and can have any changes automatically added to their report.

In this example, each object was added into a block. This makes the process easier when more objects are added. Different layout objects, including additional headers and footers, can be added to accommodate any design or regulatory changes to the reports.

Using the Layout Library

The first report in this chapter will have a list report detailing the recruitment efforts of the Great Outdoors Company organizations for a selected month. The human resources department wants to be able to see how effective different recruiting media work for different organizations. Along with capturing details about job openings by organization and branch, the managers also want to be able to find the average number of days to fill the positions by branch.

To increase the flexibility of the report, prompts should be created for organization, month, and year to allow for different views of recruiting data. Additionally, the report should take advantage of the layout library for the department's standard header and footer. The completed report should match the image in Figure 3.7.

Design

Starting with a blank report, we will not use any predefined template options. We will add page headers and footers to insert the layout component references. Otherwise, the report is a typical list report that is filtered by time and organization.

The key to integrate this report with other reports and report layouts is to use consistent naming throughout. While the layout component for the footer uses the parameter ReportID, we must explicitly define it within the report. To hide this from the report consumer, we will hide a value prompt with a default value of the report number.

Recruitment by Organization

The Great Outdoors Company
Human Resources   For Finance in 2007

Finance

City	Date	Position name	Recruitment medium	Position filled date	Days to fill
Amsterdam	Feb 1, 2007	Payroll Clerk	CV Central	Mar 6, 2007	33
Amsterdam - Summary					33
Bilbao	Jan 8, 2007	Accounting Clerk	Pathfinder Personnel	Jan 29, 2007	21
	Apr 23, 2007	Accountant 1	Referral	Jun 8, 2007	46
	Jun 25, 2007	Payroll Clerk	Unspecified		
Bilbao - Summary					34
Boston	Jan 8, 2007	Payroll Clerk	Referral	Feb 5, 2007	28
Boston - Summary					28
Distrito Federal	May 7, 2007	Payroll Clerk	Pathfinder Personnel	Jun 11, 2007	35
	Jul 9, 2007	Budget Analyst	AAA Internet Job Bank	Jul 31, 2007	22
	Jul 20, 2007	Financial Analyst	Unspecified		
Distrito Federal - Summary					28
Genève	Jan 15, 2007	Accountant 2	Local Newspaper	Feb 26, 2007	42
	Mar 9, 2007	Accountant 2	AAA Internet Job Bank	Apr 6, 2007	28
	Apr 5, 2007	Accountant 1	Professional Publication	May 8, 2007	33
	Jun 15, 2007	Financial Analyst	Unspecified		

Figure 3.7   Completed Recruitment by Organization report

Step-by-Step

The five steps in this example show how you can define multiple objects that can be integrated into reports created by other authors.

Step 1: Start the Report

1. Launch **Report Studio** and select the **GO Data Warehouse (query)** package.
2. Click on the **Create New** option.

COGNOS 8 NOTE   The option is **Create a new report or template**.

---

3. Select the **Blank** report template and click **OK**.

   We will be using the **Employee recruitment (query)** and **Employee expense (query)** namespaces inside the **HR (query)** folder.

Step 2: Set Up Recruitment by Organization Query

This query will compile recruiting information for an organization in a specified month and year. The only required filter is for the year. Later steps will change the filters from hard-coded to parameter-driven.

1. In the **Explorer Bar**, mouse over the **Query Explorer** tab and select the **Queries** folder.

2. In the **Insertable Objects** pane, drag a **Query** object into the work area.

3. In the **Properties** pane, rename **Query1** to **Recruitment_by_Organization**.

4. Double-click on the query to open the query definition.

5. From the **Source** tab of the **Insertable Objects** pane, expand the **Employee expense (query)** namespace.

6. Expand the **Organization (consolidated)** query subject and drag **Organization name** into the **Data Items** pane in the work area.

COGNOS 8 NOTE   The **Organization (consolidated)** query subject is called **Organization**.

---

7. From the **Source** tab of the **Insertable Objects** pane, drag the following items from the **Employee recruitment (query)** namespace into the **Data Items** pane in the work area:

   • **City** from **Branch**

   • **Date** from **Time**

   • **Position name** from **Position-department**

   • **Recruitment medium** from **Employee recruitment**

   • **Position filled date** and **Days to fill** from **Employee recruitment fact**

COGNOS 8 NOTE   The **Time** query subject is called **Time dimension** and the **Position-department** query subject is called **Position**. The **Recruitment medium** query item is called **Recruitment medium name**.

---

8. In the **Data Items** pane, click **Organization name** and Shift-click **Position name** to select the first four items in the query.

9. In the **Properties** pane, change the **Pre-Sort** property to **Sort ascending**.

10. In the work area, click the **City** data item to select it.

11. In the **Properties** pane, change the **Name** property to **Branch**.

12. From the **Source** tab of the **Insertable Objects** pane, drag **Year** from the **Time** query subject into the **Detail Filters** pane of the work area.

13. In the **Expression Definition** pane, add **= 2007** after the data item.

The Expression should be as follows:

```
[Employee recruitment (query)].[Time].[Year] = 2007
```

14. Click **Validate** and then **OK** if there are no errors.

15. From the **Source** tab of the **Insertable Objects** pane, drag **Month** from the **Time** query subject into the **Detail Filters** pane of the work area.

16. In the Expression Definition pane, add **= 'April'** after the data item.

The Expression should be this:

```
[Employee recruitment (query)].[Time].[Month] = 'April'
```

17. Click **Validate** and then **OK** if there are no errors.

18. With the month filter selected, change the **Usage** property to **Optional** in the **Properties** pane.

19. From the **Data Items** pane in the work area, drag **Organization name** into the **Detail Filters** pane.

20. In the **Expression Definition** pane, add **= 'Finance'** after the data item.

The Expression should be as follows:

```
[Organization name] = 'Finance'
```

21. Click **Validate** and then **OK** if there are no errors.

22. With the **Organization** name filter selected, change the **Usage** property to **Optional** in the **Properties** pane.

23. From the **Run** menu, select **View Tabular Data** to test your query. The query results should match what's shown in Figure 3.8.

Organization name	City	Date	Position name	Recruitment medium	Position filled date	Days to fill
Finance	Bilbao	Apr 23, 2007	Accountant 1	Referral	Jun 8, 2007	46
Finance	Genève	Apr 5, 2007	Accountant 1	Professional Publication	May 8, 2007	33

Figure 3.8 Recruitment_by_Organization query results

24. Close **IBM Cognos Viewer** to return to your report design.

Step 3: Add the Standard Header and Footer

Before adding any data containers, we will add the header and footer from the layout library and create the ReportID parameter.

1. In the **Explorer Bar**, mouse over the **Page Explorer** tab and select **Page1**.
2. Click in the work area to select the page body.
3. From the toolbar, click the **Headers & Footers** button and select **Page Header & Footer**. A dialog box is displayed.
4. Click the check boxes for both **Header** and **Footer**.
5. Click **OK** to close the dialog box.

   The page header and footer areas are now displayed in the work area.
6. From the **Toolbox** tab of the **Insertable Objects** pane, drag a **Layout Component Reference** object into the header area.

   The Component Reference dialog box is displayed.
7. Change the **Component Location** radio button to **Another report**.
8. Click the ellipsis button to display the Open dialog box.
9. Select the **HR Layout Library** report and click **Open**.
10. In the **Available components to reference** pane, click **ReportHeader** to select it.
11. Click **OK** to close the dialog box.
12. From the **Toolbox** tab of the **Insertable Objects** pane, drag a second **Layout Component Reference** object into the footer area.

    The Component Reference dialog box is displayed.
13. Change the **Component Location** radio button to **Another report**.
14. Click the ellipsis button to display the Open dialog box.
15. Select the **HR Layout Library** report and click **Open**.
16. In the **Available components to reference** pane, click **ReportFooter** to select it.
17. Click **OK** to close the dialog box.
18. From the **Toolbox** tab of the **Insertable Objects** pane, drag a **Text Box Prompt** object into the footer.

    The Prompt Wizard dialog is displayed.
19. Change the name of the new parameter to **ReportID**.
20. Click **Finish** to complete the wizard.

NOTE   Do not click **Next** because we will not need filters and additional queries built.

---

21. In the work area, click the prompt you just added to select it.
22. In the **Properties** pane, double-click the **Default Selections** property to open the dialog box.

23. In the lower-left corner of the dialog box, click the **Add** button.

24. In the Add dialog box, type the report ID of **HR567**.

25. Click **OK** to close the dialog box.

26. Click **OK** to close the Default Selections dialog box.

27. From the **Run** menu, select **Run Report – HTML** to test your report.

    The report output should have values similar to those shown in Figure 3.9.

Figure 3.9   Initial page design with a header and footer

28. Close **IBM Cognos Viewer** to return to your report design.

    To protect the report ID from being changed by report consumers, we will hide it.

29. With the text prompt still selected, change the **Visible** property to **No**.

Step 4: Build the List Report

A list can be created directly by dragging the query from the **Insertable Objects** pane.

1. From the **Data Items** tab of the **Insertable Objects** pane, drag the **Recruitment_by_ Organization** query into the **Page Body** in the work area.

2. In the work area, click the **List Column Header** for **Organization name** to select it.

3. From the toolbar, click the **Section** button.

4. Click the **List Column Header** for **Branch** to select it.

5. From the toolbar, click the **Group/Ungroup** button.

    The list width will be different in each section based on the length of the data returned, so we will set the width of the list to a fixed size.

6. With the **Branch** list column header selected, click the **Select Ancestor** button in the **Properties** pane.

   Notice that the section created a nested list within a list.

7. From the **Select Ancestor** list, click the **List** object closest to the **Properties** pane.

   The work area should show the inner list highlighted.

8. In the **Properties** pane, double-click the **Size & Overflow** property to open the dialog box.

9. Change the **Width** to **700 px**.

   This is an alternative to setting the size of each column.

10. Click **OK** to close the dialog box.

11. Select the **List Column Body** for **Days to fill**.

12. From the toolbar, select **Summarize** to display the list of aggregate options, and select **Automatic Summary**.

    Since the aggregation in the model is set to Average, the summary footer will inherit the function and generate an average of all details.

COGNOS 8 NOTE   The **Summarize** toolbar button is the **Aggregate** button and the **Automatic Summary** option is also **Aggregate** in IBM Cognos 8 Report Studio.

---

13. From the **Run** menu, select **Run Report – HTML** to test your report. The report output should have numbers similar to those shown in Figure 3.10.

14. Close **IBM Cognos Viewer** to return to your report design.

Step 5: Add Prompts and Titles to the Report

In this final step, the query filters will become parameter-based. Since this report will be integrated with others in this chapter, care should be given to ensure that the parameter names are consistent through the later reports.

The final tasks in this step override one of the layout component references to provide filter details in the subtitle of the report. The report title will continue to be the actual name of the page.

1. In the **Explorer Bar**, mouse over the **Query Explorer** tab and select the **Recruitment_by_Organization** query.

2. In the **Detail Filters** pane of the work area, double-click the filter for **Year**.

3. Replace **2007** with **?Selected Year?**. The expression should look like this:

   ```
   [Employee recruitment (query)].[Time].[Year] = ?Selected Year?
   ```

4. Validate the expression and click **OK** to close the Detail Filter Expression dialog box. When prompted, type **2007** for the year.

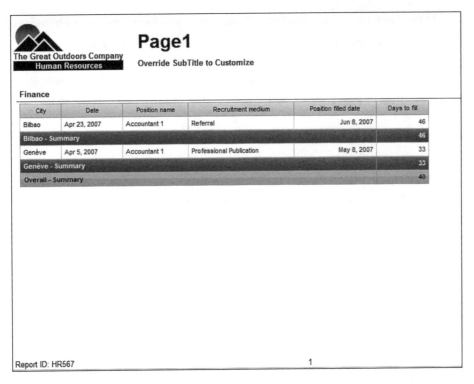

Figure 3.10   Initial list report design

5.   Double-click the filter for **Month** to open the Detail Filter Expression dialog box.

6.   Replace **'April'** with **?Selected Month?**. The expression should look like this:

    ```
    [Employee recruitment (query)].[Time].[Month] = ?Selected Month?
    ```

7.   Validate the expression and click **OK** to close the dialog box.

    This time you were not prompted for a month, since this filter was an optional one.

8.   Double-click the filter for **Organization name**.

9.   Replace **'Finance'** with **?Selected Organization?**. The expression should look like the following:

    ```
    [Organization name] = ?Selected Organization?
    ```

10.   Click **OK** to close the Detail Filter Expression dialog box.

    Now that the prompting has been added, we can add a title that shows the selected values.

11.   In the **Explorer Bar**, mouse over the **Page Explorer** tab and select the **Report Pages** folder.

12.   In the **Report Pages** pane of the work area, click **Page1** to select it.

13. In the **Properties** pane, change the **Name** property to **Recruitment by Organization**.

    When you change the page name, the layout header will automatically display this property as the title of the report.

    Now we will change the subtitle of the report to display the selected prompts for the report.

14. In the **Report Pages** pane, double-click the **Recruitment by Organization** page to display it.

15. Click the **Page Header** to select it.

    Since it is a layout component reference, you cannot change anything until you override specific parts.

16. In the **Properties** pane, double-click the **Overrides** property to display the dialog box.

17. Click the check box next to **SubTitle** to select it.

18. Click **OK** to close the dialog box.

    Now the work area changes to say **Drop item to override component child**.

19. From the **Toolbox** tab in the **Insertable Objects** pane, drag a **Layout Calculation** object into the override component box below the main report title.

    The Report Expression dialog box is displayed.

20. In the Report Expression dialog box, type the following:

    ```
    ( if ( ParamDisplayValue('Selected Organization') is not null )
    then
        ( 'For '+ParamDisplayValue('Selected Organization')+' in ' )
    else
        ( 'For all organizations in ' ) )
    +
    if ( ParamDisplayValue('Selected Month') is not null ) then
        ( ParamDisplayValue('Selected Month') + ' ' +
          ParamDisplayValue('Selected Year') )
    else
        ( ParamDisplayValue('Selected Year') )
    ```

NOTE Remember that parameters are case-sensitive, so you should be sure to verify that the parameter names match exactly those that you added to the filters.

---

21. Validate the expression and click **OK** to close the dialog box.

22. From the **Run** menu, select **Run Report – HTML** to test your report.

    When prompted, select **April**, **Finance**, and **2007**. The report output should have numbers similar to those shown in Figure 3.11.

23. Close **IBM Cognos Viewer** to return to your report design.

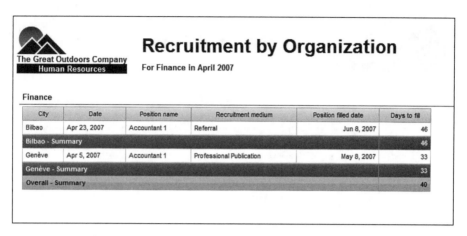

The Great Outdoors Company
Human Resources

Recruitment by Organization

For Finance in April 2007

Finance

City	Date	Position name	Recruitment medium	Position filled date	Days to fill
Bilbao	Apr 23, 2007	Accountant 1	Referral	Jun 8, 2007	46
Bilbao - Summary					46
Genève	Apr 5, 2007	Accountant 1	Professional Publication	May 8, 2007	33
Genève - Summary					33
Overall - Summary					40

Figure 3.11   Completed Recruitment by Organization report

24.   Save the report as **Recruitment by Organization**.

This report integrated the contents of the layout library with one of our three reports. The capability to use layout calculations and parameters within those components will give report writers great flexibility in designing reports using those report parts. To resolve those values, we set parameters and properties in the report itself and the values are inherited in the child objects.

Additionally, we were able to use the reporting hierarchy to set formatting of objects and use the model hierarchy to inherit aggregation properties.

Inheriting Formatting

To better track employee expenses, the human resources department would like to see an organizational report of personnel expenses by manager.

Because this report will also be added to a quarterly briefing book with the other reports in this chapter, the prompting should be identical to those in the previous example. The completed report should match what's shown in Figure 3.12.

Design

A list report will be created to track expenses by date and employee. The lists should be sectioned by both organization and manager. Additionally, the human resource department wanted to use a different style for the section headings, so the class will be changed.

The HR standard header and footer will be added into this report also.

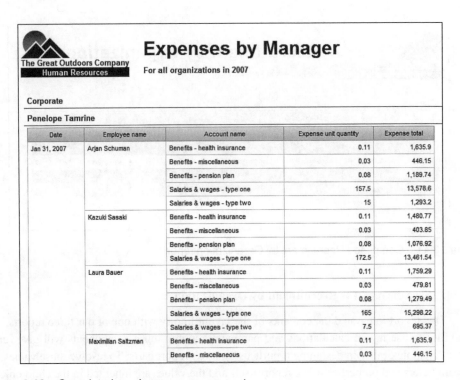

Figure 3.12   Completed employee expense report

Step-by-Step

The following steps show how you can create a report and use layout component references to link to the standard header and footer.

Step 1: Start the Report

1. Launch **Report Studio** and select the **GO Data Warehouse (query)** package.
2. Click on the **Create New** option.

COGNOS 8 NOTE   The option is **Create a new report or template**.

---

3. Select the **Blank** report template and click **OK**.

   We will be using the **Employee expense (query)** namespace inside the **HR (query)** folder.

Step 2: Set Up the Expense by Manager Query

The query will use the same filters as the recruitment report.

1. In the **Explorer Bar**, mouse over the **Query Explorer** tab and select the **Queries** folder.

2. In the **Insertable Objects** pane, drag a **Query** object into the work area.

3. In the Properties pane, rename **Query1** to **Expense_by_Manager**.

4. Double-click on the query to open the query definition.

5. From the **Source** tab of the **Insertable Objects** pane, drag the following items from the **Employee expense (query)** namespace into the **Data Items** pane in the work area:

   - **Organization name** from **Organization (consolidated)**

   - **Current Manager** from **Employee by manager**

   - **Date** from **Time**

   - **Employee name** from **Employee by manager**

   - **Account name** from **Account**

   - **Expense unit quantity** and **Expense total** from **Employee expense fact**

COGNOS 8 NOTE   The **Organization (consolidated)** query subject is called **Organization** and the **Time** query subject is called **Time dimension**.

---

6. In the **Data Items** pane, click **Organization name** and Shift-click **Employee name** to select the first four items in the query.

7. In the **Properties** pane, change the **Pre-Sort** property to **Sort ascending**.

8. In the work area, click the **Expense unit quantity** data item to select it.

9. In the **Properties** pane, change the **Aggregate Function** property to **Total**.

10. From the **Source** tab of the **Insertable Objects** pane, drag **Year** from the **Time** query subject into the **Detail Filters** pane of the work area.

11. In the **Expression Definition** pane, add **= 2007** after the data item.

    The expression should be as follows:

    ```
    [Employee expense (query)].[Time].[Year] = 2007
    ```

12. Click **Validate** and then **OK** if there are no errors.

13. From the **Source** tab of the **Insertable Objects** pane, drag **Month** from the **Time** query subject into the **Detail Filters** pane of the work area.

14. In the **Expression Definition** pane, add **= 'April'** after the data item.

    The expression should be as follows:

    ```
    [Employee expense (query)].[Time].[Month] = 'April'
    ```

15. Click **Validate** and then **OK** if there are no errors.

16. With the month filter selected, change the **Usage** property to **Optional** in the **Properties** pane.

17. From the **Data Items** pane in the work area, drag **Organization name** into the **Detail Filters** pane.

18. In the Expression Definition pane, add **= 'Finance'** after the data item.

The Expression should be this:

```
[Organization name] = 'Finance'
```

19. Click **Validate** and then **OK** if there are no errors.

20. With the organization name filter selected, change the **Usage** property to **Optional** in the **Properties** pane.

21. From the **Run** menu, select **View Tabular Data** to test your query. The query results should match what's shown in Figure 3.13.

22. Close **IBM Cognos Viewer** to return to your report design.

Organization name	Current manager	Date	Employee name	Account name	Expense unit quantity	Expense total
Finance	Alexander Schmuker	Apr 30, 2007	Bertrand Michel	Benefits - health insurance	0.11	887.05
Finance	Alexander Schmuker	Apr 30, 2007	Bertrand Michel	Benefits - miscellaneous	0.03	241.92
Finance	Alexander Schmuker	Apr 30, 2007	Bertrand Michel	Benefits - pension plan	0.08	645.13
Finance	Alexander Schmuker	Apr 30, 2007	Bertrand Michel	Salaries & wages - type one	146.25	7,488.09
Finance	Alexander Schmuker	Apr 30, 2007	Bertrand Michel	Salaries & wages - type two	11.25	576.01
Finance	Alexander Schmuker	Apr 30, 2007	Patrick Lioutau	Benefits - health insurance	0.11	800.32
Finance	Alexander Schmuker	Apr 30, 2007	Patrick Lioutau	Benefits - miscellaneous	0.03	218.27
Finance	Alexander Schmuker	Apr 30, 2007	Patrick Lioutau	Benefits - pension plan	0.08	582.05
Finance	Alexander Schmuker	Apr 30, 2007	Patrick Lioutau	Salaries & wages - type one	157.5	7,275.64
Finance	Anling Zhang	Apr 30, 2007	Bang Liú	Benefits - health insurance	0.11	314.13
Finance	Anling Zhang	Apr 30, 2007	Bang Liú	Benefits - miscellaneous	0.03	85.67
Finance	Anling Zhang	Apr 30, 2007	Bang Liú	Benefits - pension plan	0.08	228.46
Finance	Anling Zhang	Apr 30, 2007	Bang Liú	Salaries & wages - type one	157.5	2,855.77
Finance	Anling Zhang	Apr 30, 2007	Baojia Chén	Benefits - health insurance	0.11	412.5
Finance	Anling Zhang	Apr 30, 2007	Baojia Chén	Benefits - miscellaneous	0.03	112.5
Finance	Anling Zhang	Apr 30, 2007	Baojia Chén	Benefits - pension plan	0.08	300
Finance	Anling Zhang	Apr 30, 2007	Baojia Chén	Salaries & wages - type one	157.5	3,750
Finance	Anling Zhang	Apr 30, 2007	Baojia Chén	Salaries & wages - type two	7.5	500
Finance	Anling Zhang	Apr 30, 2007	Cai Huáng	Benefits - health insurance	0.11	314.13
Finance	Anling Zhang	Apr 30, 2007	Cai Huáng	Benefits - miscellaneous	0.03	85.67

Figure 3.13 Expense_by_Manager query results

Step 3: Add the Standard Header and Footer

Before adding any data containers, we will add the header and footer from the layout library and create the ReportID parameter.

1. In the **Explorer Bar**, mouse over the **Page Explorer** tab and select **Page1**.
2. Click in the work area to select the page body.
3. From the toolbar, click the **Headers & Footers** button and select **Page Header & Footer**. A dialog box is displayed.
4. Click the check boxes for both **Header** and **Footer**.
5. Click **OK** to close the dialog box.

   The page header and footer areas are now displayed in the work area.

6. From the **Toolbox** tab of the **Insertable Objects** pane, drag a **Layout Component Reference** object into the header area.

   The Component Reference dialog box is displayed.

7. Change the **Component Location** radio button to **Another report**.
8. Click the ellipsis button to display the Open dialog box.
9. Select the **HR Layout Library** report and click **Open**.
10. In the **Available components to reference** pane, click **ReportHeader** to select it.
11. Click **OK** to close the dialog box.
12. From the **Toolbox** tab of the **Insertable Objects** pane, drag a second **Layout Component Reference** object into the footer area.

    The Component Reference dialog box is displayed.

13. Change the **Component Location** radio button to **Another report**.
14. Click the ellipsis button to display the Open dialog box.
15. Select **HR Layout Library** and click **Open**.
16. In the **Available components to reference** pane, click **ReportFooter** to select it.
17. Click **OK** to close the dialog box.
18. From the **Toolbox** tab of the **Insertable Objects** pane, drag a **Text Box Prompt** object into the footer.

    The Prompt Wizard dialog is displayed.

19. Change the name of the new parameter to **ReportID**.
20. Click **Finish** to complete the wizard.

NOTE   Do not click **Next** because we will not need filters and additional queries built.

---

21. In the work area, click the prompt you just added to select it.

22. In the **Properties** pane, double-click the **Default Selections** property to open the dialog box.

23. In the lower-left corner of the dialog box, click the **Add** button.

24. In the Add dialog box, type the report ID of **HR678**.

25. Click **OK** to close the dialog box.

26. Click **OK** to close the Default Selections dialog box.

27. From the **Run** menu, select **Run Report – HTML** to test your report. The report output should have numbers similar to those shown in Figure 3.14.

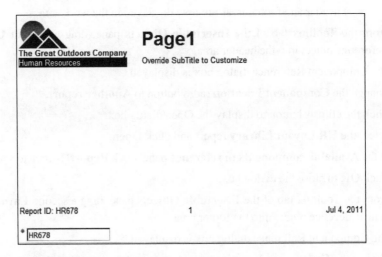

Figure 3.14   Initial page design with header and footer

28. Close **IBM Cognos Viewer** to return to your report design.

   To protect the report ID from being changed by report consumers, we will hide it.

29. With the text prompt still selected, change the **Visible** property to **No**.

Step 4: Build the List Report

This is another standard list report, but the sections of this report are going to have a different style, so the class for the section will change.

1. From the **Data Items** tab of the **Insertable Objects** pane, drag the **Expense_by_ Manager** query into the **Page Body** in the work area.

2. In the work area, Ctrl-click the **List Column Headers** for **Organization name** and **Current manager** to select them.

3. From the toolbar, click the **Section** button.

   Two different sections are created for **Organization name** and **Current manager**.

4. Ctrl-click the **List Column Headers** for **Date** and **Employee name** to select them.

5. From the toolbar, click the **Group/Ungroup** button.

   The list width will be different in each section based on the length of the data returned and should be set to a fixed amount to provide for consistency between sections.

6. Click anywhere inside the list to select a child item.

7. Click the **Select Ancestor** button in the **Properties** pane.

8. From the **Select Ancestor** list, click the **List** object closest to the **Properties** pane.

   The work area should show the inner list highlighted.

9. In the **Properties** pane, double-click the **Size & Overflow** property to open the dialog box.

10. Change the **Width** to **700 px**. This is an alternative to setting the size of each column.

11. Click **OK** to close the dialog box.

    Now we want to change the formatting of the section headers to change the color of the font used. Instead of individually formatting each section heading, we will be changing the class used by the section header.

12. In the **Explorer Bar**, mouse over the **Page Explorer** tab and select the **Classes** folder.

    A new pane appears in the work area containing both local and global classes.

    The global classes are defined by style sheets on the IBM Cognos BI server. This method will not change the global styles, but only change them for this report.

13. In the **Global Class Extensions** pane, click the **Section header cell** class to select it.

14. In the **Properties** pane, double-click the **Foreground Color** property to open the dialog box.

15. In the Foreground Color dialog box, select the **Named Color** of **Blue**.

16. Click **OK** to close the dialog box.

17. From the **Run** menu, select **Run Report – HTML** to test your report. The report output should have numbers similar to those shown in Figure 3.15.

18. Close **Cognos Viewer** to return to your report design.

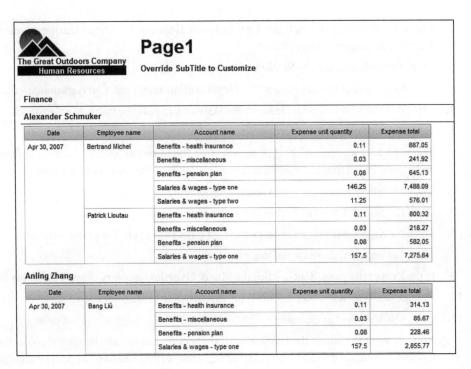

Figure 3.15   Initial list report design

Step 5: Add Prompts and Titles to the Report

To complete the report, the filters will have parameters added and the parameter selections will be added as a layout calculation.

1. In the **Explorer Bar**, mouse over the **Query Explorer** tab and select the **Expense_by_ Manager** query.

2. In the **Detail Filters** pane of the work area, double-click the filter for **Year**.

3. Replace **2007** with **?Selected Year?**. The expression should look like this:

   ```
   [Employee recruitment (query)].[Time].[Year] = ?Selected Year?
   ```

NOTE   The parameters you add here need to match the ones created in the previous report. This will allow us to quickly merge the two together in the briefing book at the end of this chapter.

4. Validate the expression and click **OK** to close the Detail Filter Expression dialog box.

5. When prompted, type **2007** for the year.

6. Double-click the filter for **Month**.

7. Replace **'April'** with **?Selected Month?**. The expression should look like this:

```
[Employee recruitment (query)].[Time].[Month] = ?Selected Month?
```

8. Validate the expression and click **OK** to close the Detail Filter Expression dialog box.

9. Double-click the filter for **Organization name**.

10. Replace **'Finance'** with **?Selected Organization?**. The expression should look like the following:

```
[Organization name] = ?Selected Organization?
```

11. Validate the expression and click **OK** to close the Detail Filter Expression dialog box.

    Now that the prompting has been added, we can add a title that shows the selected values.

12. In the **Explorer Bar**, mouse over the **Page Explorer** tab and select the **Report Pages** folder.

13. In the **Report Pages** pane of the work area, click **Page1** to select it.

14. In the **Properties** pane, change the **Name** property to **Expenses by Manager**.

    Now we will change the subtitle of the report to display the selected prompts for the report.

15. In the **Report Pages** pane, double-click the **Expenses by Manager** page to display it.

16. Click the **Page Header** to select it.

    Since it is a layout component reference, you cannot change anything until you override specific parts.

17. In the **Properties** pane, double-click the **Overrides** property to display the dialog box.

18. Click the check box next to **SubTitle** to select it.

19. Click **OK** to close the dialog box. Now the work area changes to say **Drop item to override component child**.

20. From the **Toolbox** tab in the **Insertable Objects** pane, drag a **Layout Calculation** object into the override component box below the main report title.

    The Report Expression dialog box is displayed.

21. In the Report Expression dialog box, type the following:
```
( if ( ParamDisplayValue('Selected Organization') is not null )
then
    ( 'For '+ParamDisplayValue('Selected Organization')+' in ' )
else
    ( 'For all organizations in ' ) )
+
if ( ParamDisplayValue('Selected Month') is not null ) then
    ( ParamDisplayValue('Selected Month') + ' ' +
```

```
        ParamDisplayValue('Selected Year') )
else
    ( ParamDisplayValue('Selected Year') )
```

22. Validate the expression and click **OK** to close the dialog box.

23. From the **Run** menu, select **Run Report – HTML** to test your report. When prompted, select **April**, **Finance**, and **2007**. The report output should have numbers similar to those shown in Figure 3.16.

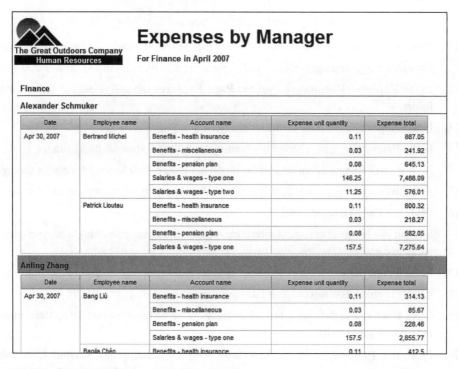

Figure 3.16   Completed Expenses by Manager report

24. Close **IBM Cognos Viewer** to return to your report design.

25. Save the report as **Expenses by Manager**.

Step 6: Save the Report as a Template

The human resources department is satisfied with the design of the report. The personnel would like to be able to quickly reproduce the layout without all the extra steps of adding all the components. To help with this task, we will convert this report to a template and make it available for the training report.

1. With the **Expenses by Manager** report design displayed, select **Convert to Template** from the **File** menu. The report design changes and should look as shown in Figure 3.17.

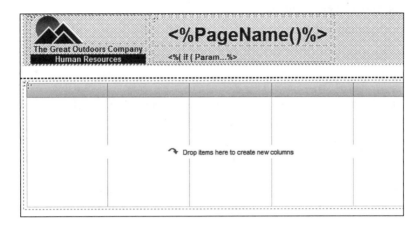

Figure 3.17   Initial HR report template

Now we will remove references to the **Expenses by Manager** report and replace them with generic directions to make the use of the template easier.

2. In the **Explorer Bar**, mouse over the **Query Explorer** and select the **Queries** folder.

3. In the work area, click the **Expense_by_Manager** query to select it.

4. In the **Properties** pane, change the **Name** property to **Query1**.

5. In the **Explorer Bar**, mouse over the **Page Explorer** and select the **Report Pages** folder. The report page still shows "Expenses by Manager."

6. In the work area, click the **Expenses by Manager** page to select it.

7. In the **Properties** pane, change the **Name** property to the following:

   ```
   Change the Page Name to Add the Report Title
   ```

8. Double-click the page to return to the page design.

   Now the ReportID should have a custom message too. First the item should be made visible and then the default selection can be changed.

9. From the toolbar, click the **Visual Aids** button to open the menu, and select **Show Hidden Objects** if it does not already have a check mark next to it.

   The text prompt is now displayed in the footer.

10. In the work area, click the **Text Prompt** in the footer to select it.

11. In the **Properties** pane, double-click the **Default Selections** property to open the dialog box.

12.   In the list of default selections, click **HR678** to select it.

13.   Click the **Delete** button below the list to remove it.

14.   Click **Add** to open the dialog box.

15.   Type the following:

```
Change the default selection in prompt and hide
```

16.   Save the template as **HR List Template**.

In addition to inheriting report components, this report showed how classes can be manipulated to ensure consistent formatting across the report. If these class changes need to be permanent across all reports, the IBM Cognos administrator can change the style sheet for the entire environment. The administrator can find more information on this in the documentation that accompanies the server installation.

With the creation of the template, several steps will be saved in the creation of the last report.

Inheriting Structure

Along with tracking recruitment and expenses, the human resources department wants to be able to track employee training in a similar manner to the other reports.

The manager would like to be able to see the results for one specific organization or all organizations for a selected time period. The completed report should match what's shown in Figure 3.18.

Design

Since the basic format is now saved as a template, the new report will be using a template stored in IBM Cognos Connection folders. By inheriting class definitions and layout component references, the report writer can focus more on query design and less on formatting.

Step-by-Step

These steps show you how to use a template and leverage the formatting done by others in the development of reports.

Step 1: Start the Report

This example will take advantage of the list template that we created with the previous report.

1.   Launch **Report Studio** and select the **GO Data Warehouse (query)** package.

2.   Click on the **Create New** option.

COGNOS 8 NOTE   The option is **Create a new report or template**.

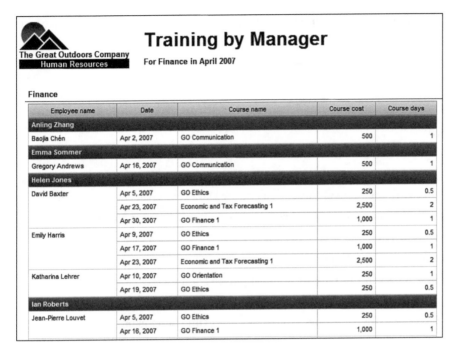

Figure 3.18   Completed employee expense report

3.   Select the **Existing...** report template and click **OK**.

An Open dialog box is displayed.

4.   Select **HR List Template** and click **Open**.

Now the template opens, but the report name in the title bar is set to New and there is a package in the Insertable Objects pane.

We will be using the **Employee expense (query)** and **Employee training (query)** namespaces inside the **HR (query)** folder.

Step 2: Set Up the Training by Manager Query

Even though the query items are coming from different namespaces, the data modeler added relationships so that the report writer can still take advantage of relationships that may not be directly shown in the package.

1.   In the **Explorer Bar**, mouse over the **Query Explorer** tab and select the **Queries** folder.

2.   In the work area, click **Query1** to select it.

3.   In the **Properties** pane, rename **Query1** to **Training_by_Manager**.

4.   Double-click on the query to open the query definition.

5. From the **Source** tab of the **Insertable Objects** pane, expand the **Employee expense (query)** namespace.

6. Expand the **Organization (consolidated)** query subject, and drag **Organization name** into the **Data Items** pane in the work area.

COGNOS 8 NOTE The **Organization (consolidated)** query subject is called **Organization**.

---

7. From the **Source** tab of the **Insertable Objects** pane, drag the following items from the **Employee training (query)** namespace into the **Data Items** pane in the work area:

   • **Current Manager** and **Employee name** from **Employee by manager**

   • **Date** from **Time**

   • **Course name** from **Employee training**

   • **Course days** and **Course cost** from **Employee training fact**

COGNOS 8 NOTE   The **Time** query subject is called **Time dimension**.

---

8. In the **Data Items** pane, click **Organization name** and Shift-click **Date** to select the first four items in the query.

9. In the **Properties** pane, change the **Pre-Sort** property to **Sort ascending**.

10. From the **Source** tab of the **Insertable Objects** pane, drag **Year** from the **Time** query subject into the **Detail Filters** pane of the work area.

11. In the Expression Definition pane, add **=2007** after the data item.

    The Expression should be this:

    ```
    [Employee training (query)].[Time].[Year] = 2007
    ```

12. Click **Validate** and then **OK** if there are no errors.

13. From the **Source** tab of the **Insertable Objects** pane, drag **Month** from the **Time** query subject into the **Detail Filters** pane of the work area.

14. In the Expression Definition pane, add **= 'April'** after the data item.

    The Expression should be as follows:

    ```
    [Employee expense (query)].[Time].[Month] = 'April'
    ```

15. Click **Validate** and then **OK** if there are no errors.

16. With the month filter selected, change the **Usage** property to **Optional** in the **Properties** pane.

17. From the **Data Items** pane in the work area, drag **Organization name** into the **Detail Filters** pane.

18. In the **Expression Definition** pane, add **= 'Finance'** after the data item.

    The Expression should be as follows:

    ```
    [Organization name] = 'Finance'
    ```

19. Click **Validate** and then **OK** if there are no errors.

20. With the **Organization name** filter selected, change the **Usage** property to **Optional** in the **Properties** pane.

21. From the **Run** menu, select **View Tabular Data** to test your query. The query results should match what's shown in Figure 3.19.

Organization name	Current manager	Employee name	Date	Course name	Course days	Course cost
Finance	Anling Zhang	Baojia Chén	Apr 2, 2007	GO Communication	1	500
Finance	Emma Sommer	Gregory Andrews	Apr 16, 2007	GO Communication	1	500
Finance	Helen Jones	David Baxter	Apr 5, 2007	GO Ethics	0.5	250
Finance	Helen Jones	David Baxter	Apr 23, 2007	Economic and Tax Forecasting 1	2	2,500
Finance	Helen Jones	David Baxter	Apr 30, 2007	GO Finance 1	1	1,000
Finance	Helen Jones	Emily Harris	Apr 9, 2007	GO Ethics	0.5	250
Finance	Helen Jones	Emily Harris	Apr 17, 2007	GO Finance 1	1	1,000
Finance	Helen Jones	Emily Harris	Apr 23, 2007	Economic and Tax Forecasting 1	2	2,500
Finance	Helen Jones	Katharina Lehrer	Apr 10, 2007	GO Orientation	1	250
Finance	Helen Jones	Katharina Lehrer	Apr 19, 2007	GO Ethics	0.5	250
Finance	Ian Roberts	Jean-Pierre Louvet	Apr 5, 2007	GO Ethics	0.5	250
Finance	Ian Roberts	Jean-Pierre Louvet	Apr 16, 2007	GO Finance 1	1	1,000
Finance	Ian Roberts	Lena Bauman	Apr 2, 2007	Accounting Concepts 2	2	2,000
Finance	Ian Roberts	Maurus Gerster	Apr 24, 2007	GO Orientation	1	250
Finance	Ian Roberts	Rolf Schirmer	Apr 13, 2007	GO Communication	1	500

Figure 3.19   Training_by_Manager query results

22. Close **IBM Cognos Viewer** to return to your report design.

Step 3: Change the Page Name and Report ID

Since the template has details about how to build the title and ReportID, we will now make those changes.

1. In the **Explorer Bar**, mouse over the **Page Explorer** and select the **Report Pages** folder. The report page still shows "Change the Page Name to Add the Report Title."

2. In the work area, click the page to select it.

3. In the **Properties** pane, change the **Name** property to the following:

    ```
    Training by Manager
    ```

4. Double-click the **Training by Manager** page to return to the page design.

    Now the ReportID should have the custom message too.

5. In the work area, click the **Text Prompt** in the footer to select it.

6. In the **Properties** pane, double-click the **Default Selections** property to open the dialog box.

7. In the list of default selections, double-click **Change the default selection in prompt and hide** to edit it.

8. In the Edit dialog box, replace the existing text with the following new report ID: **HR235**.

9. From the **Run** menu, select **Run Report – HTML** to see your changes to the template. The report output should look similar to what's shown in Figure 3.20.

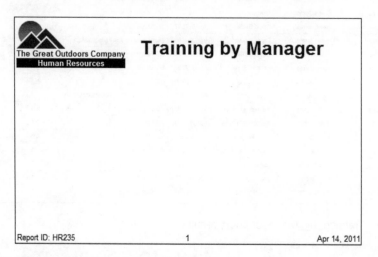

Figure 3.20   Initial page design with header and footer

10. Close **IBM Cognos Viewer** to return to your report design.

     The template has the text prompt visible as a cue to the report writer to change it.

11. Select the text box prompt and change the **Visible** property to **No**.

Step 4: Build the List Report

Now that the template has a list already created, we will add the individual query items to the report and not the entire query subject. If we were to drag the entire query subject, IBM Cognos Report Studio would embed a second list inside the first.

1. From the **Data Items** tab in the **Insertable Objects** pane, Shift-click all the items in the **Training_by_Manager** query.

2. Drag the selected items into the list in the work area.

3. In the work area, Ctrl-click the **List Column Headers** for **Organization name**, **Current manager**, and **Employee name** to select them.

4. From the toolbar, click the **Group/Ungroup** button.

5. In the work area, click the **List Column Header** for **Organization name**.

6. From the toolbar, click the **Section** button.

7. In the work area, click the **List Column Header** for **Current Manager**.

8. From the toolbar, click the **Headers & Footers** button and select **Create Header**.

9. Now that the manager name has been added to the header, click the **Delete** button on the toolbar to remove the column.

   The list width has already been set as a result of using the template, and the section formatting is complete also.

10. From the **Run** menu, select **Run Report – HTML** to test your report. The report output should have numbers similar to those shown in Figure 3.21.

11. Close **IBM Cognos Viewer** to return to your report design.

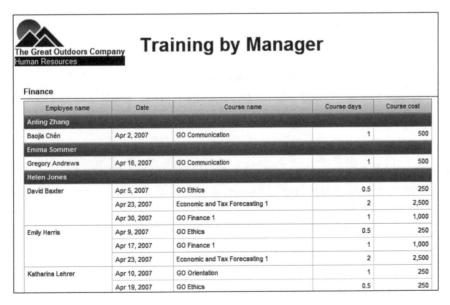

Finance

Employee name	Date	Course name	Course days	Course cost
Anling Zhang				
Baojia Chén	Apr 2, 2007	GO Communication	1	500
Emma Sommer				
Gregory Andrews	Apr 16, 2007	GO Communication	1	500
Helen Jones				
David Baxter	Apr 5, 2007	GO Ethics	0.5	250
	Apr 23, 2007	Economic and Tax Forecasting 1	2	2,500
	Apr 30, 2007	GO Finance 1	1	1,000
Emily Harris	Apr 9, 2007	GO Ethics	0.5	250
	Apr 17, 2007	GO Finance 1	1	1,000
	Apr 23, 2007	Economic and Tax Forecasting 1	2	2,500
Katharina Lehrer	Apr 10, 2007	GO Orientation	1	250
	Apr 19, 2007	GO Ethics	0.5	250

Figure 3.21   Initial list report design

Step 5: Add Prompts and Titles to the Report

The parameter names that you use in this step need to match the parameters used in the previous report because the template is assuming that the parameters are the same. You may see an additional prompt page if the parameter names do not match.

1. In the **Explorer Bar**, mouse over the **Query Explorer** tab and select the **Training_by_Manager** query.

2. In the **Detail Filters** pane of the work area, double-click the filter for **Year**.

3. Replace **2007** with **?Selected Year?**. The expression should look like this:

```
[Employee training (query)].[Time].[Year] = ?Selected Year?
```

NOTE   The parameters you add here need to match the ones created in the first report. This will allow us to quickly merge the reports together in the briefing book at the end of this chapter.

---

4. Validate the expression and click **OK** to close the Detail Filter Expression dialog box.

5. When prompted, type **2007** for the year.

6. Double-click the filter for **Month**.

7. Replace **'April'** with **?Selected Month?**. The expression should look like this:

```
[Employee training (query)].[Time].[Month] = ?Selected Month?
```

8. Click **OK** to close the Detail Filter Expression dialog box.

9. Double-click the filter for **Organization name**.

10. Replace **'Finance'** with **?Selected Organization?**. The expression should look like this:

```
[Organization name] = ?Selected Organization?
```

11. Click **OK** to close the Detail Filter Expression dialog box.

12. From the **Run** menu, select **Run Report – HTML** to test your report.

    When prompted, select **April**, **Finance**, and **2007**. The report output should have numbers similar to those shown in Figure 3.22.

13. Close **IBM Cognos Viewer** to return to your report design.

14. Save the report as **Training by Manager**.

This report showed how templates can be used by report authors to reuse formatting across reports. Like the global styles, the IBM Cognos BI administrator could add this template so that it would appear in the new report dialog box for every user.

The Great Outdoors Company
Human Resources

Training by Manager

For Finance in April 2007

Finance

Employee name	Date	Course name	Course days	Course cost
Anling Zhang				
Baojia Chén	Apr 2, 2007	GO Communication	1	500
Emma Sommer				
Gregory Andrews	Apr 16, 2007	GO Communication	1	500
Helen Jones				
David Baxter	Apr 5, 2007	GO Ethics	0.5	250
	Apr 23, 2007	Economic and Tax Forecasting 1	2	2,500
	Apr 30, 2007	GO Finance 1	1	1,000
Emily Harris	Apr 9, 2007	GO Ethics	0.5	250
	Apr 17, 2007	GO Finance 1	1	1,000
	Apr 23, 2007	Economic and Tax Forecasting 1	2	2,500
Katharina Lehrer	Apr 10, 2007	GO Orientation	1	250
	Apr 19, 2007	GO Ethics	0.5	250

Figure 3.22   Completed training by manager report

Creating the Briefing Book

Now that the human resources department is using these reports individually, you find out that they compile all of these reports together as a yearly summary. To save time, you offer to compile all the reports into one and add a table of contents to allow for easy navigation. The completed table of contents should match what's shown in Figure 3.23.

Design

With the actual content already built into three different reports, we will copy and paste the queries and then import the report pages from the original reports into the new briefing book.

With the report pages added, a table of contents can be added to the first page of the report, and table of contents entries can be placed in the report details.

Step-by-Step

As you learn more about how the report specifications are stored, you can merge the contents of several reports into one master report. This saves you time in developing complex reports and saves time for the report consumers since the reports are already merged and collated.

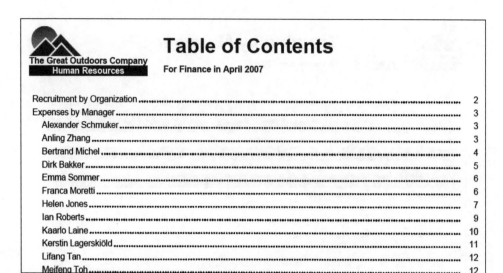

Table of Contents

The Great Outdoors Company
Human Resources   For Finance in April 2007

Figure 3.23   Completed HR briefing book table of contents

Step 1: Start the Report

1. Launch **Report Studio** and select the **GO Data Warehouse (query)** package.

2. Click on the **Create New** option.

COGNOS 8 NOTE   The option is **Create a new report or template**.

---

3. Select the **Blank** report template and click **OK**.

    We will be using the **Employee training (query)** namespace inside the **HR (query)** folder. The only data items we will be using are the attributes used by the prompts, so any namespace should work.

    We will not be using the template in this example since the table of contents will not be using a list data container.

Step 2: Import the Recruitment by Organization Report

When you cut or copy report parts onto the clipboard, you are manipulating XML code that can be placed in other reports. Since the data containers on the page refer to queries, we will make sure that the queries are copied to the new report first.

1. In the **Explorer Bar**, mouse over the **Query Explorer** tab and select the **Queries** folder.

   The queries will be coming from the other reports created in this chapter, so you will want to open a second IBM Cognos Report Studio session.

2. Navigate in another browser session from **IBM Cognos Connection** and launch **Report Studio**.

   Even though you will be opening a report, you still need to select a package. When prompted for a package, you can select any one. A typical problem that new users have with IBM Cognos Report Studio is that they try to open a report from the Select a Package dialog.

3. Select the **GO Data Warehouse (query)** package.

4. Click on **Open Existing** option.

   The Open dialog box is displayed.

COGNOS 8 NOTE   The option is **Open an existing report or template**.

---

5. Open the **Recruitment by Organization** report.

6. In the **Explorer Bar**, mouse over the **Query Explorer** tab and select the **Queries** folder.

7. Right-click on the **Recruitment_by_Organization** query in the work area.

8. Select **Copy** from the shortcut menu.

9. Navigate to the new report window.

10. In the work area of the **Query Explorer**, right-click and select **Paste** from the shortcut menu.

11. Navigate back to the **Recruitment by Organization** report.

12. In the **Explorer Bar**, mouse over the **Page Explorer** tab and select the **Report Pages** folder.

13. Right-click on the **Recruitment by Organization** page in the work area.

14. Select **Copy** from the shortcut menu.

15. Navigate back to the new report window.

16. In the **Explorer Bar**, mouse over the **Page Explorer** tab and select the **Report Pages** folder.

17. In the **Report Pages** pane of the work area, right-click below **Page1** and select **Paste** from the shortcut menu.

    The Report Pages pane should match what's shown in Figure 3.24.

18. Save the report as **HR Briefing Book**.

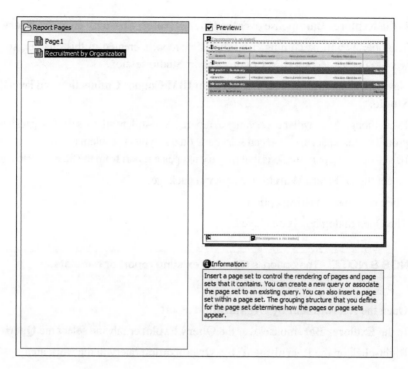

Figure 3.24   Briefing book page list

Step 3: Import the Expenses by Manager Report

When you copy entire queries and then report pages, nothing needs to change in these objects. The report writer can focus on the placement of the pages.

1. In the **Explorer Bar** of the HR Briefing Book, mouse over the **Query Explorer** tab and select the **Queries** folder.

2. Navigate to the **Recruitment by Organization** report session.

3. From the toolbar, select the **Open** button.

4. Open the **Expenses by Manager** report.

5. In the **Explorer Bar**, mouse over the **Query Explorer** tab and select the **Queries** folder.

6. Right-click on the **Expense_by_Manager** query in the work area.

7. Select **Copy** from the shortcut menu.

8. Navigate to the **HR Briefing Book** report.

9. In the **Explorer Bar**, mouse over the **Query Explorer** tab and select the **Queries** folder.

10. In the work area of the **Query Explorer**, right-click in the work area below **Recruitment_by_Organization** and select **Paste** from the shortcut menu.

   The work area should match what's shown in Figure 3.25.

Figure 3.25   Briefing book query list

11. Navigate back to the **Expenses by Manager** report.

12. In the **Explorer Bar**, mouse over the **Page Explorer** tab and select the **Report Pages** folder.

13. Right-click on the **Expenses by Manager** page in the work area.

14. Select **Copy** from the shortcut menu.

15. Navigate back to the **HR Briefing Book** report window.

16. In the **Explorer Bar**, mouse over the **Page Explorer** tab and select the **Report Pages** folder.

17. In the **Report Pages** pane of the work area, right-click below **Recruitment by Organization** and select **Paste** from the shortcut menu.

   The Report Pages pane should match what's shown in Figure 3.26.

18. Save the **HR Briefing Book** report.

Step 4: Import the Training by Manager Report

One more query and report need to be copied into the briefing book report.

1. In the **Explorer Bar** of the HR Briefing Book, mouse over the **Query Explorer** tab and select the **Queries** folder.

2. Navigate to the **Expenses by Manager** report session.

3. From the toolbar, select **Open**.

4. Open the **Training by Manager** report.

5. In the **Explorer Bar**, mouse over the **Query Explorer** tab and select the **Queries** folder.

6. Right-click on the **Training_by_Manager** query in the work area.

7. Select **Copy** from the shortcut menu.

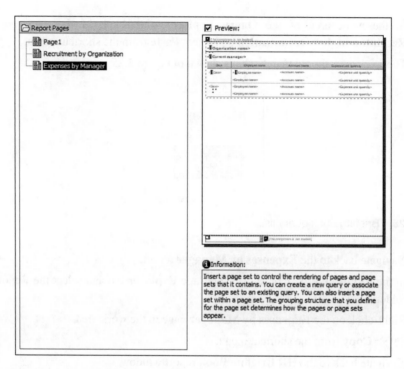

Figure 3.26   Updated briefing book page list

8. Navigate to the **HR Briefing Book** report.

9. In the **Explorer Bar**, mouse over the **Query Explorer** tab and select the **Queries** folder.

10. In the work area of the **Query Explorer**, right-click in the work area below **Expense_by_Manager** and select **Paste** from the shortcut menu.

    The work area should match what's shown in Figure 3.27.

Figure 3.27   Updated briefing book query list

11. Navigate back to the **Training by Manager** report.

12. In the **Explorer Bar**, mouse over the **Page Explorer** tab and select the **Report Pages** folder.

13. Right-click on the **Training by Manager** page in the work area.

14. Select **Copy** from the shortcut menu.

15. From the **File** menu, select **Exit** to close the **Training by Manager** report session.

16. Navigate back to the **HR Briefing Book** report session.

17. In the **Explorer Bar**, mouse over the **Page Explorer** tab and select the **Report Pages** folder.

18. In the **Report Pages** pane of the work area, right-click below **Expenses by Manager** and select **Paste** from the shortcut menu.

    The Report Pages pane should match what's shown in Figure 3.28.

19. Save the **HR Briefing Book** report.

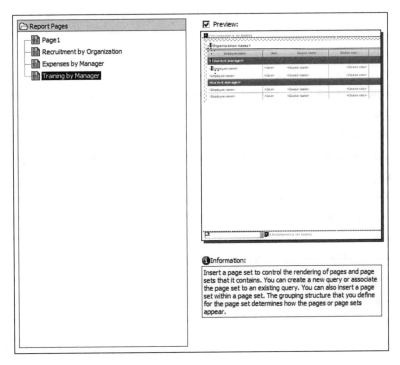

Figure 3.28   Updated briefing book page list

Step 5: Create the Table of Contents

Now that the report detail pages have been added, the original page that was created with this report can be converted into the table of contents.

1. In the **Explorer Bar**, mouse over the **Page Explorer** tab and select **Report Pages**.

2. In the work area, click **Page1** to select it.

3. In the **Properties** pane, change the **Name** property to **Table of Contents**.

4. In the **Report Pages** pane of the work area, double-click the **Table of Contents** page to open it.

5. Click in the work area to select the **Page Body**.

6. From the toolbar, click the **Headers & Footers** button and select **Page Header & Footer**. A dialog box is displayed.

7. Click the check boxes for both **Header** and **Footer**.

8. Click **OK** to close the dialog box.

   The page header and footer areas are now displayed in the work area.

9. From the **Toolbox** tab of the **Insertable Objects** pane, drag a **Layout Component Reference** object into the header area.

   The Component Reference dialog box is displayed.

10. Change the **Component Location** radio button to **Another report**.

11. Click the ellipsis button to display the Open dialog box.

12. Select **HR Layout Library** and click **Open**.

13. In the **Available components to reference** pane, click **ReportHeader** to select it.

14. Click **OK** to close the dialog box.

15. From the **Toolbox** tab of the **Insertable Objects** pane, drag a second **Layout Component Reference** object into the footer area. The Component Reference dialog box is displayed.

16. Change the **Component Location** radio button to **Another report**.

17. Click the ellipsis button to display the Open dialog box.

18. Select **HR Layout Library** and click **Open**.

19. In the **Available components to reference** pane, click **ReportFooter** to select it.

20. Click **OK** to close the dialog box.

21. From the **Toolbox** tab in the **Insertable Objects** pane, drag a **Text Box Prompt** object into the footer.

   The Prompt Wizard dialog is displayed.

22. Change the name of the new parameter to **ReportID**.

23. Click **Finish** to complete the wizard.

NOTE   Do not click **Next** because we will not need filters and additional queries built.

---

24. In the work area, click the prompt you just added to select it.

25. In the **Properties** pane, double-click the **Default Selections** property to open the dialog box.

26. In the lower-left corner of the dialog box, click the **Add** button.

27. In the Add dialog box, type the report ID of **HRYEARLY**.

28. Click **OK** to close the dialog box.

29. Click **OK** to close the Default Selections dialog box.

30. With the text prompt still selected, change the **Visible** property to **No**.

31. From the **Run** menu, select **Run Report – HTML** to test your report. The report output should have numbers similar to those shown in Figure 3.29.

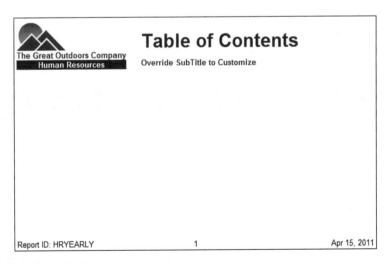

Figure 3.29   Initial page design with a header and footer

As you page through the report, note that the ReportID is HRYEARLY for all pages. The first prompt with a Default Selection in the report sets the default value for all other prompts in the report. This helps to prove that report parameters are shared throughout the report and not just on a report page.

32. Close **IBM Cognos Viewer** to return to your report design.

33. From the **Toolbox** tab of the **Insertable Objects** pane, drag a **Table of Contents** object into the **Page Body** in the work area.

34. Save the report.

Step 6: Build the Table of Contents Entries

When you add a Table of Contents object onto a report, you will add Table of Contents Entries to build the list on the table of contents page. The entries are linked to a specific table of contents and are assigned as a specific level.

1. In the **Explorer Bar**, mouse over the **Page Explorer** tab and select **Recruitment by Organization**.

2. From the **Toolbox** tab of the **Insertable Objects** pane, drag a **Table of Contents Entry** object to the left side of the header layout component reference. The page should resemble what's shown in Figure 3.30.

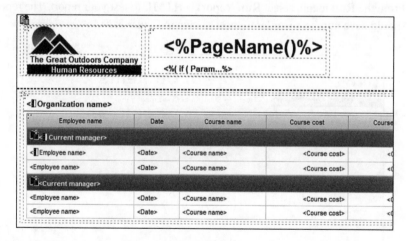

Figure 3.30 Page design with table of contents entry

3. In the **Explorer Bar**, mouse over the **Page Explorer** tab and select **Expenses by Manager**.

4. From the **Toolbox** tab of the **Insertable Objects** pane, drag a **Table of Contents Entry** object to the left side of the header layout component reference.

To add sections for each manager, we will add a level 2 table of contents entry.

5. From the toolbar, select the **Unlock (currently locked)** button.

6. From the **Toolbox** tab in the **Insertable Objects** pane, drag a **Table of Contents Entry** directly to the left of **Current manager** in the **Page Body**.

7. In the work area, click the newly added **Table of Contents Entry** to select it.

8. In the **Properties** pane, change the **Heading Level** property to **2**.

    This means that the entry will be a subheading rather than the heading in the table of contents.

9. In the **Explorer Bar**, mouse over the **Page Explorer** tab and select **Training by Manager**.

10. From the **Toolbox** tab of the **Insertable Objects** pane, drag a **Table of Contents Entry** object to the left side of the header layout component reference.

11. Drag a **Table of Contents Entry** directly to the left of **Current manager** in the **Page Body**.

12. In the work area, click the newly added **Table of Contents Entry** to select it.

13. In the **Properties** pane, change the **Heading Level** property to **2**.

14. In the **Explorer Bar**, mouse over the **Page Explorer** tab and select the **Table of Contents** page.

With the references to all the newly added entries, the page should match what's shown in Figure 3.31.

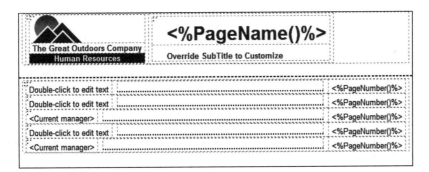

Figure 3.31   Table of contents page with entries

Step 7: Complete the Design of the Table of Contents

On the Table of Contents page, there are three empty text fields. We want to replace the empty text with the page name of each page. The two entries that say Current manager are level-two headings and should be indented. Finally, the subtitle should display the same parameter information as the three detail report pages.

1. In the work area, click the first text item in the **Table of Contents** to select it.

2. In the **Properties** pane, change the **Source Type** property to **Report Expression**.

3. Double-click the **Report Expression** property to open the dialog box.

4. In the **Expression Definition** pane, type **PageName()** to display the name of the page containing the table of contents entry.

5. Validate the expression and click **OK** to close the dialog box.

   You may be prompted to select a year. Type **2007** and click **OK**.

6. In the work area, click the second text item in the **Table of Contents** to select it.

7. In the **Properties** pane, change the **Source Type** property to **Report Expression**.

8. Double-click the **Report Expression** property to open the dialog box.

9. In the **Expression Definition** pane, type **PageName()** to display the name of the page containing the table of contents entry.

10. Validate the expression and click **OK** to close the dialog box.

11. In the work area, click the third text item (the first one that uses **Current manager**) in the **Table of Contents** to select it.

12. In the **Properties** pane, double-click the **Padding** property to open the dialog box.

13. Change the left padding value to **15 px**.

14. Click **OK** to close the dialog box.

15. In the work area, click the fourth text item in the **Table of Contents** to select it.

16. In the **Properties** pane, change the **Source Type** property to **Report Expression**.

17. Double-click the **Report Expression** property to open the dialog box.

18. In the **Expression Definition** pane, type **PageName()** to display the name of the page containing the table of contents entry.

19. Validate the expression and click **OK** to close the dialog box.

20. In the work area, click the fifth text item (the second one that uses **Current manager**) in the **Table of Contents** to select it.

21. In the **Properties** pane, double-click the **Padding** property to open the dialog box.

22. Change the left padding value to **15 px**.

23. Click **OK** to close the dialog box.

24. Now that the entries are finished, click **Lock (currently unlocked)** on the toolbar.

25. Click the page header to select it.

26. In the **Properties** pane, double-click the **Overrides** property to display the dialog box.

27. Click the check box next to **SubTitle** to select it.

28. Click **OK** to close the dialog box.

29. From the **Toolbox** tab in the **Insertable Objects** pane, drag a **Layout Calculation** object to the right of the text in the title. The Report Expression dialog box is displayed.

30. In the Report Expression dialog box, type the following:

```
( if ( ParamDisplayValue('Selected Organization') is not null )
 then
    ( 'For '+ParamDisplayValue('Selected Organization')+' in ' )
 else
    ( 'For all organizations in ' ) )
+
if ( ParamDisplayValue('Selected Month') is not null ) then
    ( ParamDisplayValue('Selected Month') + ' ' +
       ParamDisplayValue('Selected Year') )
else
    ( ParamDisplayValue('Selected Year') )
```

31. Validate the expression and click **OK** to close the dialog box.

32. From the **Run** menu, select **Run Report – PDF** to test your report.

When prompted, select **April**, **Finance**, and **2007**. The report table of contents should have numbers similar to those shown in Figure 3.32.

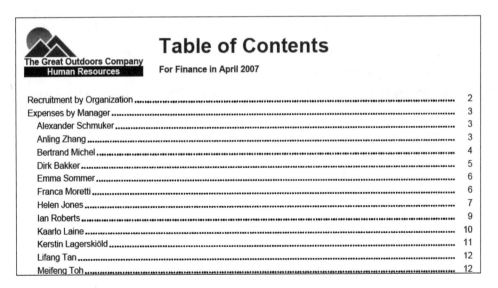

Figure 3.32 Completed HR briefing book report

33. Close **IBM Cognos Viewer** to return to your report design.

34. Save the report.

Now we have built a single report that integrates all the details of three reports. Additionally, with common parameters, different organizations can request reports for different months.

Summary

In this chapter, we wanted to develop a better understanding of the hierarchical relationship that is built into IBM Cognos BI 10. Objects can be nested inside other objects. The properties are inherited from higher levels until they are overridden in child objects. This concept can simplify the report-creation process and make maintaining reports easier.

The first example shows that you can create customized components using layout component references. We used the term *layout library* to mean a report that contains one or more layout components that could be used in multiple reports. In the references, you can use either layout calculations or report parameters since there is no query associated with the items. If you need to customize items in the layout library, you can create named items and override them in the target report.

With the layout library created, three additional reports were built with a number of hierarchical features.

With different reports built, the human resources department asked that these reports be integrated into a quarterly report. By copying and pasting queries and then pages, we accomplished this task. Using consistent parameters and layout component references, the reports were integrated easily. We used the table of contents functionality to create a very complex organization to the report.

Some techniques that you may want to integrate into other reports include the following:

- Using layout libraries to create a set of standard report layout pieces
- Creating templates to remove many of the formatting tasks from report creation
- Integrating layout calculations and parameters into libraries for powerful references
- Leveraging and overriding classes to simplify formatting report objects
- Copying and pasting queries and report pages from one report to another

CHAPTER 4

Overriding the Data Model

Even after going through IBM Cognos Report Studio Fundamentals and Advanced classes, our students sometimes find it challenging to relate the topics learned in class to their own environment because their data just isn't organized the same way as the sample data in class.

Formatting of the reports is not as difficult as it is time-consuming; however, having the most dazzling report does not matter one bit if it is not displaying the correct data. Getting the correct data sometimes requires creating complex queries. This could include querying the database multiple times and combining the results in ways that were not possible during the creation of reporting models (packages). This might have been done intentionally by the developer of the model to design a package that can provide predictable results to match most of the team's reporting needs.

Modelers should follow certain best practices that do not involve customizing the package for each report. Their objective rather is to build a package that can be used to create as many reports as possible within the scoped requirements.

Another issue that can come up is that the models are not meeting report requirements fully due to lack of development time, modeler inexperience, or incomplete business requirements. Report developers cannot wait for the model to change; they have to work within the existing model and override aspects of the model instead of expecting the model to change.

The design technique of overriding the data model is not limited to a specific type of the report and does not separate one report from the other. This technique is used in conjunction with all other techniques discussed in this book to create a very functional, highly formatted, and easily maintained report.

We have selected techniques to present in this chapter in order to demonstrate the solution for the most common challenges that students bring up in class. These challenges involve the ability to ensure that all items are counted in all warehouses even if none are currently available and the ability to perform data audits when building data warehouses.

In our first example, we will demonstrate the usage of query unions to overcome the constraints of the reporting package. Our second example will use query joins to create relationships between data elements that were not defined in the model.

NOTE   If you want some help with the files and typing involved in this chapter, go to www.ibmpressbooks.com/title/9780132656757 and download the supplements.zip file from the Downloads section under **More Information**.

Creating a Union

Your customer wants a report to view the inventory at each location to help with the monthly audit. The modeler defined a relationship such that products will be listed only if they are available at the warehouse location. The report should have a list of all the products in the ficticious Great Outdoors Company catalog, not just the items that are in inventory. This will help track the items that are available and the ones that are not available for distribution.

The report will prompt the user for a month and year. The prompt will also allow the report consumer to view reports for all warehouses or for a specific warehouse.

After the prompt, the title will display the warehouse location. The products available will be placed into sections by the product types. The detail lines will contain a column for the product, one for the stated inventory, and one final column to allow for inventory audit staff to write the number on hand.

The final report should match what's shown in Figure 4.1.

Design

The model is designed so that you see inventory on hand at a given location because the modeler created an inner join between the facts (inventory numbers) and the dimensions (product information).

It will not allow us to also see the items that are not in inventory.

Instead of asking the modeler to change the model, we are going to create two queries: one that gives us inventory on hand and one that gives us all the products. By doing the union, we will be showing all products whether or not they are on hand.

This is a common report query challenge that students describe in class. The problem is an inability to report on certain items or events that did not happen (i.e., there was no sale, or there were no events).

Boston

January 2004

Product type	Product	Closing inventory	Inventory on Hand
Binoculars	Seeker 35	2,443	
	Seeker 50	874	
	Seeker Extreme	631	
	Seeker Mini	805	
Climbing Accessories	Firefly Charger	0	
	Firefly Climbing Lamp	0	
	Firefly Rechargeable Battery	0	
	Granite Belay	0	
	Granite Carabiner	0	
	Granite Chalk Bag	0	
	Granite Pulley	0	
Cooking Gear	TrailChef Canteen	11,967	
	TrailChef Cook Set	7,049	
	TrailChef Cup	9,308	
	TrailChef Deluxe Cook Set	5,570	
	TrailChef Double Flame	3,201	
	TrailChef Kettle	11,736	
	TrailChef Kitchen Kit	8,990	
	TrailChef Single Flame	6,738	
	TrailChef Utensils	5,075	

Figure 4.1   Completed inventory count report

The most common request is to show zero values in the report for items that otherwise would not show in the report. Report developers will often think that the problem lies with the model, and they are only partially correct to think that.

The way data has been modeled will cause this issue, but it is not necessarily a problem that needs to be resolved. It is actually caused by the modeler following the best practices for meta-data modeling.

Step-by-Step

There are 11 steps involved in the creation of the queries, the formatting of the report, and the building of the prompt page.

Step 1: Start the Report

1. Launch **Report Studio** and select the **GO Data Warehouse (query)** package.
2. Click on the **Create new** option.

COGNOS 8 NOTE   The option is **Create a new report or template**.

---

   3.   Select **List** report template and click **OK**.

      We will be using the **Inventory (query)** namespace inside the **Sales and Marketing (query)** folder.

Step 2: Set Up Report Queries

This step creates a main query that is a union of two queries.

   1.   In the **Explorer Bar**, hover over the **Query Explorer** tab and select the **Queries** folder.

   2.   Rename **Query1** to **Main_Query**.

   3.   Drag a **Union** object from the **Insertable Objects** pane and place it to the right of the **Main_Query**.

      The work area for the queries should look like Figure 4.2.

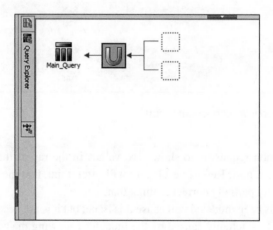

Figure 4.2   Union query object

   4.   Drag two **Query** objects from the **Insertable Objects** pane, one into each of the place-holders to the right of the **Union** object.

   5.   Rename the two new **Query** objects: **Query1** to **All_Products** and **Query2** to **Products_in_Inventory**.

Step 3: Build the Products_in_Inventory Query

   1.   Double-click the **Products_in_Inventory** query. The Query Definition dialog box is displayed.

2. From the **Source** tab of the **Insertable Objects** pane, drag the following query items into the query from the **Sales and Marketing (query)** folder and **Inventory (query)** namespace:

   - The **City** query item from the **Branch** query subject
   - The **Product type** query item from the **Products** query subject
   - The **Product** query item from the **Products** query subject
   - The **Closing inventory** query item from the **Inventory fact** query subject

COGNOS 8 NOTE   The **Products** query subject is called **Product**, and the **Product** query item is called **Product Name**.

3. Click the **City** data item in the **Data Items** pane of the query design window, and change the **Pre-Sort** property to **Sort ascending**.

4. Click the **Product type** data item in the **Data Items** pane of the query design window, and change the **Pre-Sort** property to **Sort ascending**.

5. Click the **Product** query subject in the **Data Items** pane of the query design window, and change the **Pre-Sort** property to **Sort ascending**.

6. From the **Toolbox** tab of the **Insertable Objects** pane, drag the **Filter** object into the **Detail Filters** area of the query design window.

7. In the **Detail Filter Expression** dialog box, create the following expression using the **Year** and **Month (numeric)** query items from the **Time** query subject:

   ```
   [Inventory (query)].[Time].[Year] = 2004 and
   [Inventory (query)].[Time].[Month (numeric)] = 1
   ```

NOTE   We will change this filter later when we are ready to build the prompt page.

COGNOS 8 NOTE   The **Time** query subject is called **Time Dimension**.

8. From the **Run** menu, select **View Tabular Data** to test your query. Figure 4.3 shows the output from the query.

COGNOS 8 NOTE   The **Closing inventory** query item has the default aggregate property of average in IBM Cognos 8. To get the numbers to match, you can change the **Aggregate Function** property to **Total**.

City	Product type	Product	Closing inventory
Boston	Binoculars	Seeker 35	2,443
Boston	Binoculars	Seeker 50	874
Boston	Binoculars	Seeker Extreme	631
Boston	Binoculars	Seeker Mini	805
Boston	Cooking Gear	TrailChef Canteen	11,967
Boston	Cooking Gear	TrailChef Cook Set	7,049
Boston	Cooking Gear	TrailChef Cup	9,308
Boston	Cooking Gear	TrailChef Deluxe Cook Set	5,570
Boston	Cooking Gear	TrailChef Double Flame	3,201
Boston	Cooking Gear	TrailChef Kettle	11,736
Boston	Cooking Gear	TrailChef Kitchen Kit	8,990
Boston	Cooking Gear	TrailChef Single Flame	6,738
Boston	Cooking Gear	TrailChef Utensils	5,075
Boston	Cooking Gear	TrailChef Water Bag	23,838
Boston	Eyewear	Polar Extreme	141
Boston	Eyewear	Polar Ice	382
Boston	Eyewear	Polar Sports	387
Boston	Eyewear	Polar Sun	277
Boston	Eyewear	Polar Wave	205
Boston	First Aid	Aloe Relief	3,413

Figure 4.3   Initial query results

Notice that Boston has inventory for Binoculars and Cooking Gear.

9. Close **IBM Cognos Viewer** to return to your report design.

Step 4: Build the All_Products Query

1. From the **Query Explorer** tab, select the **All_Products** query.

2. From the **Source** tab of the **Insertable Objects** pane, drag the following query items into the query from the **Sales and Marketing (query)** folder and **Inventory (query)** namespace:
   - The **City** query item from the **Branch** query subject
   - The **Product type** query item from the **Product** query subject
   - The **Product** query item from the **Product** query subject

3. From the **Toolbox** tab of the **Insertable Objects** pane, drag a **Data Item** object below the **Product name** in the **Data Items** section of the query design.

4. Type **0** (zero) in the Data Item Expression dialog box and click **OK**.

5. Rename the **Data Item1** data item to **Closing inventory**.

6. Click the **City** data item in the **Data Items** pane of the query design window, and change the **Pre-Sort** property to **Sort ascending**.

7. Click the **Product type** data item in the **Data Items** pane of the query design window, and change the **Pre-Sort** property to **Sort ascending**.

8. Click the **Product** query subject in the **Data Items** pane of the query design window, and change the **Pre-Sort** property to **Sort ascending**.

9. From the **Run** menu, select **View Tabular Data** to test your query. Verify that your query results match what's shown in Figure 4.4.

City	Product type	Product	Closing inventory
Boston	Binoculars	Seeker 35	0
Boston	Binoculars	Seeker 50	0
Boston	Binoculars	Seeker Extreme	0
Boston	Binoculars	Seeker Mini	0
Boston	Climbing Accessories	Firefly Charger	0
Boston	Climbing Accessories	Firefly Climbing Lamp	0
Boston	Climbing Accessories	Firefly Rechargeable Battery	0
Boston	Climbing Accessories	Granite Belay	0
Boston	Climbing Accessories	Granite Carabiner	0
Boston	Climbing Accessories	Granite Chalk Bag	0
Boston	Climbing Accessories	Granite Pulley	0
Boston	Cooking Gear	TrailChef Canteen	0
Boston	Cooking Gear	TrailChef Cook Set	0
Boston	Cooking Gear	TrailChef Cup	0
Boston	Cooking Gear	TrailChef Deluxe Cook Set	0
Boston	Cooking Gear	TrailChef Double Flame	0
Boston	Cooking Gear	TrailChef Kettle	0
Boston	Cooking Gear	TrailChef Kitchen Kit	0
Boston	Cooking Gear	TrailChef Single Flame	0
Boston	Cooking Gear	TrailChef Utensils	0

Figure 4.4   All_Products query results

Notice that now Boston has Climbing Accessories in between Binoculars and Cooking Gear.

Because the modeler defined an inner join between Products and Inventory Fact, the Products_in_Inventory query will contain only products that have inventory at that location. If you do not include any fact information in your query, you will not be constrained by the inner join.

By creating a "fake" Closing inventory data item in the All_Products query, we are creating the records needed to set up the display of the products that are not in inventory.

10. Close **IBM Cognos Viewer** to return to your report design.

Step 5: Build the Main_Query

1. From the **Query Explorer** tab, select **Main_Query**.

2. Drag **Union1** into the **Data Items** pane.

   You could have also chosen to drag all data items individually into the **Data Items** pane.

3. Click the **City** data item in the **Data Items** pane of the query design window, and change the **Pre-Sort** property to **Sort ascending**.

4. Click the **Product type** data item in the **Data Items** pane of the query design window, and change the **Pre-Sort** property to **Sort ascending**.

5. Click the **Product** query subject in the **Data Items** pane of the query design window, and change the **Pre-Sort** property to **Sort ascending**.

6. From the **Run** menu, select **View Tabular Data** to verify that your query results match what's shown in Figure 4.5. Click **OK** to dismiss the warning message.

City	Product type	Product	Closing inventory
Boston	Binoculars	Seeker 35	0
Boston	Binoculars	Seeker 35	2,443
Boston	Binoculars	Seeker 50	0
Boston	Binoculars	Seeker 50	874
Boston	Binoculars	Seeker Extreme	0
Boston	Binoculars	Seeker Extreme	631
Boston	Binoculars	Seeker Mini	0
Boston	Binoculars	Seeker Mini	805
Boston	Climbing Accessories	Firefly Charger	0
Boston	Climbing Accessories	Firefly Climbing Lamp	0
Boston	Climbing Accessories	Firefly Rechargeable Battery	0
Boston	Climbing Accessories	Granite Belay	0
Boston	Climbing Accessories	Granite Carabiner	0
Boston	Climbing Accessories	Granite Chalk Bag	0
Boston	Climbing Accessories	Granite Pulley	0
Boston	Cooking Gear	TrailChef Canteen	0
Boston	Cooking Gear	TrailChef Canteen	11,967
Boston	Cooking Gear	TrailChef Cook Set	0
Boston	Cooking Gear	TrailChef Cook Set	7,049
Boston	Cooking Gear	TrailChef Cup	0

Figure 4.5   Main_Query query results

Because we defined a union, our result shows two records for each product that had inventory, and one zero record for any product that did not have inventory.

The aggregation of inventory numbers was handled by the modeler in the Products_in_Inventory query. The projection list has the Aggregate Function property set to Automatic for each of the data items. We want to remove the duplicate records without affecting the inventory numbers.

7. Close **IBM Cognos Viewer** to return to your report design.

8. Click **City** and Shift-click **Product** to select the first three data items in the query. Change the **Aggregate Function** property to **None**.

9. Click **Closing inventory** and change the **Aggregate Function** property to **Total**.

10. From the **Run** menu, select **View Tabular Data** to test your query. Click **OK** to dismiss the warning message. Figure 4.6 shows the two details merged into one.

City	Product type	Product	Closing inventory
Boston	Binoculars	Seeker 35	2,443
Boston	Binoculars	Seeker 50	874
Boston	Binoculars	Seeker Extreme	631
Boston	Binoculars	Seeker Mini	805
Boston	Climbing Accessories	Firefly Charger	0
Boston	Climbing Accessories	Firefly Climbing Lamp	0
Boston	Climbing Accessories	Firefly Rechargeable Battery	0
Boston	Climbing Accessories	Granite Belay	0
Boston	Climbing Accessories	Granite Carabiner	0
Boston	Climbing Accessories	Granite Chalk Bag	0
Boston	Climbing Accessories	Granite Pulley	0
Boston	Cooking Gear	TrailChef Canteen	11,967
Boston	Cooking Gear	TrailChef Cook Set	7,049
Boston	Cooking Gear	TrailChef Cup	9,308
Boston	Cooking Gear	TrailChef Deluxe Cook Set	5,570
Boston	Cooking Gear	TrailChef Double Flame	3,201
Boston	Cooking Gear	TrailChef Kettle	11,736
Boston	Cooking Gear	TrailChef Kitchen Kit	8,990
Boston	Cooking Gear	TrailChef Single Flame	6,738
Boston	Cooking Gear	TrailChef Utensils	5,075

Figure 4.6   Query with merged results

By doing a union query, we are not changing the relationships defined by the modeler between the **Products** data and the **Inventory** numbers.

Step 6: Create the List Report

Now that the queries have been built and tested, we will create the report using that query. The report will perform page breaks for every city and list product type, product, and closing inventory.

1. From the **Page Explorer** tab, select the **Page1** object.

2. From the **Data Items** tab of the **Insertable Objects** pane, drag the **Product type**, **Product**, and **Closing inventory** data items from **Main_Query** into the **List** object.

3. Click on the **Product type** column body, and on the toolbar, click the **Group/Ungroup** button to group the products by product type.

Step 7: Create Page Breaks and the Title

1. From the **Page Explorer** tab, select the **Report Pages** folder.

2. From the **Toolbox** tab, drag the **Page Set** object into the **Report Pages** pane.

3. Click on the **Page Set1** page set.

4. Change the **Query** property to **Main_Query**.

5. Double-click the **Grouping & Sorting** property.

   The Grouping & Sorting dialog box is displayed.

6. Within the **Grouping & Sorting** dialog box, drag the **City** data item from the **Data Items** pane to the **Groups** folder of the **Groups** pane.

7. Drag the **City** data item from the **Data Items** pane to the **Sort List** folder under the **City** group.

8. Click **OK** to close the dialog box.

9. Drag the **Page1** object into the **Detail Pages** folder of **Page Set1**.

10. Double-click the **Page1** object to go back to the page design.

11. Click on the report title text to select it.

12. Change the **Source Type** property from **Text** to **Data Item Value**.

13. Change the **Data Item Value** property to **City**.

14. Run the report to test the page breaks and titles, as demonstrated in Figure 4.7.

15. Close **IBM Cognos Viewer** to return to your report design.

Step 8: Complete the Report Body

1. Click on the page body background and center the report content on the page by clicking the **Center** button in the toolbar.

   To assist inventory auditors, document any differences in the actual inventory on hand versus the report; we will add an empty column at the end to serve as a placeholder.

2. From the **Insertable Objects** pane, drag a **Text Item** object as the last column of the **List**. The Text dialog box is displayed.

Figure 4.7   Merged results with title

3. Click **OK** in the Text dialog box because we will not be typing in any static text. This column should be empty.

4. Double-click on the **Text Item** column title of the last column and change the text to **Inventory on Hand**.

Step 9: Create the Year and Month Prompt

Now that the report format is complete, we will create a prompt page to make the results of the report dynamic based on user choices. The report consumer will be able to choose the time period and warehouse locations.

1. From the **Query Explorer** tab, select the **Products_in_Inventory** query.

2. Double-click the filter defined in the **Detail Filters** pane. The Expression Definition dialog box is displayed.

3. In the **Detail Filter Expression** window, replace **2004** with **?Year?** and **1** with **?MonthNum?**, and click **OK**. Here is the updated filter expression:

```
[Inventory (query)].[Time].[Year] = ?Year? and
[Inventory (query)].[Time].[Month (numeric)] = ?MonthNum?
```

Our filter is now parameterized and we are ready to create prompt controls to link with the parameters.

4. From the **Page Explorer** tab, select **Prompt Pages** folder.

5. From the **Insertable Objects** pane, drag and drop a **Page** object into the **Prompt Pages** area.

6. Double-click **Prompt Page1** to activate the prompt page design.

7. Change the prompt page title to **Prompt Page**.

8. From the **Insertable Objects** pane, drag and drop a **Table** object into the page body of the prompt page, and in the **Insert Table** dialog box, uncheck the **Maximize width** property and click **OK**.

   A new table with one row and two columns is created. By unchecking Maximize width, you are making the width of each column only long enough for the items placed inside the cells.

9. From the **Insertable Objects** pane, drag a **Text Item** object into each of the two cells in the newly created table object. The text in each of the text boxes will be **Select Year:** and **Select Month:**, respectively.

10. From the **Insertable Objects** pane, drag a **Value Prompt** object into the first cell of the table to the right of the **Select Year:** text item.

11. In the **Prompt Wizard–Choose Parameter** dialog box, select the radio button for **Use existing parameter**, and in the drop-down menu, select the **Year** parameter. Click the **Next** button.

12. In the **Prompt Wizard–Populate Control** dialog box, change **Query1** to **YearPrompt** and click the **Finish** button.

13. Click the new **Value Prompt** object to select it and change the **Select UI** property to **ListBox**.

14. From the **Insertable Objects** pane, drag another **Value Prompt** object into the second cell of the table to the right of the **Select Month:** text item.

15. In the **Prompt Wizard–Choose Parameter** dialog box, select the radio button for **Use existing parameter**, and in the drop-down menu, select **MonthNum** parameter. Click the **Next** button.

16. In the **Prompt Wizard–Populate Control** dialog box, change **Query1** to **MonthPrompt**.

17. Click the ellipsis button next to the **Values to display** property and navigate to the **Inventory (query)** namespace inside the **Sales and Marketing (query)** folder. Select the **Month** query item from the **Time** query subject. Click **OK** and then click **Finish**.

18. Click the new value prompt object in the second table cell and change the **Select UI** property to **ListBox**.

19. Click the ellipsis button within the **Sorting** property of the selected prompt object, and in the Sorting dialog box, drag **Month (numeric)** from the **Data Items** pane to the **Sort List** pane. Click **OK**.

    This property will sort the months in the prompt control from January to December. Otherwise, the months will be sorted alphabetically.

20. Click the page body background and center all the content on the page by clicking the **Center** button on the toolbar.

21. Click the footer background and center all the footer content on the page by clicking the **Center** button again. All the prompt page action buttons will be centered on the page too.

22. Click any of the table cells and click the **Select Ancestor** button. Select the **Table** object.

NOTE   There is a new feature in Cognos 10 that can be used instead of the Select Ancestor button in this situation. You could have clicked on the three red dots in the upper-left corner of the table object.

---

23. Change the **Margin** property to add **15** pixels of bottom margin.

24. Run the report to test the prompts. Verify that the prompt page resembles Figure 4.8.

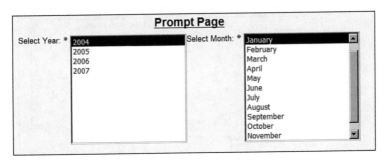

Figure 4.8   Year and month prompt

25. Close the **IBM Cognos Viewer** window after verifying that the report runs.

Step 10: Create the City Prompt

Now that you have filtered the report for a specific month, you will prompt the report consumer for the time frame as well as the city.

1. From the **Query Explorer** tab, select the **All_Products** query.
2. Create the following detail filter:
   `[City] in (?City?)`
3. From the **Query Explorer** tab, select the **Products_in_Inventory** query.
4. Create the following detail filter:
   `[City] in (?City?)`
5. From the **Page Explorer** tab, select the **Prompt Page1** page.
6. From the **Toolbox** tab of the **Insertable Objects** pane, drag a **Text Item** object under the table object. Type **Select City:** as text. Remember to add a space after the colon.
7. From the **Insertable Objects** pane, drag a **Value prompt** object next to the newly added text item.
8. In the **Prompt Wizard–Choose Parameter** dialog box, select the radio button for **Use existing parameter**, and in the drop-down menu select the **City** parameter. Click on the **Next** button.
9. In the **Prompt Wizard–Populate Control** dialog box, change **Query1** to **CityPrompt** and click on the **Finish** button.
10. Click on the new value prompt object and verify that the **Select UI** property is set to **ListBox**.
11. Run the report to test the prompts. The report prompt page should look like Figure 4.9.

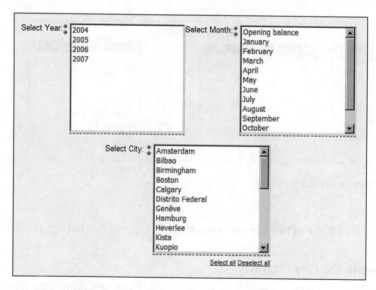

Figure 4.9   Report prompt page

Step 11: Modify the Report Title to Dynamically Show the Selected Year and Month

1. From the **Page Explorer** tab, select the **Page1** object.

2. From the **Insertable Objects** pane, drag a **Block** object under the existing **Block** in the **Page Header** area.

3. Click on the inserted **Block** object to select it, and click on the ellipsis button next to the **Classes** property (this property is the last property in the property list). In the Classes dialog box, select **Subtitle area** in the **Global classes** pane and move it into the **Selected classes** pane by clicking on the green arrow. Click **OK**.

4. From the **Insertable Objects** pane, drag a **Layout Calculation** object into the subtitle area block in the page header.

5. In the Report Expression dialog box, create the following expression:

```
ParamDisplayValue('MonthNum') + ' ' + ParamDisplayValue('Year')
```

6. Validate the expression and click **OK**.

The report should match the final report design shown in Figure 4.10.

Product type	Product	Closing inventory	Inventory on Hand
Binoculars	Seeker 35	2,443	
	Seeker 50	874	
	Seeker Extreme	631	
	Seeker Mini	805	
Climbing Accessories	Firefly Charger	0	
	Firefly Climbing Lamp	0	
	Firefly Rechargeable Battery	0	
	Granite Belay	0	
	Granite Carabiner	0	
	Granite Chalk Bag	0	
	Granite Pulley	0	
Cooking Gear	TrailChef Canteen	11,967	
	TrailChef Cook Set	7,049	
	TrailChef Cup	9,308	
	TrailChef Deluxe Cook Set	5,570	
	TrailChef Double Flame	3,201	
	TrailChef Kettle	11,736	
	TrailChef Kitchen Kit	8,990	
	TrailChef Single Flame	6,738	
	TrailChef Utensils	5,075	

Boston

January 2004

Figure 4.10 Final report

By creating a query that has attributes and zero-valued facts, you can ensure that all the items are listed regardless of join relationships between dimension tables and fact tables.

Joining SQL and Model Queries

When you convert a traditional report to using a new IBM Cognos data model, you want to verify that the new report query returns the same results as the original. This should help report consumers who are concerned that a new reporting process still matches the existing reports.

A challenge to this approach of report development is that you need special capabilities to create customized SQL. Your IBM Cognos BI administrator will determine whether you are permitted to create these types of queries.

One way is to create a report that runs the original query and the query using the new package. When the two queries are joined together, the results can be audited in a report that shows details that match and details that do not. This report could have a summary cover page (see Figure 4.11) and also display detailed results for direct comparison (see Figure 4.12).

Forecast Audit Report

This report compares the results of the Revenue Forecast Report from the previous reporting tool to the results of the new data model for Report Studio. This page will display the summary results and the following pages will show the details of query results that are different and those that match in both queries.

Record status	Expected volume	New expected volume	Forecast revenue	New forecast revenue
1. Totals are different between the two queries	160,550,400	23,856,220	$9,951,864,926.05	$1,412,538,239.50
4. Volume and revenue match	51,640,790	51,640,790	$2,861,757,832.60	$2,861,757,832.60

Figure 4.11   Completed query audit cover page

Design

The audit report will need to run two queries and perform a full outer join that merges all the results from the original query and the new query.

The new query will need a calculation to categorize the merged results in the following ways:

- There are matching results in both queries.
- The totals are different between the queries.
- Details exist in only the original query.
- Details exist in only the new query.

The report should have page breaks on each category.

A cover page should summarize the results of the queries, including links to the appropriate sections.

Forecast Audit Report

Year	Month	Country	Product	Expected volume	Forecast revenue	New expected volume	New forecast revenue
1. Totals are different between the two queries							
2004	April	Austria	Mountain Man Analog	120	$5,086.80	40	$1,695.60
			Mountain Man Deluxe	80	$6,969.60	40	$3,484.80
			Polar Ice	60	$5,805.00	30	$2,902.50
			Polar Sports	210	$25,907.70	30	$3,701.10
			Polar Sun	400	$23,104.00	50	$2,888.00
2004	April	Brazil	Mountain Man Analog	225	$9,537.75	75	$3,179.25
			Mountain Man Deluxe	160	$13,939.20	80	$6,969.60
			Polar Ice	100	$9,675.00	50	$4,837.50
			Polar Sports	350	$43,179.50	50	$6,168.50
			Polar Sun	360	$20,793.60	45	$2,599.20
2004	April	Canada	Mountain Man Analog	570	$24,162.30	190	$8,054.10
			Mountain Man Deluxe	310	$27,007.20	155	$13,503.60
			Polar Ice	160	$15,480.00	80	$7,740.00

Figure 4.12   Completed query audit report

Step-by-Step

The following steps describe the process of designing the two queries that will be joined together and generating the report that displays the results of the comparison.

Step 1: Start the Report

1. Launch **Report Studio** and select the **GO Data Warehouse (query)** package.
2. Click on the **Create new** option.
3. Select the **List** report template and click **OK**.

   We will be using the **Product forecast (query)** namespace inside the **Sales and Marketing (query)** folder.

Step 2: Set Up Report Queries

This step details the steps to create a main query that consists of a join between two other queries. The first query in the join is based on the SQL from the original report. The second one is based on the new data model.

1. In the **Explorer Bar**, hover over the **Query Explorer** tab and select the **Queries** folder.
2. Rename **Query1** to **Main_Query**.
3. Drag a **Join** object from the **Insertable Objects** pane and place it to the right of the **Main_Query**.

4.   Drag two **Query** objects from the **Insertable Objects** pane, one into each of the place-
     holders to the right of the **Join** object.

5.   Rename the two new **Query** objects–**Query1** to **New_Model_Query** and **Query2** to
     Legacy_Query.

6.   Drag a **SQL** object from the **Insertable Objects** pane to the right of the **Legacy_Query**.

     After completing these steps, your queries pane should look like Figure 4.13.

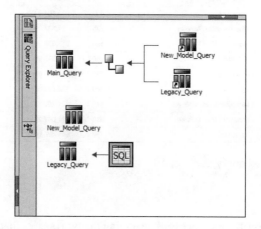

Figure 4.13   All queries in a join relationship

Step 3: Build New_Model_Query

1.   Double-click **New_Model_Query**.

2.   From the **Source** tab of the **Insertable Objects** pane, drag the following query items
     into the query from the **Sales and Marketing (query)** folder and **Product forecast
     (query)** namespace:

     • **Year** and **Month** query items from the **Time** query subject

     • The **Country** query item from the **Branch** query subject

     • The **Product** query item from the **Products** query subject

     • **Expected volume** and **Forecast revenue** query items from the Product forecast fact
       query subject

3.   In the **Data Items** pane, click **Year** and Shift-click **Product**.

4.   Change the **Pre-Sort** property to **Sort ascending** to ensure that the query itself is sorted
     by **Product** name.

5.   From the **Toolbox** tab of the **Insertable Objects** pane, drag the **Filter** object into the
     Detail Filters pane.

6. In the Detail Filter Expression dialog box, create the following expression using the **Month key** query item from the **Time dimension** query subject:

```
[Product forecast (query)].[Time].[Month key]
IN (200505, 200506)
```

NOTE We will be removing this filter after testing is complete for this query. To make sure that the report will actually return different data, we will query on months that are similar (May 2005) and ones that are in only one query (June 2005).

---

7. Validate the expression and click **OK** to close the dialog box.
8. From the **Run** menu, select **View Tabular Data** to test your query. The results should match what's shown in Figure 4.14.

Year	Month	Country	Product	Expected volume	Forecast revenue
2005	June	Australia	Aloe Relief	55	322.85
2005	June	Australia	Bear Edge	90	3,661.20
2005	June	Australia	Bear Survival Edge	35	3,482.50
2005	June	Australia	Blue Steel Max Putter	70	14,041.30
2005	June	Australia	Blue Steel Putter	85	7,286.20
2005	June	Australia	BugShield Extreme	1,570	11,932.00
2005	June	Australia	BugShield Lotion	345	2,270.10
2005	June	Australia	BugShield Lotion Lite	215	1,588.85
2005	June	Australia	BugShield Natural	715	3,939.65
2005	June	Australia	BugShield Spray	355	2,215.20
2005	June	Australia	Calamine Relief	50	300.50
2005	June	Australia	Canyon Mule Carryall	260	21,572.20
2005	June	Australia	Canyon Mule Climber Backpack	225	16,996.50
2005	June	Australia	Canyon Mule Cooler	340	10,995.60
2005	June	Australia	Canyon Mule Extreme Backpack	45	19,044.90
2005	June	Australia	Canyon Mule Journey Backpack	100	33,337.00
2005	June	Australia	Canyon Mule Weekender Backpack	95	23,952.35
2005	June	Australia	Compact Relief Kit	75	1,816.50
2005	June	Australia	Course Pro Gloves	285	3,462.75
2005	June	Australia	Course Pro Golf Bag	35	7,326.20

Figure 4.14 Forecast query using the new model

Step 4: Build Legacy_Query

The legacy query will contain the code from the previous version of the report.

1. In the **Explorer Bar**, hover over the **Query Explorer** tab and select the **Queries** folder.
2. Click the **SQL** object pointing to the **Legacy_Query** query.

3.   In the **Properties** pane, double-click the **Data Source** property.

This shows that reports do not need to be related directly to a package. As long as the data source is available in the IBM Cognos Connection environment, certain report authors can create their own SQL and query the database directly.

This feature may be limited by your IBM Cognos Administrator.

4.   Select **great_outdoors_sales** and click **OK**.

5.   Double-click the **SQL** property. The SQL dialog box is displayed.

6.   Enter the following code:

```
select UNIQUE_MONTH.CURRENT_YEAR,
       UNIQUE_MONTH.MONTH_EN,
       COUNTRY.COUNTRY_EN,
       UNIQUE_PRODUCT.PRODUCT_NAME,
       sum(PRODUCT_FORECAST.EXPECTED_VOLUME) as EXPECTED_VOLUME,
       sum(PRODUCT_FORECAST.UNIT_PRICE *
         PRODUCT_FORECAST.EXPECTED_VOLUME) as FORECAST_REVENUE
from
       (select distinct MONTH_KEY,
             min(CURRENT_YEAR) as CURRENT_YEAR,
             min(CURRENT_MONTH)as CURRENT_MONTH,
             min(MONTH_EN) as MONTH_EN
        from GOSALES.TIME_DIMENSION
        group by MONTH_KEY) UNIQUE_MONTH,
       GOSALES.COUNTRY COUNTRY,
       (select PRODUCT.BASE_PRODUCT_NUMBER AS
                  BASE_PRODUCT_NUMBER,
             PRODUCT_NAME_LOOKUP.PRODUCT_NAME AS PRODUCT_NAME
        from GOSALES.PRODUCT PRODUCT,
           GOSALES.PRODUCT_NAME_LOOKUP PRODUCT_NAME_LOOKUP
        where PRODUCT.PRODUCT_NUMBER =
             PRODUCT_NAME_LOOKUP.PRODUCT_NUMBER
          and PRODUCT_NAME_LOOKUP.PRODUCT_LANGUAGE = N'EN')
       UNIQUE_PRODUCT,
       GOSALES.PRODUCT_FORECAST PRODUCT_FORECAST,
       GOSALES.BRANCH BRANCH
  where PRODUCT_FORECAST.SALES_YEAR = UNIQUE_MONTH.CURRENT_YEAR
    and PRODUCT_FORECAST.SALES_MONTH = UNIQUE_MONTH.CURRENT_MONTH
    and PRODUCT_FORECAST.BRANCH_CODE = BRANCH.BRANCH_CODE
    and COUNTRY.COUNTRY_CODE = BRANCH.COUNTRY_CODE
    and PRODUCT_FORECAST.BASE_PRODUCT_NUMBER =
```

```
        UNIQUE_PRODUCT.BASE_PRODUCT_NUMBER
    and UNIQUE_MONTH.MONTH_KEY IN (200504, 200505)
group by UNIQUE_MONTH.CURRENT_YEAR,
         UNIQUE_MONTH.MONTH_EN,
         COUNTRY.COUNTRY_EN,
         UNIQUE_PRODUCT.PRODUCT_NAME
order by 1 asc , 2 asc , 3 asc , 4 asc
```

This SQL command is available from the book's website (www.ibmpressbooks.com/title/9780132656757) in the accompanying supplements.zip file as Product Forecast.sql.

NOTE   To make sure that the report will actually return different data, we will query on months that are similar (May 2005) and ones that are in only one query (April 2005). At the end of the testing of the report, you will remove the following line: and UNIQUE_MONTH .MONTH_KEY IN (200504, 200505).

---

7. Click **Validate** to check the syntax on the database server. Click **OK** if no messages appear.

8. Double-click **Legacy_Query**.

    Now we want to make sure that the legacy query uses the same names as the query using the new package..

9. From the **Properties** pane, rename the following data items:

    - **CURRENT_YEAR** to **Year**
    - **MONTH_EN** to **Month**
    - **COUNTRY_EN** to **Country**
    - **PRODUCT_NAME** to **Product**
    - **EXPECTED_VOLUME** to **Expected volume**
    - **FORECAST_REVENUE** to **Forecast revenue**

10. Click **Year** and Shift-click **Forecast revenue**. Change the **Aggregate Function** property to **None**.

    This is designed to turn off the automatic aggregation for the query in IBM Cognos Report Studio. This is done because the legacy query handled all the aggregation.

11. Click **Year**.

    This is done to select a single data item in order to test the query. Any one data item can be selected in this instance. If you do not click on a data item in the Data Items pane, you might get an error message in the next step.

12. From the **Run** menu, select **View Tabular Data** to test your query. Verify that your results match what's shown in Figure 4.15.

Year	Month	Country	Product	Expected volume	Forecast revenue
2,005	April	Australia	Aloe Relief	60	352.2
2,005	April	Australia	Bear Edge	90	3,661.2
2,005	April	Australia	Bear Survival Edge	40	3,980
2,005	April	Australia	Blue Steel Max Putter	95	19,056.05
2,005	April	Australia	Blue Steel Putter	75	6,429
2,005	April	Australia	BugShield Extreme	1,255	9,538
2,005	April	Australia	BugShield Lotion	415	2,730.7
2,005	April	Australia	BugShield Lotion Lite	230	1,699.7
2,005	April	Australia	BugShield Natural	785	4,325.35
2,005	April	Australia	BugShield Spray	565	3,525.6
2,005	April	Australia	Calamine Relief	45	270.45
2,005	April	Australia	Canyon Mule Carryall	185	15,349.45
2,005	April	Australia	Canyon Mule Climber Backpack	240	18,129.6
2,005	April	Australia	Canyon Mule Cooler	350	11,319
2,005	April	Australia	Canyon Mule Extreme Backpack	65	27,509.3
2,005	April	Australia	Canyon Mule Journey Backpack	105	35,003.85
2,005	April	Australia	Canyon Mule Weekender Backpack	120	30,255.6
2,005	April	Australia	Compact Relief Kit	70	1,695.4
2,005	April	Australia	Course Pro Gloves	895	10,874.25
2,005	April	Australia	Course Pro Golf Bag	35	7,326.2

Figure 4.15   Results of the SQL query

Step 5: Join Queries to Main_Query

1. From the **Query Explorer** tab, select **Queries**.

2. Double-click on the **Join Relationships** icon pointing to **Main_Query**.

3. From the Join Relationships dialog box, click **New Link** to create a join between the **Year** data items.

   The two queries should be joined on all the attributes in order to validate the numbers.

4. Click **New Link** and then click **Month** in both **New_Model_Query** and **Legacy_Query**.

5. Click **New Link** and then click **Country** in both **New_Model_Query** and **Legacy_Query**.

6. Click **New Link** and then click **Product** in both **New_Model_Query** and **Legacy_Query**.

7. Change both **Cardinality** drop-down boxes to **0..1**.

   This will allow the full outer join between the two query subjects to validate the data in both queries.

8. Click **OK**.

9. Double-click **Main_Query**.

   Now that the two queries have a join relationship between them, we need to define the fields to be returned.

Step 6: Build Main_Query

1. From the **Insertable Objects** pane, drag **Legacy_Query** to the **Data Items** pane.

   The attributes of year, month, country, and product name will be displayed only if expected volume or forecast revenue values are a part of both queries, so these attributes need to be displayed if results exist in either query.

2. In the **Data Items** pane, double-click **Year**. Change the **Expression Definition** to coalesce([Legacy_Query].[Year],[New_Model_Query].[Year]) and click **Validate** and **OK**.

3. Double-click **Month**. Change the **Expression Definition** to coalesce([Legacy_ Query].[Month],[New_Model_Query].[Month]) and click **Validate** and **OK**.

4. Double-click **Country**. Change the **Expression Definition** to coalesce([Legacy_ Query].[Country],[New_Model_Query].[Country]) and click **Validate** and **OK**.

5. Double-click **Product**. Change the **Expression Definition** to coalesce([Legacy_ Query].[Product],[New_Model_Query].[Product]) and click **Validate** and **OK**.

6. From the **Insertable Objects** pane, drag **Expected volume** and **Forecast revenue** from New_Model_Query to the **Data Items** pane.

7. In the **Data Items** pane, click **Expected volume**. Change the **Name** and **Label** properties to **New expected volume**.

8. Click **Forecast revenue**. Change the **Name** and **Label** properties to **New forecast revenue**.

9. Click **Year** and Shift-click **Product**. Change the **Aggregate Function** property to **None**.

10. Click **Expected Volume** and Shift-click **New forecast revenue**. Change the **Aggregate Function** property to **Total**.

11. From the **Toolbox** tab in the **Insertable Objects** pane, drag a **Data Item** to the **Data Items** pane.

12. In the Data Item Expression dialog box, enter the following statement:

```
TRIM(
CASE
WHEN [Expected volume] = [New expected volume]
  AND [Forecast revenue] = [New forecast revenue]
THEN '4. Volume and revenue match'
WHEN [Expected volume] IS NULL
  OR [Forecast revenue] IS NULL
THEN '3. Details only exist in new model query'
WHEN [New expected volume] IS NULL
  OR [New forecast revenue] IS NULL
```

```
THEN '2. Details only exist in legacy query'
ELSE '1. Totals are different between the two queries'
END
)
```

This data item will evaluate the differences between the queries based on whether the numbers match or the numbers exist in one query and not the other.

13. Click **Validate**. If no errors are returned, click **OK**.

14. In the **Properties** pane, change the name from **Data Item1** to **Record status**. Change the **Aggregate Function** to **None**.

15. From the **Run** menu, select **View Tabular Data** to test the query. Click **OK** to dismiss the warning message that will appear. The results of the query should match what's shown in Figure 4.16.

16. Close **IBM Cognos Viewer** to return to your report design.

Year	Month	Country	Product	Expected volume	Forecast revenue	Expected volume	Forecast revenue	Record status
2,005	April	Australia	Aloe Relief	60	352.2			2. Details only exist in legacy query
2,005	April	Australia	Bear Edge	90	3,661.2			2. Details only exist in legacy query
2,005	April	Australia	Bear Survival Edge	40	3,980			2. Details only exist in legacy query
2,005	April	Australia	Blue Steel Max Putter	95	19,056.05			2. Details only exist in legacy query
2,005	April	Australia	Blue Steel Putter	75	6,429			2. Details only exist in legacy query
2,005	April	Australia	BugShield Extreme	1,255	9,538			2. Details only exist in legacy query
2,005	April	Australia	BugShield Lotion	415	2,730.7			2. Details only exist in legacy query
2,005	April	Australia	BugShield Lotion Lite	230	1,699.7			2. Details only exist in legacy query
2,005	April	Australia	BugShield Natural	785	4,325.35			2. Details only exist in legacy query
2,005	April	Australia	BugShield Spray	565	3,525.6			2. Details only exist in legacy query
2,005	April	Australia	Calamine Relief	45	270.45			2. Details only exist in legacy query
2,005	April	Australia	Canyon Mule Carryall	185	15,349.45			2. Details only exist in legacy query
2,005	April	Australia	Canyon Mule Climber Backpack	240	18,129.6			2. Details only exist in legacy query
2,005	April	Australia	Canyon Mule Cooler	350	11,319			2. Details only exist in legacy query
2,005	April	Australia	Canyon Mule Extreme Backpack	65	27,509.3			2. Details only exist in legacy query
2,005	April	Australia	Canyon Mule Journey Backpack	105	35,003.85			2. Details only exist in legacy query
2,005	April	Australia	Canyon Mule Weekender Backpack	120	30,255.6			2. Details only exist in legacy query
2,005	April	Australia	Compact Relief Kit	70	1,695.4			2. Details only exist in legacy query
2,005	April	Australia	Course Pro Gloves	895	10,874.25			2. Details only exist in legacy query
2,005	April	Australia	Course Pro Golf and Tee Set	420	4,779.6			2. Details only exist in legacy query

Figure 4.16   Report query with categories

Step 7: Create the Report Page

1. From the **Page Explorer** tab, select the **Page1** object.

2. Double-click the **Text Item** in the title block. Type **Forecast Audit Report** and click **OK**.

3. From the **Data Items** tab of the **Insertable Objects** pane, drag all the items in **Main_Query** into the **List** object.

The first step is to organize the results by record status.

4. In the work area, click the **List Column Body** for **Record status**. On the toolbar, click **Group/Ungroup**.

5. From the **Structure** menu, select **Headers & Footers** and then click **List Headers & Footers**.

6. Check the **List page header** box and click **OK**.

   While this will not show when the actual break will occur, a page set will be added to perform a page break for each status.

7. Click the **List Cell** for the **List Page Header**. Change the **Source Type** property to **Data Item Value**.

8. Change the **Data Item Value** property to **Record Status**.

9. Click the **List Column Body** for **Year** and Shift-click the **List Column Body** for **Country**. Click the **Group/Ungroup** button on the toolbar.

10. Click the **List Column Body** for **Year**. Change the **Group Span** property to **Country**.

11. Click the **List Column Body** for **Month**. Change the **Group Span** property to **Country**.

12. From the **Run** menu, select **Run Report** to view the results.

13. Click **Page down** to page 7 and notice that the Record status column changes from 1 to 2, as displayed in Figure 4.17.

14. Close **IBM Cognos Viewer** to return to your report design.

Forecast Audit Report

Year	Month	Country	Product	Expected volume	Forecast revenue	Expected volume	Forecast revenue	Record status
1. Totals are different between the two queries								
2,005	May	United States	Polar Sports	1,365	189,421.05	195	27,060.15	1. Totals are different between the two queries
			Polar Sun	11,280	710,188.8	1,410	88,773.60	
2,005	April	Australia	Aloe Relief	60	352.2			2. Details only exist in legacy query
			Bear Edge	90	3,661.2			
			Bear Survival Edge	40	3,980			
			Blue Steel Max Putter	95	19,056.05			
			Blue Steel Putter	75	6,429			
			BugShield Extreme	1,255	9,538			
			BugShield Lotion	415	2,730.7			
			BugShield Lotion Lite	230	1,699.7			
			BugShield Natural	785	4,325.35			
			BugShield Spray	565	3,525.6			
			Calamine Relief	45	270.45			
			Canyon Mule Carryall	185	15,349.45			
			Canyon Mule Climber Backpack	240	18,129.6			
			Canyon Mule Cooler	350	11,319			
			Canyon Mule Extreme Backpack	65	27,509.3			
			Canyon Mule Journey Backpack	105	35,003.85			
			Canyon Mule Weekender Backpack	120	30,255.6			
			Compact Relief Kit	70	1,695.4			

Figure 4.17 Report query with categories

Step 8: Create Page Breaks

In the previous example, we used a page set to create a customized page break. For this example, we will look at another way to change pages.

1. Click the **List Column Body** for **Record status** to select it.

2. From the **Structure** menu, select **Set Page Break**.

   You should receive a confirmation message stating that a new page will be displayed for each value of record status. This process will automatically create a page set for you based on the record status.

   For simple page breaks, this option is handy because it creates all the page-breaking elements in the report automatically for the report developer. We have just avoided the need to manually create a page set, define the page-break group, and associate the page with the page set. This manual technique was showcased in previous chapters. You can mouse over the **Page Explorer** tab and click on the **Report Pages** folder to verify that the **Page Set** has been created.

3. Click the **List Column Body** for **Record status**.

4. From the toolbar, click **Cut** to remove the column from the report.

5. From the **Run** menu, select **Run Report** to view the results.

6. Click **Page down** to page 7 and notice that only the record status of 1 is displayed. Figure 4.18 shows the results after the page set has been added.

7. Close **IBM Cognos Viewer** to return to your report design.

				Forecast Audit Report			
Year	Month	Country	Product	Expected volume	Forecast revenue	Expected volume	Forecast revenue
1. Totals are different between the two queries							
2,005	May	United States	Polar Sports	1,365	189,421.05	195	27,060.15
			Polar Sun	11,280	710,188.8	1,410	88,773.60

Figure 4.18   Report query with page breaks

Step 9: Format the Detail Page

1. From the page layout, click in the **List Cell** for the **Record status**.

2. On the toolbar, click **Bold**.

3. Click in the **List Column Body** for **Year**.

   To make sure that the year is not displayed as a number with a thousands separator, we will change the format.

4. On the toolbar, click **Data Format**.

5. In the **Data Format** dialog box, select the **Number** for the **Format Type**, and in the Properties pane, change the **Use Thousands Separator** to **No**.

6. Click **OK** to close the dialog.

The facts (volume and revenue numbers) need to be properly aligned and formatted also.

7. Click in the **List Column Body** for **Expected volume**. Shift-click in the **List Column Body** for **New forecast revenue** to select all four columns.

8. In the **Properties** pane, change the **Horizontal Alignment** property to **Right**.

9. Click the **List Column Body** for **Forecast revenue**. Ctrl-click the **List Column Body** for **New forecast revenue** to select the two columns.

10. Double-click on the **Data Format** property.

11. Change the **Format Type** to **Currency**.

12. Click **OK**.

13. From the **Run** menu, select **Run Report** and compare the results to those shown in Figure 4.19.

14. Close **IBM Cognos Viewer** to return to your report design.

Forecast Audit Report

Year	Month	Country	Product	Expected volume	Forecast revenue	Expected volume	Forecast revenue
1. Totals are different between the two queries							
2005	May	Australia	Mountain Man Analog	510	$21,603.60	170	$7,201.20
			Mountain Man Deluxe	80	$6,352.00	40	$3,176.00
			Polar Ice	100	$11,244.00	50	$5,622.00
			Polar Sports	245	$33,998.65	35	$4,856.95
			Polar Sun	1,680	$105,772.80	210	$13,221.60
2005	May	Austria	Mountain Man Analog	630	$26,686.80	210	$8,895.60
			Mountain Man Deluxe	100	$7,940.00	50	$3,970.00
			Polar Ice	90	$10,119.60	45	$5,059.80
			Polar Sports	245	$33,998.65	35	$4,856.95
			Polar Sun	2,040	$128,438.40	255	$16,054.80
2005	May	Belgium	Mountain Man Analog	450	$19,062.00	150	$6,354.00
			Mountain Man Deluxe	100	$7,940.00	50	$3,970.00
			Polar Ice	120	$13,492.80	60	$6,746.40
			Polar Sports	245	$33,998.65	35	$4,856.95
			Polar Sun	2,040	$128,438.40	255	$16,054.80
2005	May	Brazil	Mountain Man Analog	705	$29,863.80	235	$9,954.60
			Mountain Man Deluxe	140	$11,116.00	70	$5,558.00
			Polar Ice	120	$13,492.80	60	$6,746.40
			Polar Sports	245	$33,998.65	35	$4,856.95
			Polar Sun	2,320	$146,067.20	290	$18,258.40

Figure 4.19 Formatted report

Step 10: Create the Cover Page

Instead of expecting the report reader to look at all the details, a cover page summarizing the results will be built.

1. From the **Page Explorer** tab, select **Report Pages**.

2. From the **Insertable Objects** pane, drag a **Page** object from the **Toolbox** tab to the **Report Pages** pane above the page set **Record status**.

3. In the **Properties** pane, change the **Name** property to **Cover Page**.

4. In the **Report Pages** pane, double-click **Cover Page** to display it.

5. From the **Insertable Objects** pane, drag a **Table** object from the **Toolbox** tab into the **Page Body**.

6. In the Insert Table dialog box, change the **Number of Columns** to **1** and the **Number of Rows** to **3**.

7. Click **OK**.

8. Click in a **Table Cell**. In the **Properties** pane, click **Select Ancestor**. Select **Table** to change the selected object.

9. Double-click the **Margin** property.

10. Type **150** for the number of pixels to add to the upper margin of the table.

11. From the **Page Explorer** tab, select **Page1**.

12. Click in the title block area to select it. From the toolbar, click **Copy**.

13. From the **Page Explorer** tab, select **Cover Page**.

14. Click in the top **Table Cell**. From the toolbar, click **Paste**.

15. Click in the middle **Table Cell**.

16. In the **Property** pane, double-click the **Padding** property.

17. In the Padding dialog box, make all the values **25** pixels.

18. Click **OK**.

19. From the **Insertable Objects** pane, drag a **Text Item** object from the **Toolbox** tab to the middle **Table Cell**. Type some summary text describing the report.

20. Click **OK**.

21. Click the bottom **Table Cell**.

22. In the **Properties** pane, change the **Horizontal Alignment** property to **Center**.

Step 11: Add Cover Page Data

1. From the **Insertable Objects** pane, drag a **List** object from the **Toolbox** tab to the bottom **Table Cell**.

2. Click an item in the **List**. In the Properties pane, click **Select Ancestor**.

3. Select the **List** object.

4. In the **Properties** pane for the **List**, change the **Query** property to **Main_Query**.

5. From the **Insertable Objects** pane, drag the following items from the **Main_Query** in the **Data Items** tab:

   • **Record status**

   • **Expected volume**

   • **New expected volume**

   • **Forecast revenue**

   • **New forecast revenue**

6. Click the **List Column Body** for **Expected volume**.

7. Shift-click in the **List Column Body** for **New forecast revenue** to select all four columns.

8. In the **Properties** pane, change the **Horizontal Alignment** property to **Right**.

9. Click the **List Column Body** for **Forecast revenue**. Ctrl-click the **List Column Body** for **New forecast revenue** to select the two columns.

10. In the **Properties** pane, double-click on the **Data Format** property.

    The Data Format dialog box is displayed.

11. Change the **Format Type** to **Currency**.

12. Click **OK**.

13. From the **Run** menu, select **Run Report** to view the results. Figure 4.20 shows the new cover page.

14. Close **IBM Cognos Viewer** to return to your report design.

Forecast Audit Report

This report compares the results of the Revenue Forecast Report from the previous reporting tool to the results of the new data model for Report Studio. This page will display the summary results and the following pages will show the details of query results that are different and those that match in both queries.

Record status	Expected volume	Expected volume	Forecast revenue	Forecast revenue
1. Totals are different between the two queries	3,413,315	495,685	$194,962,300.30	$27,230,370.85
2. Details only exist in legacy query	4,281,120		$231,706,761.45	
3. Details only exist in new model query		1,632,885		$91,341,224.65
4. Volume and revenue match	1,086,360	1,086,360	$55,797,722.15	$55,797,722.15

Figure 4.20 Formatted cover page

Step 12: Create Interactive Links in the Report

1. From the **Insertable Objects** pane, drag a **Bookmark** object from the **Toolbox** tab to the left of the report title.

2. Click the newly placed **Bookmark** object to select it.

3. In the **Properties** pane, double-click the **Label** property.

    The Label dialog box is displayed.

4. Type **Cover** in the dialog box.

    This will act as a drill-through target for links from the other report pages.

5. Click **OK**.

6. Click the **List Column Body** for **Record status**.

7. In the **Properties** pane, double-click the **Drill-Through Definitions** property.

    A dialog box is displayed.

8. In the **Drill-Through Definitions** dialog box, click **New Drill-Through Definition**.

9. Click the **Bookmark** tab.

10. Change the **Source Type** to **Data Item Value**.

11. Change the **Data Item** to **Record status**.

12. Click **OK** to close the Drill-Through Definition dialog box.

13. From the **Page Explorer** tab, select **Page1**.

14. From the toolbar, click **Unlock (currently locked)**.

15. From the **Insertable Objects** pane, drag a **Bookmark** object from the **Toolbox** tab to the immediate left of the **Record status** data item.

16. Click the newly placed **Bookmark** object to select it.

17. In the **Properties** pane, change the **Source Type** property to **Data Item Value**.

18. Change the **Data Item Value** property to **Record status**.

19. In the work area, click the **Record status** text item.

20. In the **Properties** pane, double-click the **Drill-Through Definitions** property.

21. In the Drill-Through Definitions dialog box, click **New Drill-Through Definition**.

22. Click the **Bookmark** tab.

23. Change the **Source Type** property to **Text**.

24. Click the ellipsis next to **Text**.

25. In the Text dialog box, type **Cover**.

26. Click **OK**.

27. Click **OK** to close the Drill-Through Definitions dialog box.

28. From the toolbar, click **Lock (currently unlocked)**.

29. From the **Run** menu, select **Run Report – PDF** to view the results. Figure 4.21 illustrates the new cover page.

Forecast Audit Report

This report compares the results of the Revenue Forecast Report from the previous reporting tool to the results of the new data model for Report Studio. This page will display the summary results and the following pages will show the details of query results that are different and those that match in both queries.

Record status	Expected volume	Expected volume	Forecast revenue	Forecast revenue
1. Totals are different between the two queries	3,413,315	495,685	$194,962,300.30	$27,230,370.85
2. Details only exist in legacy query	4,281,120		$231,706,761.45	
3. Details only exist in new model query		1,632,885		$91,341,224.65
4. Volume and revenue match	1,086,360	1,086,360	$55,797,722.15	$55,797,722.15

Figure 4.21 Cover page

NOTE In order for the drill-throughs to work, all report pages need to be built. HTML rendering builds only one page at a time. PDF will build the entire report every time.

Now each record status on the cover page has a link to the specific record status pages in the detail report. Also, the list headings on every page of the detail report have a link to the top of the cover page.

30. Close **IBM Cognos Viewer** to return to your report design.

Step 13: Remove the Filters to Run a Full Comparison of the Queries

This last step is optional. We are just completing the report by removing the filters that create a condition in which we will see all four record status options.

1. In the **Explorer Bar**, hover over the **Query Explorer** tab and select the **Queries** folder.

2. In the work area, double-click the **SQL** object attached to the **Legacy_Query** to display the SQL code.

3. Remove the line from the **WHERE** clause that filters on the months (**and UNIQUE_ MONTH.MONTH_KEY IN (200504, 200505)**) and then validate the SQL statement.

4. In the **Explorer Bar**, hover over the **Query Explorer** tab and select the **New_Model_ Query** object.

5. In the work area, click the filter in the **Detail Filters** pane and delete it.

NOTE   Because you are running a full comparison in the database, this query will run a long time. It will generate a large PDF of over 800 megabytes with more than 2,000 report pages.

---

6. From the **Run** menu, select **Run Report – PDF** to view the results. Figure 4.22 illustrates the cover page with the unfiltered results.

Forecast Audit Report

This report compares the results of the Revenue Forecast Report from the previous reporting tool to the results of the new data model for Report Studio. This page will display the summary results and the following pages will show the details of query results that are different and those that match in both queries.

Record status	Expected volume	New expected volume	Forecast revenue	New forecast revenue
1. Totals are different between the two queries	160,550,400	23,856,220	$9,951,864,926.05	$1,412,538,239.50
4. Volume and revenue match	51,640,790	51,640,790	$2,861,757,832.60	$2,861,757,832.60

Figure 4.22   Completed cover page

7. Close **IBM Cognos Viewer** to return to your report design.

By being able to compare the results of two queries, you can see that there are still some differences between the two queries. This means that you will need to spend some time analyzing the differences and see whether the query needs to change or whether the legacy query returned invalid results that you just uncovered.

Summary

In this chapter, you had an opportunity to create queries that were designed to override the relationships defined in the data model.

The first example looks at ensuring that all the products are listed for each warehouse when the data modeler has created relationships that will display products only if they exist in the warehouse.

The second example helps ease concerns by report consumers who want to see whether a report created with the new data model will work exactly the same as the query used in the legacy system.

Some techniques that you may want to integrate into other reports include the following:

•   Creating fixed-value filters and converting the filters to prompt report consumers after testing is complete

- Using the Pre-Sort property to sort values in your query and not in the data container
- Changing the Aggregate Function property in the query from Automatic to ensure that you will get the desired results from the query
- Selecting multiple items in a query to change sort and aggregation properties
- Customizing the prompt buttons at the bottom of the prompt page to improve the design
- Using the Group Span property to repeat (or display) items when there is a group break
- Using existing class styles to give a consistent look to reports
- Drilling through to bookmarks to add interactivity to published reports

CHAPTER 5

Additional Examples

As we have shown in previous chapters, report developers can use a number of methods to present complex data that is still readable and presentable. Additionally, report consumers want to be able to analyze information in a manner that they have come to expect by using other tools, such as spreadsheets.

IBM Cognos Report Studio uses HTML technology in presenting reports. As a report writer, you can take advantage of this functionality to enhance the presentation of your report in a web browser. In class, we discuss how you are limited only by your understanding of creating web pages. As you add more custom code to your report, you will begin to override some of the default functionality that makes IBM Cognos Report Studio a powerful tool, like drill-through definitions.

Some of the primary goals for your reports are that they are user-friendly, presentable, and interactive. For example, many spreadsheet applications have features that users now expect is reports. The first report in this chapter addresses one of these concerns.

The other report in the chapter addresses the situation where report developers will require additional data processing that has not been done in the database because it was not possible or feasible to incorporate all the data slicing in the reporting database design.

In this chapter, we will present the two most commonly requested functionalities that our students bring up in class: tab-like navigation through report content, and the capability to process data sets multiple times in order to satisfy report user requirements.

NOTE   If you want some help with the files and typing involved in this chapter, go to www.ibmpressbooks.com/title/9780132656757 and download the supplements.zip file from the Downloads section under **More Information**.

Using HTML to Enhance Functionality

Many users of reports are accustomed to analyzing data using spreadsheets. They prefer the ability to see worksheets in a tabbed format and would like to see this functionality in a report. We would like to be able to click on each tab to show the desired presentation of our data and at the same time make the user feel as though they are in a spreadsheet environment. This example will be presenting the quantity shipped by product line and year. The results will be displayed as a crosstab in one tab and a chart in another. This will be accomplished by the simulation of "active" and "not active" tabs with the use of borders and cell shading (i.e., white and gray).

The HTML coding will infuse functionality by making certain areas of the report actionable, while careful formatting will add to the proper look and feel of tabs that are being activated and navigated through.

Final Product

The final result we are trying to achieve should look similar to Figure 5.1.

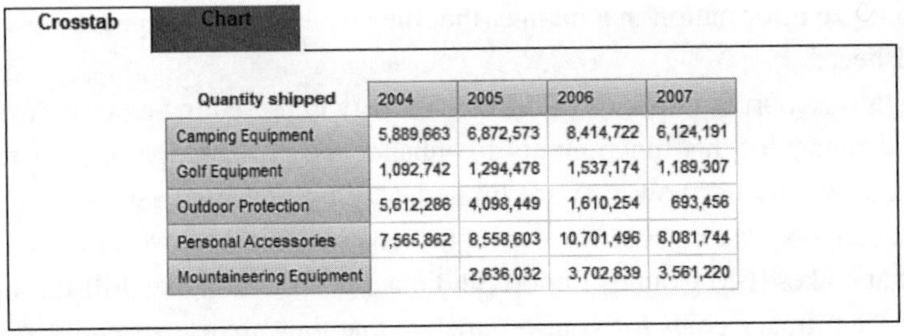

Quantity shipped	2004	2005	2006	2007
Camping Equipment	5,889,663	6,872,573	8,414,722	6,124,191
Golf Equipment	1,092,742	1,294,478	1,537,174	1,189,307
Outdoor Protection	5,612,286	4,098,449	1,610,254	693,456
Personal Accessories	7,565,862	8,558,603	10,701,496	8,081,744
Mountaineering Equipment		2,636,032	3,702,839	3,561,220

Figure 5.1   Completed tab example

Design

This report should be rendered in HTML format to make it interactive and have some HTML coding added to make it behave like a spreadsheet.

The key to this report is to place the block objects and HTML tags in the correct order.

The two main HTML tags that will create the desired effects will be the <DIV> and <SPAN> tags:

- <DIV> tags are used to identify the section of a web page in order to apply some common formatting. This tag provides some visual changes (the look and feel) to the parts of the web page that are enclosed within the tag.

- `<SPAN>` tags are used to provide interactive actions to the section of the web page enclosed within the tag. Most common usages of the tag are to provide mouse-over actions (tooltips) or some kind of actions if users click on the section of the web page.

In addition, the functionality of clicking through desired tabs will be accomplished by the inclusion of a small bit of JavaScript code within the `<SPAN>` tag.

Step-by-Step

The five steps in this example focus on formatting report elements in a tabbed format and then adding the presentation of the data in each of the tabs.

Step 1: Start the Report

1. Launch **Report Studio** and select the **GO Data Warehouse (query)** package.
2. Click on the **Create new** option.

COGNOS 8 NOTE   The option is **Create a new report or template**.

---

3. Select the **Blank** report template and click **OK**.

We will be using the **Inventory (query)** namespace inside the **Sales and Marketing (query)**.

Step 2: Set Up the Initial Block Objects

We will create several blocks in the report to define various zones where we can apply custom content.

1. From the **Toolbox** tab of the **Insertable Objects** pane, drag and drop a **Block** object to the report design area.
2. Click on the inserted **Block** object to select it.
3. Change the **Horizontal alignment** property to **Left**.
4. Double-click the **Size & Overflow** property.

   The Size & Overflow dialog box is displayed.
5. Change the **Width** to **820** pixels. Verify that the **Content is not clipped** radio button is selected.

Your **Size & Overflow** property window should look like Figure 5.2.

This will be our main **Block**.

Figure 5.2   Size & Overflow dialog box

6. Click **OK** to close the dialog box.

    We will now create the shape of our first tab.

7. Stack four more **Blocks** within the main **Block**.

NOTE   Be careful not to embed any of the four within each other.

The first three blocks will act as the tab area for our first worksheet. The last block will become the content area for the crosstab.

8. Click on the first **Block** to select it.

9. Double-click the **Border** property. The Border dialog box is displayed.

10. Click on the diagram in the bottom of the dialog box to add a **1 point**, **solid**, **black line** around the top, left, and right edges.

    The dialog box should look like Figure 5.3.

11. Click **OK** to close the dialog box and return to the work area.

12. Change the **Background Color** property to **White**.

13. Change the **Horizontal Alignment** property to **Center**.

14. Double-click the **Size & Overflow** property to open the dialog box.

15. Change the **Height** to **30** pixels.

16. Change the **Width** to **100** pixels.

17. Click **OK** to close the dialog box.

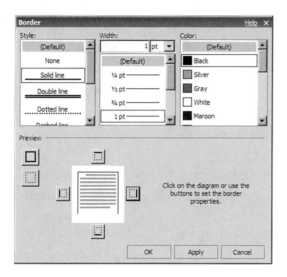

Figure 5.3 Border dialog box

18. Double-click the **Floating** property. The Floating dialog box is displayed.

    Students are usually surprised about this property since blocks are typically used to stack vertical layers on a report.

19. In the **Float** section, click the middle image to have the other blocks flow to the right of this block.

20. Verify that the **Clear** section has **Allow floating objects on both sides** selected. The dialog box should resemble Figure 5.4.

Figure 5.4 Floating dialog box

21. Click **OK** to close the dialog box.

    Now we will make the second block the next tab for our example.

22. Click on the second block to select it.

23. Change the **Background Color** property to **Gray**.

24. Change the **Horizontal Alignment** property to **Center**.

25. Double-click the **Size & Overflow** property to open the dialog box.

26. Change the **Height** to **30** pixels.

27. Change the **Width** to **100** pixels.

28. Click **OK** to close the dialog box.

29. Double-click the **Floating** property to display the dialog box.

30. In the **Float** section, click the middle image to have the other blocks flow to the right of this block.

31. Click **OK** to close the dialog box.

   Now that the second tab is complete, the third block will be used to display the rest of the top row.

32. Click on the third block to select it.

33. Double-click the **Border** property.

   The Border dialog box is displayed.

34. Click on the diagram in the bottom of the dialog box to add a **1 point**, **solid**, **black line** along the **bottom edge** only.

35. Click **OK** to close the dialog box and return to the work area.

36. Change the **Horizontal Alignment** property to **Center**.

37. Double-click the **Size & Overflow** property to open the dialog box.

38. Change the **Height** to **30** pixels.

39. Change the **Width** to **400** pixels.

40. Click **OK** to close the dialog box.

   No floating will be applied to this block so that the content of our tab will be displayed below these three blocks.

41. Click on the fourth block to select it.

42. Double-click the **Border** property.

   The Border dialog box is displayed.

43. Click on the diagram in the bottom of the dialog box to add a **1 point**, **solid**, **black line** around the **left**, **right**, **and bottom edges**.

44. Click **OK** to close the dialog box and return to the work area.

45. Double-click the **Padding** property to open the Padding dialog box.

46. Change all the padding to **20** pixels to ensure some whitespace on all sides.

47. Click **OK** to close the dialog box.

48. Change the **Background Color** property to **White**.

49. Change the **Horizontal Alignment** property to **Center**.

50. Double-click the **Size & Overflow** property to open the dialog box.

51. Change the **Height** to **500** pixels.

52. Change the **Width** to **600** pixels.

53. Select **Use scrollbars only when necessary** to provide an option for a scrollbar to appear within the block if the contents exceed the size of the block.

54. Click **OK** to close the dialog box.

Your report design page should look similar to the design shown in Figure 5.5.

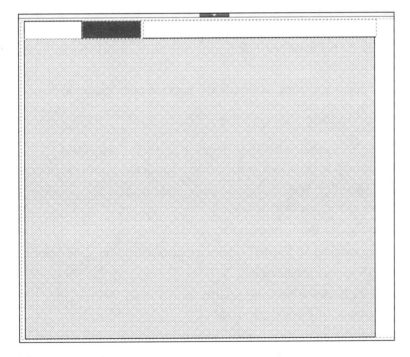

Figure 5.5   First tab design

Step 3: Set Up Additional Block Objects

We will now create the shape of our second tab.

You can repeat Step 2, tasks 7 through 54, or follow these alternative steps for the same results:

1. From the **View** menu, select **Page Structure**.

    You will see each of the four blocks inside of the main block. The work area should look like Figure 5.6.

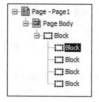

Figure 5.6   Page structure of the first tab design

2. With the first inner block selected, Shift-click the fourth inner block to select all four blocks.

3. Ctrl-click the last block and drag down to copy all four blocks inside the main block.

NOTE   You could also copy and paste the selected block by using copy and paste commands.

---

4. From the **View** menu, select **Page Design** to see the two sets of tabs.

    We will now format the look of the second group of blocks. We only need to change the look of the current tabs.

5. Click on the first new block to select it.

6. Double-click the **Border** property to open the dialog box.

7. Click the **Remove All Borders** button on the lower-left side of the dialog box.

8. Click **OK** to close the dialog box.

9. Change the **Background Color** to **Gray**.

10. Click on the second new block to select it.

11. Double-click the **Border** property to open the dialog box.

12. Click on the diagram in the bottom of the dialog box to add a **1 point, solid, black line** around the **top, left, and right edges**.

13. Click **OK** to close the dialog box.

14. Change the **Background Color** to **White**.

Your report design should look similar to what's shown in Figure 5.7.

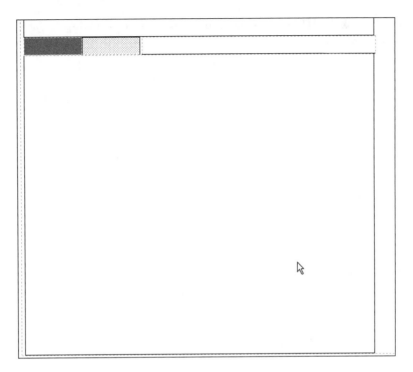

Figure 5.7   Second tab added

Step 4: Create HTML Objects

We will insert seven HTML items into the report from the **Toolbox** tab of the **Insertable Objects** pane.

1. From the **Insertable Objects** pane, drag an **HTML item** from the **Toolbox** tab into the main block and before the first inner block.

2. Click on the newly inserted **HTML item**, and in the **Properties** pane, double-click the **HTML** property.

3. Type the following HTML code inside the **HTML** dialog box:

```
<DIV ID="Tab1"
STYLE="visibility:visible;position:absolute;
height:480px;width:800px;">
```

4. Click **OK**.

   This HTML tag creates the section named Tab1.

5. Drag an **HTML item** inside the first inner block (which is white).

6. Double-click the **HTML item** and add the following code to display Tab1 if you click on the word Crosstab:

```
<span style="font-weight: bold;cursor: hand;"
onclick="javascript:document.all['Tab1'].style.visibility=
'visible';document.all['Tab2'].style.visibility='hidden';">
Crosstab </span>
```

7. Click **OK** to close the dialog box.

8. Drag an **HTML item** into the second inner block (which is gray).

9. Double-click the **HTML item** and add the following code to display Tab2 if you click on the word Chart:

```
<span style="font-weight: bold;cursor: hand;" onclick=
"javascript:document.all['Tab1'].style.visibility='hidden';
document.all['Tab2'].style.visibility='visible';">Chart</span>
```

10. Drag an **HTML item** below the fourth large inner block.

11. Double-click the **HTML item** and add the following code to mark the end of Tab1 and the start of Tab2:

```
</div><DIV ID="Tab2"
STYLE="visibility:hidden;position:absolute;
height:480px;width:800px;">
```

12. Drag an **HTML item** inside the first inner block of Tab2 (which is gray).

13. Double-click the **HTML item** and add the following code to display Tab1 if you click on the word Crosstab:

```
<span style="font-weight: bold;cursor: hand;"
onclick="javascript:document.all['Tab1'].style.visibility=
'visible';document.all['Tab2'].style.visibility='hidden';">
Crosstab</span>
```

14. Click **OK** to close the dialog box.

15. Drag an **HTML item** into the second inner block of Tab2 (which is white).

16. Double-click the **HTML item** and add the following code to display Tab2 if you click on the word Chart:

```
<span style="font-weight: bold;cursor: hand;" onclick=
"javascript:document.all['Tab1'].style.visibility='hidden';
document.all['Tab2'].style.visibility='visible';">Chart</span>
```

17. Drag an **HTML item** below the last large inner block.

18. Double-click the **HTML item** and add the following code to mark the end of Tab2:

```
</div>
```

Your report design should look like Figure 5.8 at this point.

Figure 5.8   Tabs with HTML objects

The HTML has been enhanced to have two sections (Tab1 and Tab2), and you can toggle between them if you click on the smaller blocks that act as tabs.

Step 5: Insert Data Containers and Data Content

A crosstab will be added to the first tab and a chart will be added to the second tab such that both will reference the same query.

1. From the **Toolbox** tab of the **Insertable Objects** pane, drag and drop a **Crosstab** container into the large inner block inside Tab1.

2. From the **Toolbox** tab of the **Insertable Objects** pane, drag and drop a **Chart** container into the large inner block inside Tab2.

3. Select **Pie with 3-D Effects** and click **OK**.

4. Populate the crosstab by dragging the following items from the **Source** tab of the **Insertable Objects** pane within the **Inventory (query)** namespace:

- The **Product Line** query item from the **Products** query subject to rows
- The **Year** query item from the **Time** query subject to columns
- **Quantity shipped** from the **Inventory Fact** query subject to measures

---

IBM COGNOS 8 NOTE   The **Products** query subject is called **Product** in IBM Cognos 8, and the **Time** query subject is called **Time Dimension**.

---

5. Click on the **Chart** and change the **Query** property to **Query1**.

6. From the **Data Items** tab of the **Insertable Objects** pane, drag the following data items to the chart container:

   - **Product Line** to **Series (pie slices)**
   - **Year** to **Categories (pies)**
   - **Quantity shipped** to **Default measure**

7. Run your report in HTML to see results similar to those shown in Figure 5.9.

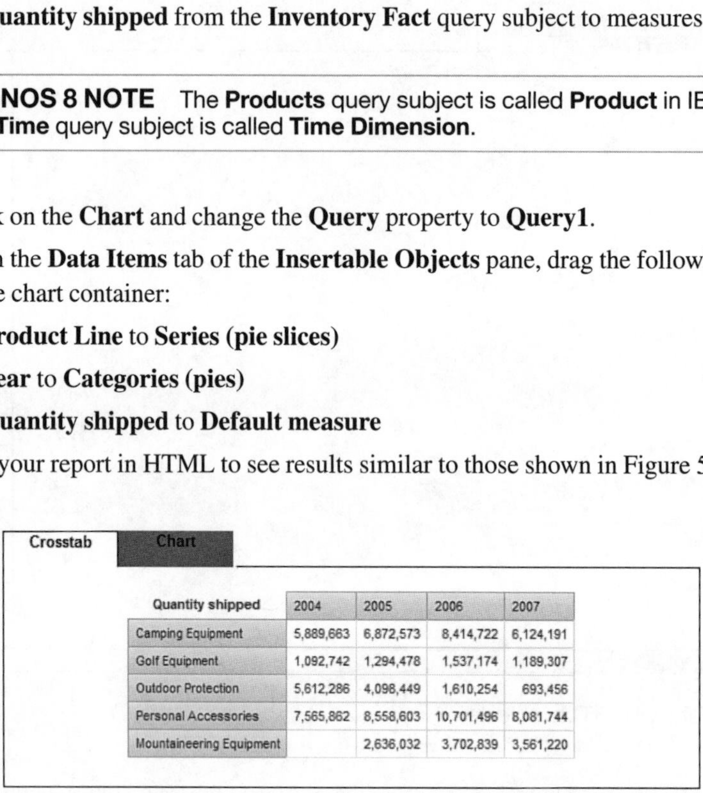

Quantity shipped	2004	2005	2006	2007
Camping Equipment	5,889,663	6,872,573	8,414,722	6,124,191
Golf Equipment	1,092,742	1,294,478	1,537,174	1,189,307
Outdoor Protection	5,612,286	4,098,449	1,610,254	693,456
Personal Accessories	7,565,862	8,558,603	10,701,496	8,081,744
Mountaineering Equipment		2,636,032	3,702,839	3,561,220

Tabs: Crosstab | Chart

Figure 5.9   First tab—Crosstab

8. Click on the **Chart** tab to see the results in a pie chart display similar to that shown in Figure 5.10.

9. Return to the crosstab by clicking on the **Crosstab** tab. Notice how the active tab will have a white background while the inactive tab will be grayed out.

Our report design is finished at this point. The design can be expanded by copying and pasting parts of the report to add tabs, and the HTML objects can be expanded to add click functionality for the additional tabs.

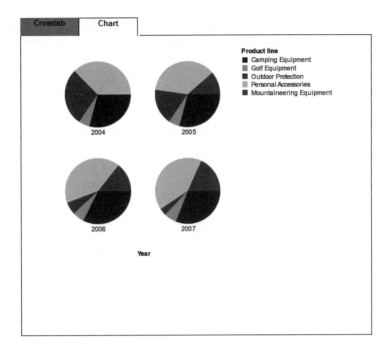

Figure 5.10 Second tab—Chart

Integrating Multiple Queries into a Complex Report

One of the common assumptions that new report developers make is that everything needs to exist in one query. Given that assumption, it is very difficult for them to mold the data into one query design, which becomes worse as the reporting requirements include "massaging" the data in different views. This additional data processing is necessary because it was not possible to think of all the scenarios during the data modeling of the report package.

One of the most common problems our students bring up in class is grouping transaction records based on some kind of date range and then summarizing the results into dashboard presentations.

The following example will show you how to query the same data set multiple times, select records according to the business rules, and summarize the new business logic groupings for the dashboard presentation.

Our assumption for this example is that the report users would like to analyze the time it takes to close orders and group them into special categories that were not defined at the time the reporting database was built. They would like to classify the orders into three different categories (less than 10 days to close, 10 to 20 days to close, and more than 20 days to close). In addition, they would like to see whether there is a difference between various retailer types to look for trends that need to be addressed by the sales and distribution teams.

Finally, we would like to take this example further by enhancing the design with multipage navigation.

Final Product

The final result we are trying to achieve should look similar to Figure 5.11.

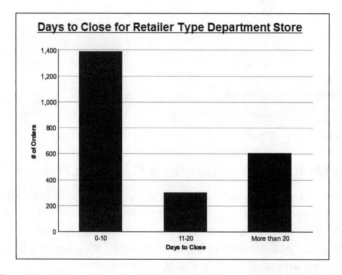

Figure 5.11   Completed integration of multiple queries into a complex report example

Design

The trick to solving this problem will be to create a union of three queries at the same time. Each query will process the same data set from the database; however, the logic in each query will categorize the records differently.

One of the little-known design capabilities of query unions in IBM Cognos Report Studio is that you can actually union as many queries as you need at one time. Usually, new developers will think that they can union only two queries at the time because when they drag a union object into the query design, they see only two placeholders for the queries. This leads them to think that they work with only two query joins at a time and that a lot of unions have to be performed, which can be tedious.

IBM Cognos Report Studio was designed so that developers can stack the queries in one union to create a clean design that is easy to maintain or expand.

Step-by-Step

Here is our suggested approach to solving the described report problem by creating a union of multiple queries.

Step 1: Start the Report

1. Launch **Report Studio** and select the **GO Data Warehouse (query)** package.
2. Click on the **Create new** option.

COGNOS 8 NOTE   The option is **Create a new report or template**.

---

3. Select the **Chart** report template and click **OK**.
4. Select the first default **Column** chart type and click **OK**.

    We will be using the **Sales (query)** namespace inside the **Sales and Marketing (query)**.

Step 2: Set Up the Initial Report Queries

1. In the **Explorer Bar**, mouse over the **Query Explorer** tab and select the **Queries** folder.

    For this example, we will take the time to rename the queries in order to keep track of what each query calculates.

2. Rename **Query1** to **FinalQuery**.
3. From the **Toolbox** tab of the **Insertable Objects** pane, drag a **Union** object to the right of the **FinalQuery**.

    Your Query Explorer design window will look similar to Figure 5.12.

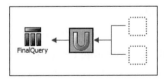

Figure 5.12   FinalQuery with a Union object

4. From the **Toolbox** tab of the **Insertable Objects** pane, drag a **Query** object to the top query reference window to the right of the union icon.
5. Rename **Query1** to **0-10**.

This query will contain logic that will count the number of orders that took under ten days to close.

Step 3: Build the Query Logic

1. Double-click the **0-10** query to access the query build window.

2. From the **Source** tab of the **Insertable Objects** pane, drag the **Date** query item from the **Time** query subject into the **Data Items** pane.

IBM COGNOS 8 NOTE   The **Time** query subject is called **Time Dimension**.

---

3. Drag the **Date (close date)** query item from the **Time (close day)** query subject into the **Data Items** pane.

COGNOS 8 NOTE   The **Date (close date)** query item is called **Date (close day)**.

---

4. From the **Toolbox** tab of the **Insertable Objects** pane, drag a **Data Item** into the **Data Items** pane.

   The Data Item Expression dialog box opens.

5. Create the following expression:

   ```
   _days_between([Date (close date)],[Date])
   ```

   This expression will return the number of days it took to close the order.

TIP   You can type the expression or drag and drop the **_days_between** function from the functions tab in the available components pane and the two data items that are used as the arguments in the function from the data items tab of the available components pane.

---

6. Validate the expression and click **OK**.

7. Rename the **DataItem1** data item to **DaysBetween**.

8. From the **Toolbox** tab of the **Insertable Objects** pane, drag another **Data Item** into the Data Items pane below the **DaysBetween** data item.

9. In the Data Item Expression dialog box, create the following expression:

   ```
   if([DaysBetween]<11)
   then (1)
   else (0)
   ```

   This expression will count the record if there have been fewer than 11 days between the time the order was placed and the time it was closed. The function will be applied to every single record as it is being pulled from the database. Every database record will be evaluated.

10. Validate the expression and click **OK**.

11. Rename the **DataItem1** data item to **Count**.

12. From the **Toolbox** tab of the **Insertable Objects** pane, drag another **Data Item** into the Data Items pane below the **Count** data item.

13. Create the following expression in the dialog box:

```
'0-10'
```

This expression will serve as a label for the unioned set that we will use as a column in a crosstab or a chart.

14. Validate the expression and click **OK**.

15. Rename the **DataItem1** data item to **Range**.

16. From the **Toolbox** tab of the **Insertable Objects** pane, drag **Filter** object into the **Detail Filters** pane.

   The Detail Filter Expression dialog box is displayed.

17. Create the following expression:

```
[Count]>0
```

We would like to optimize this query to deal with only the records that match our count criteria.

18. Validate the expressions and click **OK**.

   Our first query has been created.

19. From the **Run** menu, select **View Tabular Data** for results similar to those shown in Figure 5.13.

20. Close the **IBM Cognos Viewer** window to return to IBM Cognos Report Studio.

NOTE   We are using a building-block approach to solve a common report query problem. This approach is easy to follow and understand. However, in case your record count is high, the database query that this report will generate may not be the most optimized. By bringing in the date fields into the query, we are making the queries too detailed, and some of the aggregation is happening after the records have been pulled from the database.

The more efficient query would be to perform all the days between calculations and the `if then else` logic of the record counter in one query calculation. The aggregation of the query would have to be turned on and the `Count` calculation would have to use the `Total` aggregate function. This will push all the query execution to the database level and the query would return only one record, which would show the exact number of records that fit the desired range of days it took to close the order.

Date	Date (close date)	DaysBetween	Count	Range
Jan 16, 2004	Jan 17, 2004	1	1	0-10
Jan 21, 2004	Jan 22, 2004	1	1	0-10
Jan 24, 2004	Jan 25, 2004	1	1	0-10
Feb 18, 2004	Feb 19, 2004	1	1	0-10
Apr 17, 2004	Apr 18, 2004	1	1	0-10
Jun 15, 2004	Jun 16, 2004	1	1	0-10
Sep 18, 2004	Sep 19, 2004	1	1	0-10
Feb 11, 2005	Feb 12, 2005	1	1	0-10
Apr 16, 2005	Apr 17, 2005	1	1	0-10
Apr 27, 2005	Apr 28, 2005	1	1	0-10
Jun 23, 2005	Jun 24, 2005	1	1	0-10
Oct 19, 2005	Oct 20, 2005	1	1	0-10
Feb 24, 2006	Feb 25, 2006	1	1	0-10
May 11, 2006	May 12, 2006	1	1	0-10
May 23, 2006	May 24, 2006	1	1	0-10
Oct 21, 2006	Oct 22, 2006	1	1	0-10
Nov 10, 2006	Nov 11, 2006	1	1	0-10
Mar 14, 2007	Mar 15, 2007	1	1	0-10
Mar 30, 2007	Mar 31, 2007	1	1	0-10
Jun 19, 2007	Jun 20, 2007	1	1	0-10

Figure 5.13   Tabular data view of the 0-10 query

Step 4: Create Additional Queries

1. Mouse over **Query Explorer** and click on the **Queries** folder.

    To speed up the development of this report, we will copy the **0-10** query to create the additional two queries for the union.

2. Select the **0-10** query, and click on the **Copy** button on the toolbar (or press Ctrl+C on the keyboard).

3. Click on the background area of the **Query Explorer** design window (any whitespace) and click on the **Paste** button on the toolbar twice (or press Ctrl+V twice).

4. This action creates two new queries and their initial names are 0-11 and 0-12.

5. Rename query **0-11** to **11-20**.

6. Rename query **0-12** to **More than 20**.

7. Drag the **11-20** query to the bottom query reference window to the right of the union icon.

8. Drag the **More than 20** query below the **11-20** query within the same union.

HINT   You will get an insertion point.

Your query design window should now look similar to the design shown in Figure 5.14.

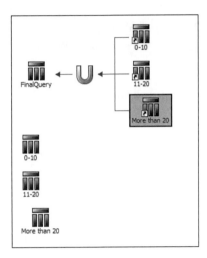

Figure 5.14 Three queries union design

The three queries that will be used have been created. They will need to be customized and the union relationship defined before the data items are ready to be added to the final query.

Step 5: Modify the Additional Queries

1. Double-click the **11-20** query to access the data items.

   We need to modify the **Count** and **Range** data items.

2. Double-click the **Count** data item and modify the data item expression to this:
   ```
   if( [DaysBetween] > 10 and [DaysBetween] <= 20)
   then ( 1 )
   else ( 0 )
   ```

3. Validate the expression and click **OK**.

4. Double-click the **Range** data item and modify the data item expression to this:

   ```
   '11-20'
   ```

5. Validate the expressions and click **OK**.

6. Mouse over the **Query Explorer** tab and click on the **More than 20** query to access the data items.

   We need to modify the **Count** and **Range** data items in this query too.

7. Double-click the **Count** data item and modify the data item expression to the following:
   ```
   if([DaysBetween]>20)
   then (1)
   else (0)
   ```

8. Validate the expression and click **OK**.

9. Double-click the **Range** data item and modify the data item expression to the following:

```
'More than 20'
```

10. Validate the expressions and click **OK**.

Step 6: Build the FinalQuery

1. Mouse over the **Query Explorer** tab and click on the **FinalQuery** query to access the data items.

> **NOTE**   Because all three queries have the same query item names in the same order, we did not have to modify **Union** properties and project the data item names.

2. Ctrl-click **Range** and **Count** data items and drag them into the **Data Items** area of the query design pane.

3. From the **Data Items** pane, select the **Range** data item and change the **Aggregate Function** property to **None**.

4. Select the **Count** data item and change the **Aggregate Function** property to **Total**.

We want to add up all the records so that the end result will have only three records. These records will represent the total number of orders that closed within the three specified ranges.

5. From the **Run** menu, select **View Tabular Data** for results similar to those shown in Figure 5.15. Click **OK** in the warning message window.

Range	Count
0-10	1919
11-20	1204
More than 20	2731

Figure 5.15   Tabular data view of the FinalQuery

6. Close the **IBM Cognos Viewer** window to return to IBM Cognos Report Studio.

Step 7: Set Up the Chart

1. In the **Explorer Bar**, mouse over the **Page Explorer** tab and select **Page1**.

2. From the **Data Items** tab of the **Insertable Objects** pane, expand the **FinalQuery** data items and drag the **Range** data item into the **Categories (x-axis)** drop zone of the **Chart**.

3. Drag the **Count** data item from the **Data Items** tab into the **Default measure (y-axis)** drop zone of the **Chart**.

4. Run the report and compare your results to those shown in Figure 5.16.

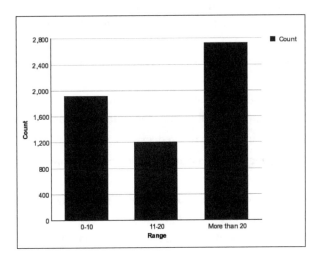

Figure 5.16   Graph of calculated values

5. Close the **IBM Cognos Viewer** window to return to IBM Cognos Report Studio.

Our three-query union is completed and the results are in a bar chart.

We will enhance the report with additional modifications to the chart and queries to showcase page breaking of the multidimensional containers (in this case, charts).

Step 8: Enhance the Queries with Retailer Type Information

The chart by itself looks good, but the report request needs to look at how our different retailer types are performing in the number of days to close sales.

1. Mouse over the **Query Explorer** tab and click on the **0-10** query to access the data items.

   We will add retailer type information to each of the union queries and place them in the same position in all three queries in order to avoid having to modify **Union** properties and project the data item names.

2. From the **Source** tab of the **Insertable Objects** pane, drag the **Retailer type** query item from the **Retailer type** query subject into the **Data Items** pane, above the **Date** data item.

IBM COGNOS 8 NOTE   The **Retailer type** query item is found in the **Retailer** query subject.

The **Retailer Type** data item will now be first, at the top, of all query data items.

We will repeat the preceding steps for the other two queries that are part of our union.

3. Mouse over the **Query Explorer** tab and click on the **11-20** query to access the data items.

4. From the **Source** tab of the **Insertable Objects** pane, drag the **Retailer type** query item from the **Retailer type** query subject into the **Data Items** pane, above the **Date** data item.

5. Mouse over the **Query Explorer** tab and click on the **More than 20** query to access the data items.

6. From the **Source** tab of the **Insertable Objects** pane, drag the **Retailer type** query item from the **Retailer type** query subject into the **Data Items** pane, above the **Date** data item.

    We are now ready to update the report query.

7. Mouse over the **Query Explorer** tab and click on the **FinalQuery** query to access the data items.

8. From the **Source** tab of the **Insertable Objects** pane, drag the **Retailer type** data into the **Data Items** pane, above the **Range** data item.

9. In the **Properties** pane, change the **Aggregation Function** to **None**.

Step 9: Finish the Chart and Set Up a Page Break

1. In the **Explorer Bar**, mouse over the **Page Explorer** tab and select **Page1**.

2. From the **Data Items** tab of the **Insertable Objects** pane, drag the **Retailer Type** query item from the **FinalQuery** query into the **Series** drop zone.

3. Click on the just-inserted **Retailer Type** data item in the **Series** drop zone, and from the **Structure** menu of IBM Cognos Report Studio, select **Set Page Break** option.

4. Click **OK** in the message window that pops up.

5. In the work area, expand the **Axis titles area** of the chart.

    We will now modify the default axis titles to be more user-friendly.

6. Click on the first **Default Axis Title** to select it (this one is for the horizontal axis).

7. In the **Properties** pane, change the **Default Title** property from **Yes** to **No**.

8. Double-click on the horizontal axis title and, in the text window, type the following text:

    ```
    Days to Close
    ```

9. Click on the second **Default Axis Title** to select it (this one is for the vertical axis).

10. In the **Properties** pane, change the **Default Title** property from **Yes** to **No**.

11. Double-click on the vertical axis title and, in the text window, type the following text:

    ```
    # of orders
    ```

12. In the work area, click the **Legend** icon within the **Chart**.

13. In the **Properties pane**, change the **Visible** property to **No**.

We will display the **Retailer Type** titles at the top of the page instead of within the chart legend because of the page break.

Your chart design within IBM Cognos Report Studio should look similar to the one shown in Figure 5.17.

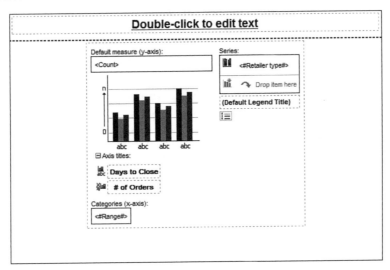

Figure 5.17   Final chart design

Step 10: Finish the Report Page Design

1. In the work area, click on the report background to select the **Page Body**.

2. From the IBM Cognos Report Studio toolbar, click the **Center** button to center all the report body content on the page.

3. Double-click on the report title text.

The Text dialog box is displayed.

4. Type the title of the report:

```
Days to Close for Retailer Type
```

Remember to add a space at the end of the phrase so that you can add the **Retailer type** query item.

5. Click **OK**.

6. From the **Toolbox** in the **Insertable Objects** pane, drag a **Layout Calculation** object to the right of the text you just added.

The Report Expression dialog box is displayed.

7. From the **Available Components** pane, drag the **Retailer Type** query item from **FinalQuery** into the **Expression Definition**.

8. Validate the expression and click **OK**.

   Since the page break setup has already associated the **FinalQuery** with the **Page** object, there are no other settings that need to be changed at this point.

9. Click the **Layout Calculation** you just created to select it.

10. Change the **Class** property to **Report Title Text**.

   Your report design within IBM Cognos Report Studio should look similar to the one shown in Figure 5.18.

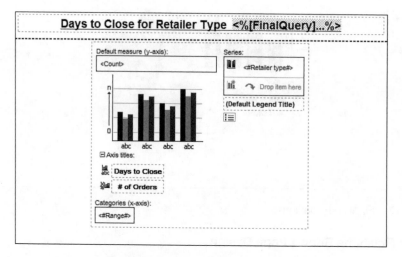

Figure 5.18   Final report page design

11. Run your report in HTML to see results similar to those shown in Figure 5.19.

As you page through the different retailer types, you will notice that Outdoors Shops have extremely high numbers of long days to close as compared to the other retailer types. At this point, you could design a drill-though process to get to more specific information, such as individual orders for the retailer type grouped by days to close.

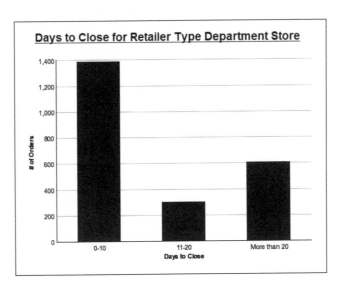

Figure 5.19 Final report chart for a retailer type

Summary

In this chapter, you had an opportunity to create reports that were designed to provide some additional examples that you could use in your everyday report development.

The first example helps you design reports in IBM Cognos Report Studio that have the capability to render data in different presentations and provide the "look and feel" of tabbing through the report. As you have probably noticed, the only limitation to our suggested solution is that we are limited to HTML output because the reporting environment is web-based and the only way we can achieve the desired functionality is to render the report as a web page.

The second example helps to ease concerns by report developers who are overwhelmed by the users' requests to present data in such a way that it is not captured in the reporting databases.

Some techniques that you may want to integrate into other reports include the following:

- Placing block or table objects to achieve the desired report design with modification of various object properties, such as Horizontal Alignment, Size & Overflow, Floating, Border, and Background Colors
- Adding of HTML items to enhance report presentation
- Using a variety of copy-and-paste options to reuse queries and report objects
- Using a one-click page break setup to speed report development

CHAPTER 6

New Techniques in Version 10

The earlier chapters of this book have focused on practical report samples that could be used in both the previous version of IBM Cognos Business Intelligence and the current release. We wanted to highlight minor differences between the releases and give those report authors who have not upgraded an opportunity to see how they can use IBM Cognos Report Studio effectively.

This chapter gives you some examples of the key enhancements to IBM Cognos Report Studio in version 10. There are four main enhancements in IBM Cognos Report Studio that were introduced in the new version of IBM Cognos Business Intelligence:

- **Active Reports:** Active reports allow report consumers to view interactive report output without connecting to the server. In IBM Cognos 10, this new IBM Cognos Report Studio feature allows IBM Cognos Report Studio report developers to create interactive report controls that in the past would have required extensive HTML and JavaScript coding to achieve a similar level of interaction in reports.

- **Capability to add your own data:** Sometimes report developers have the need to easily maintain the report prompt selections they would like to use without having to maintain the selection lists in the database. Also, the additional data that report authors need to incorporate into their reports may not be available in the current systems their reports are sourcing. The answer to this problem is the new Add Datasource feature, available only in IBM Cognos Report Studio reports.

- **New Charting Engine:** New charting options have been introduced to allow for more complex representations of your data. Report authors are allowed to select creating charts using the version 8 styles by changing an option in the report settings.

- **Statistical Reports:** A new add-in was introduced using the IBM SPSS® query engine to retrieve complex statistical analyses within IBM Cognos Report Studio. You are able to perform a number of functions from descriptive analytics, regression and correlation analysis, and parametric and nonparametric testing, which allows report consumers to delve deeper into the numbers.

This chapter presents examples for each of these new IBM Cognos Report Studio features and takes a look at some of the other features that will allow you to present data in new ways.

NOTE   If you want some help with the files and typing involved in this chapter, go to www.ibmpressbooks.com/title/9780132656757 and download the supplements.zip file from the Downloads section under **More Information**.

Using Active Reports to Replace HTML Code

In Chapter 5, "Additional Examples," we demonstrated how to utilize HTML functionality to simulate a tabbed report with multiple display options.

The new Active Reports controls make the creation of the same functionality that required HTML coding of the report in prior versions much easier.

The final result we are trying to achieve should look similar to Figure 6.1.

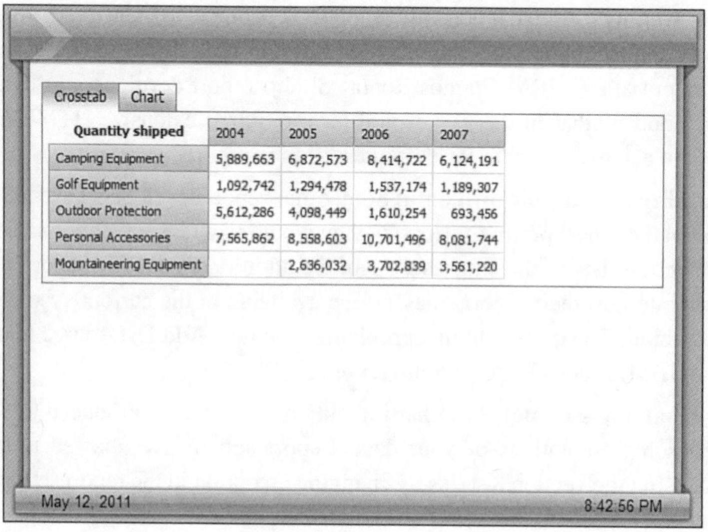

Quantity shipped	2004	2005	2006	2007
Camping Equipment	5,889,663	6,872,573	8,414,722	6,124,191
Golf Equipment	1,092,742	1,294,478	1,537,174	1,189,307
Outdoor Protection	5,612,286	4,098,449	1,610,254	693,456
Personal Accessories	7,565,862	8,558,603	10,701,496	8,081,744
Mountaineering Equipment		2,636,032	3,702,839	3,561,220

Figure 6.1   Completed alternative tab example

Design

This report can be rendered only in HTML.

The report will utilize the Tab Active Report control to achieve the desired report interactivity, and the report data containers will be the same ones used in Chapter 5.

Step-by-Step

The three quick steps in this example will demonstrate how report development is much faster and easier with the new toolbox objects. A significant amount of effort is reduced over the technique that had to be used in the previous version to achieve the desired report user experience.

Step 1: Start the Report

1. Launch **Report Studio** and select the **GO Data Warehouse (query)** package.
2. Click on the **Create new** option.
3. Select the **Active Report** template and click **OK**.

We will be using the **Inventory (query)** namespace inside the **Sales and Marketing (query)**.

Step 2: Set Up Tab Control

After the active report template has been selected, the Toolbox tab area of the Insertable Objects pane will contain additional controls specific to active reports. These new controls will significantly reduce the amount of time it takes to develop an interactive report.

1. From the **Toolbox** tab of the **Insertable Objects** pane, drag and drop a **Tab Control** object into the design area of the report.
2. Double-click **Tab Label 1** in the **Tab Control**.

   The Label dialog box is displayed.
3. Change the **Default Text** property to **Crosstab**.
4. Click **OK** to close the dialog box.
5. Double-click **Tab Label 2** in the **Tab Control**.

   The Label dialog box opens.
6. Change the **Default Text** property to **Chart**.
7. Click **OK** to close the dialog box.
8. Right-click **Tab Label 3** in the **Tab Control** and select **Delete**.

   Your report design should look similar to Figure 6.2.

This initial control is similar in function to the conditional blocks described earlier, but is enhanced for use in active reports. As you worked in the toolbox tab, you likely noticed that a number of other new controls can enhance the functionality and appearance of active reports.

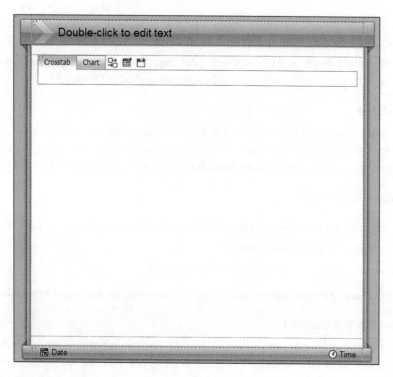

Figure 6.2   Tab control setup

Another thing you might have noticed is that the labels of the tabs can be customized for multilingual report design.

Step 3: Insert Data Containers and Data Content

With the two tabs, a crosstab will be added to the first tab and a chart will be added to the second tab such that both will reference the same query.

1. Ensure that the **Crosstab** tab of the **Tab Control** object is selected.

2. From the **Toolbox** tab of the **Insertable Objects** pane, drag a **Crosstab** object into the **Crosstab** tab.

3. Click on the **Chart** tab of the **Tab Control** object.

NOTE   At this point we will assume you are using the new chart engine of IBM Cognos 10 Report Studio. To make sure you are not using "legacy charting" mode, check your settings in IBM Cognos Report Studio. From the menu, click on **Tools** and select **Options**. In Options dialog box, click on the **Advanced** tab and make sure **Use legacy chart authoring** is not selected. If it is, uncheck it and click **OK**.

---

4. From the **Toolbox** tab of the **Insertable Objects** pane, drag and drop a **Chart** object into the **Chart** tab.

    The Insert Chart dialog box is displayed.

5. In the left pane, click **Pie, Donut** to select it.

6. In the right pane of the dialog box, select **Pie with 3-D** effects.

NOTE   The dialog box has a check box for **Fill with data**. While this sounds as though it might link the two data containers together, it will create a second query and add the data items from the first query.

---

7. Click **OK** to close the dialog box.

    Now we will add the data items to the query and data containers.

8. Click the **Crosstab** tab to show the crosstab container.

9. Using the **Inventory (query)** namespace, populate the crosstab data container by dragging the following items from the **Source** tab of the **Insertable Objects** pane:

    *   The **Product line** query item from the **Products** query subject to the rows
    *   The **Year** query item from the **Time** query subject to the columns
    *   **Quantity shipped** from the **Inventory fact** query subject to the measures

10. Click on the **Chart** tab to show the chart data container.

11. Click the **Chart** data container to select it.

12. In the Properties pane, change the **Query** property to **Query1**.

13. From the **Data Items** tab of the **Insertable Objects** pane, drag the following data items to the chart container:

    *   **Product line** to **Series (pie slices)**
    *   **Year** to **Categories (pies)**
    *   **Quantity shipped** to **Default measure**

14. From the **Run** menu, select **Run Active Report** to test your report.

    The **Run** menu changed for active reports. The only format for an active report is HTML, and you are given the option to view the results or to receive a file download dialog to save the report locally. The results should be similar to Figure 6.3.

15. Click the **Chart** tab to see the results in a pie chart display similar to the one shown in Figure 6.4.

Notice how the active tab has a different background from the inactive tab. This functionality required some HTML programming in our Chapter 5 example. The functionality of tab navigation is now built into this control.

Quantity shipped	2004	2005	2006	2007
Camping Equipment	5,889,663	6,872,573	8,414,722	6,124,191
Golf Equipment	1,092,742	1,294,478	1,537,174	1,189,307
Outdoor Protection	5,612,286	4,098,449	1,610,254	693,456
Personal Accessories	7,565,862	8,558,603	10,701,496	8,081,744
Mountaineering Equipment		2,636,032	3,702,839	3,561,220

Crosstab   Chart

May 12, 2011   8:42:56 PM

Figure 6.3   First tab—Crosstab

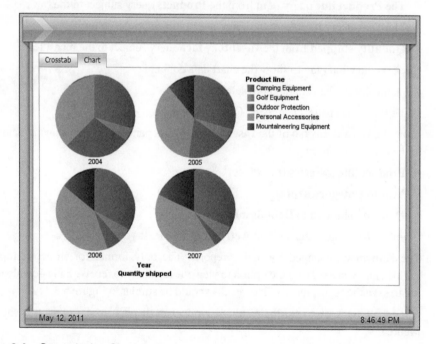

Figure 6.4   Second tab—Chart

Adding Local Data Sources to Reports

The customer service manager wants to have a report of problem orders, meaning that the reps have taken calls on these orders and the customer was not satisfied. This way the manager can follow up later to check for resolution.

The list of problem orders keeps changing. The manager gets a new list in a file every day from the call center. Currently, the call center database for customer complaints is not integrated with the sales database, and the only way to get the list of orders to follow up with is to create a prompted report and select all orders that are on the list.

Selecting such orders, of which there are always several dozen, from a long list of existing orders is always tedious, and there is a big potential that some can be missed. The manager would like to upload the list of orders he gets from the call center every day and run a report with the information he needs about these orders only.

The final result we should look similar to Figure 6.5.

Problem Orders Report

Order #:	100003
Retailer:	Universo Acampando
Retailer Contact:	PedroGomes
Retailer Phone:	55-11-32535232 ext. 121
Retailer E-mail:	Pedro.Gomes@Univ208.com

Ordered by Alexandre Pereira on Jan 12, 2004

Product number	Product	Quantity	Unit sale price	Revenue	Gross profit
72110	Polar Extreme	19	143.85	2,733.15	1,355.65
79110	Seeker 50	88	124.72	10,975.36	2,828.32
90110	BugShield Extreme	3,252	6.51	21,170.52	13,300.68
95110	Sun Shield	1,107	5.76	6,376.32	3,321
Overall - Total		4,466		41,255.35	20,805.65

Figure 6.5   Completed problem order report

Design

The report will utilize the new IBM Cognos 10 Report Studio's capability to allow advanced report authors to import their own external data sources (e.g., text files and spreadsheets). We will also use a Repeater Table object to achieve automatic paging though the order detail information.

Step-by-Step

The initial steps will be used to set up the external data source before the order selection data source is added. After the external data is added, it will be incorporated into the report for order selection purposes. Finally, we will demonstrate how a new file can be provided with the updated order list and how the report results will change.

Step 1: Start the Report

1. Launch **Report Studio** and select the **GO Data Warehouse (query)** package.
2. Click on the **Create new** option.
3. Select the **Repeater Table** template and click **OK**.

Step 2: Set Up the External Data Source

1. In the **Source** tab of the **Insertable Objects** pane, click on the **Manage External Data** button, as shown in Figure 6.6. The External Data wizard dialog is displayed.

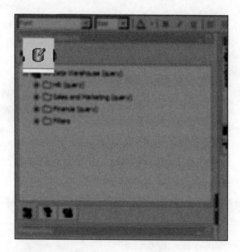

Figure 6.6   Manage External Data button

NOTE   The capability to add an external data source is an advanced feature given to report authors. If you do not see this button, you will need to ask the administrator whether you can have access to this feature.

---

2. In the **Select Data** pane, click the **Browse** button to select the import file.

   The Choose file dialog box opens.

3. Select the **Orders.txt** file and click **Open**.

This file can be located in the file that can be found on the accompanying website (www. ibmpressbooks.com/title/9780132656757).

4. Click on the check box next to the **Allow the server to automatically load the file** option.

This will ensure that the server will always look in the same location every time for the selected file. If you want to force the report user to choose a location, do not select the check box.

The External Data–Select Data dialog box should resemble the one shown in Figure 6.7.

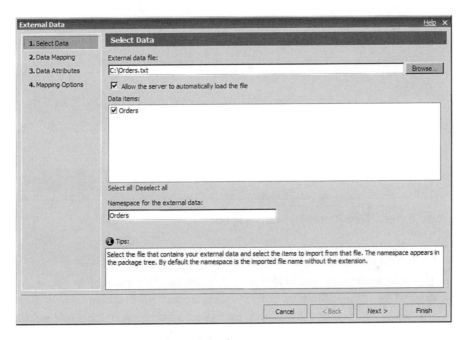

Figure 6.7   External Data–Select Data dialog box

5. Click **Next** to display the Data Mapping pane.

6. Below the **Existing query subject/report** section, click on the ellipsis and select the **Choose Query Subject** option.

The Choose Query Subject dialog box opens. We will be using the **Sales (query)** namespace inside the **Sales and Marketing (query)** to link to the external data source.

7. Select the **Sales order** query subject from the **Sales (query)** namespace and click **OK**.

8. Click on the **New Link** button to establish the connection between the newly added external data source and the **Sales order** query subject.

Since the order number is the first field for both data sets, it will be used as a joining field by default.

The External Data–Data Mapping dialog box should look like Figure 6.8.

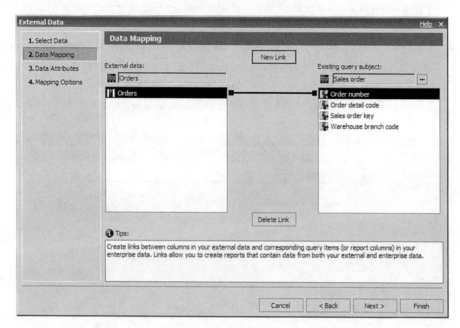

Figure 6.8   External Data–Data Mapping dialog box

9. Click **Next** to display the **Data Attributes** pane.

This pane would allow you to change some of the basic attributes of the data items in the external data source. Since the order numbers are numeric in the data warehouse and we will not be aggregating the numbers, we will not change any of the settings in the Data Attributes window.

The External Data–Data Attributes dialog box should look similar to Figure 6.9.

10. Click **Next** to display the **Mapping Options** pane.

11. Under the **Existing query subject items section:** (right side of the dialog window), select the **Some values exist more than once** radio button.

There may be more than one order detail record for the orders we are selecting. Your External Data–Mapping Options dialog box should look like the one in Figure 6.10.

12. Click **Finish**.

The Manage External Data dialog box is now visible with the **Orders** external data source included.

13. Click **Publish**.

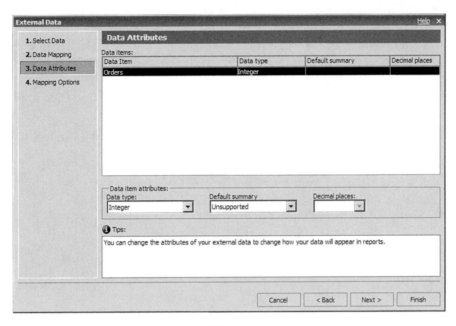

Figure 6.9   External Data–Data Attributes dialog box

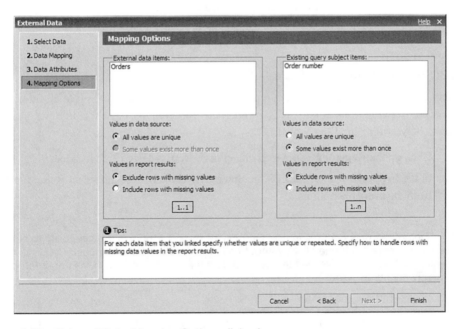

Figure 6.10   External Data–Mapping Options dialog box

You will notice that the Source tab of the Insertable Objects pane contains a slightly different package now. The new package is a combination of the original package and the text file we have added. By default, this new package will be saved under your own My Folders tab with the name GO Data Warehouse (query) External Data.

The new text file has been imported under a new namespace called Orders, as a new query subject called Orders, which has one column called Orders.

Your Source tab of the Insertable Objects pane should now resemble Figure 6.11.

Figure 6.11   Source tab of the Insertable Objects pane

Step 3: Set Up the Repeater Table

Our plan is to make the repeater object repeat only one cell per page and place all information about one order within that cell. This is an alternative to creating page sets like we created in Chapter 4, "Overriding the Data Model."

1. Click on the **Repeater Table Cell** object in the report design area to select it.

2. In the **Properties** pane, click on the **Select Ancestor** button and select **Repeater Table** from the available options.

TIP   One of the new features in IBM Cognos 10 Report Studio is the capability to select parent containers "with one click" without having to use the Select Ancestor button. This one-click option is available via the three red dots that you will notice in the upper-left corner of any container object.

---

3. In the **Properties** pane, change the **Across** property value to **1** and the **Down** property value to **1**.

These properties control how many repeater table cells will be displayed on each page.

4. From the **Toolbox** tab of the **Insertable Objects** pane, drag a **Table** object into the **Repeater Table Cell**.

   The Insert Table dialog box opens.

5. Set the **Number of columns** to **2** and the **Number of rows** to **5**.

6. Clear the **Maximize width** check box and click **OK**.

7. From the **Toolbox** tab of the **Insertable Objects** pane, drag a **List** object into the **Repeater Table Cell** below the **Table**.

8. Click on the **three red dots** in the upper-left corner of the newly inserted **List** object to select the whole list object.

9. In the **Properties** pane, change the **Query** property to **Query1**.

10. Double-click the **Margin** property.

    The Margin property dialog box opens.

11. Add **15** pixels to the top margin and click **OK**.

12. Shift-click on the first cell in the first column of the **Table** object and on the last cell in the first column.

NOTE Because we removed the **Maximize Width** check box for the table, you might accidentally click the three red dots.

13. Double-click the **Classes** property.

    The Classes property dialog box opens.

14. Scroll down the **Global classes** pane to find the **List inner footer cell** class.

15. Double-click on the **List inner footer cell** class to add it into the **Selected classes** pane.

16. Click **OK**.

17. Shift-click on the first cell in the second column of the **Table** object and on the last cell in the second column.

18. Double-click on the **Classes** property.

    The Classes property dialog box opens.

19. Scroll down the **Global classes** pane to find the **List outer header cell** class.

20. Double-click on the **List outer header cell** class to add it into the **Selected classes** pane.

21. Click **OK**.

22. From the **Toolbox** tab of the **Insertable Objects** pane, drag a **Text** object into the first cell of the first column.

    The Text dialog box opens.

23. Type in the text **Order #:** and click **OK**.

24. From the **Toolbox** tab of the **Insertable Objects** pane, drag a **Text** object into the second cell of the first column.

The Text dialog box opens.

25. Type in the text **Retailer:** and click **OK**.

26. From the **Toolbox** tab of the **Insertable Objects** pane, drag a **Text** object into the third cell of the first column.

The Text dialog box is displayed.

27. Type in the text **Retailer Contact:** and click **OK**.

28. From the **Toolbox** tab of the **Insertable Objects** pane, drag a **Text** object into the fourth cell of the first column.

The Text dialog box opens.

29. Type in the text **Retailer Phone:** and click **OK**.

30. From the **Toolbox** tab of the **Insertable Objects** pane, drag a **Text** object into the last cell of the first column.

The Text dialog box is displayed.

31. Type in the text **Retailer E-mail:** and click **OK**.

32. Double-click the **Report Title** and change it to **Problem Orders Report**.

Your initial repeater table design should look like Figure 6.12.

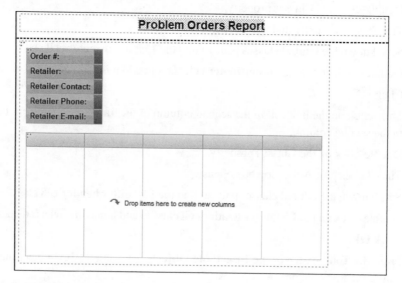

Figure 6.12   Repeater table design

Step 4: Build the Report Query

We will be using the **Sales (query)** namespace inside the **Sales and Marketing (query)**, as well as the newly added **Orders** namespace, to create the data items for the report.

1. In the **Explorer Bar**, mouse over the **Query Explorer** tab and select the **Query1** query.

2. In the **Properties** pane, change the name of **Query1** to **MainQuery**.

3. From the **Source** tab of the **Insertable Objects** pane, drag the **Orders** query item from the **Orders** query subject (they are under the **Orders** namespace) into the **Data Items** pane.

4. From the **Source** tab of the **Insertable Objects** pane under the **go_data_warehouse** namespace, drag the following query items into the **Data Items** pane:

   - **Employee name** from the **Employee by manager** query subject
   - **Retailer**, **Contact first name**, **Contact last name**, **Contact phone number**, **Contact extension**, and **Contact e-mail** from the **Retailers** query subject
   - **Date** from the **Time** query subject
   - **Product number** from the **Codes** folder in the **Products** query subject
   - **Product** from the **Products** query subject
   - **Quantity**, **Unit Sale Price**, **Revenue**, and **Gross Profit** from the **Sales fact** query subject

5. From the **Toolbox** tab of the **Insertable Objects** pane, drag a **Query Calculation** into the **Data Items** pane.

   The Create Calculation dialog box is displayed.

6. Type **Full contact number** for the name of the calculation.

7. Click **OK**.

   The Data Item Expression window opens. We want to create a calculation that will concatenate the phone number and extension. However, if the extension is blank, we want to eliminate the use of the extension field.

8. Create the following expression in the **Expression Definition** window:

```
IF ( [Contact extension] IS NULL) THEN
    ( [Contact phone number] )
ELSE
    ( [Contact phone number] + ' ext. ' + [Contact extension])
```

9. Validate the expression and click **OK**.

Step 5: Insert Data into the Report

1. In the **Explorer Bar**, mouse over the **Page Explorer** tab and select the **Page1** object.

2. From the **Data Items** tab of the **Insertable Objects** pane, drag the following query items from the **MainQuery** into the **List** object in the report work area:

   Employee name, **Date**, **Product number**, **Product**, **Quantity**, **Unit sale price**, **Revenue**, and **Gross profit**.

3. From the **Data Items** tab of the **Insertable Objects** pane, drag the following query items from the **MainQuery** into the **Table** object in the report work area:

   • The **Orders** data item into the first cell of the second column in the table

   • The **Retailer** data item into the second cell of the second column

   • **Contact first name** and **Contact last name** into the third cell of the second column

   • **Full contact number** into the fourth cell of the second column

   • **Contact email** into the fifth and last cell of the second column

   Your report design should look similar to what's shown in Figure 6.13 at this point.

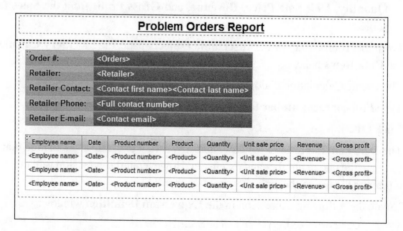

Figure 6.13   Report design

4. From the **Toolbox** tab of the **Insertable Objects** pane, drag a **Text Item** object into the work area between **Contact first name** and **Contact last name**.

   We need to add a little spacing between the names.

5. In the dialog box, type a space and click **OK**.

Step 6: Finalize Report Formatting

1. Click on any column inside the **List** object to select it.
2. In the **Toolbar** click on the **Headers & Footers** button, and from the drop-down menu, select the **Create Header** option.

   An Overall header will show up under the column titles in the List.
3. Click on the three red dots in the upper-left corner of the **List** to select the whole object.
4. In the **Properties** pane, change the **Column Titles** property from **At start of list** to **At start of details**.
5. In the toolbar, click on the **Unlock (currently locked)** button to unlock the **List** cells.

   We will be replacing the word Overall with the name of the employee and the date of the order. Since every page has one order, we will not need to group the order attributes.
6. Click on the **Overall** text item in the **List header** and delete it.
7. In the **Employee name** column body, click on the **Employee name** data item without selecting the entire cell.
8. Drag the **Employee name** data item into the **List header**.
9. In the **Date** column body, click on the **Date** data item without selecting the entire cell.
10. Drag the **Date** data item into the **List Header** to the right of the **Employee name** data item.
11. From the **Toolbox** tab of the **Insertable Objects** pane, drag a **Text** object in between the **Employee name** and **Date** data items in the **List** header.

    The Text input dialog box opens.
12. Type the word **on** in the box, along with leading and trailing spaces.
13. Click **OK**.
14. From the **Toolbox** tab of the **Insertable Objects** pane, drag a **Text** object in front of the **Employee name** data item in the **List** header.

    The Text input dialog box opens.
15. Type the following text in the box, with a trailing space:

    Ordered by
16. Click **OK**.
17. In the **Toolbar** click on the **Lock (currently unlocked)** button to lock the report.
18. In the **List** object Ctrl-click the **Employee name** and **Date** list column bodies and delete them.
19. Ctrl-click the **Quantity**, **Revenue**, and **Gross Profit** column bodies to select them.
20. From the **Toolbar**, click on the **Summarize** button and select the **Total** option.

    Your final report design should look like Figure 6.14.

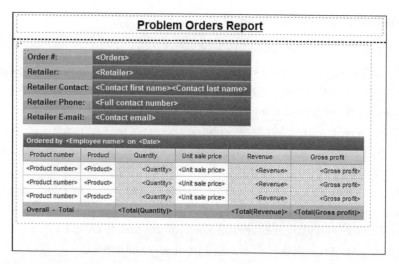

Figure 6.14   Final report design

21. From the **Run** menu, select **Run Report – PDF** to view the report.

Your results should resemble those shown in Figure 6.15.

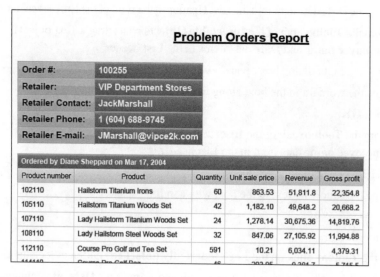

Figure 6.15   Report results

There will be 11 pages, and the results should be for those orders that were listed in the Orders.txt file.

22. Close the **IBM Cognos Viewer** window to return to IBM Cognos Report Studio.

23. Save your report as **Problem Orders Report** and exit IBM Cognos Report Studio.

Our report design is finished at this point. Before ending this example, we would like to show how easy it is to change the external data source and rerun the report.

Step 7: Test the Report with New Source Data

We will use a new source file to provide a new list of orders. This new source file is called Orders1.txt in the chapter file that can be found on the accompanying website (www.ibmpressbooks. com/title/9780132656757).

The easiest process for report developers would be to simply replace the original file with the new one and keep the name the same. This way no other adjustment of the package or reimporting of the file needs to happen. You do not have to return to IBM Cognos Report Studio for the next set of tasks; however, we do recommend that during development you log in again in order to clear the cache for the report to be able to see the new results.

Depending on the web browser that you choose, you might need to completely exit all instances of the browser and reopen it to be sure that any caches have been cleared.

1. Rename the original **Orders.txt** file to **OrdersOld.txt**.

2. Rename the new source file **Orders1.txt** to **Orders.txt**.

We are ready to rerun the report now.

3. From IBM Cognos Connection, run the report in PDF format.

Your results should look like Figure 6.16.

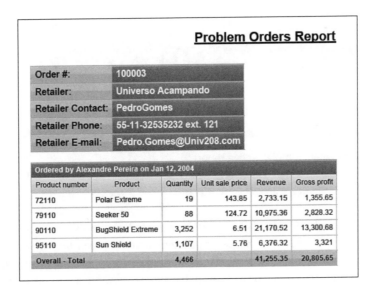

Figure 6.16 New report results

There will be 9 pages. The results should be for those orders that were listed in the Orders1.txt file before we renamed it.

New Charting Options and Active Reports

You need to create a new IBM Cognos BI 10 version of the Shipping dashboard (from Chapter 2, "Matching the Report to the Analysis") because your manager wants to see a showcase of new features with the introduction of new charts and active reports. He heard that he can now "take his reports on the road" and that there are some new chart options in the new version of the software.

The data you present will stay the same, but you want to adapt your report development approach to leverage the new capabilities.

The final result should look like what's shown in Figure 6.17.

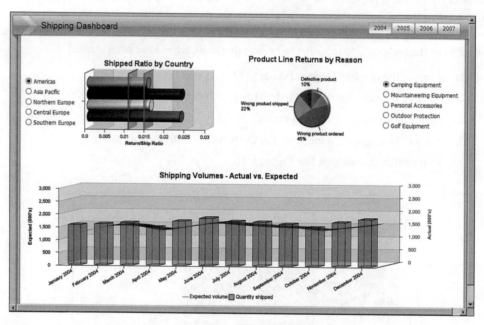

Figure 6.17   Completed complex active report

Design

The report will utilize the new IBM Cognos 10 Report Studio's capability to easily create report web page controls to achieve a higher level of interactivity between the objects on the report, making it highly dynamic and easy to use. We will also take the opportunity to utilize some of the new chart objects and options that became available with the new release of the Cognos reporting software.

Step-by-Step

The initial steps will be used to set up report dynamic control layout and link the controls to establish the capability to filter multiple chart objects at the same time in the active report. After the report queries have been added for the chart objects, we will finalize the report by formatting the chart objects.

Step 1: Start the Report

1. Launch **Report Studio** and select the **GO Data Warehouse (analysis)** package.

2. Click on the **Create new** option.

3. Select the **Active Report** template and click **OK**.

We will be using the **Inventory**, **Product forecast**, **Returned items**, and **Sales** namespaces inside the **Sales and Marketing (analysis)** folder.

Step 2: Insert Active Report Controls

1. From the **Toolbox** tab of the **Insertable Objects** pane, drag a **Data Button Bar** object into the right table cell of the report header area (next to the report title).

   The Data Button Bar control will be inserted to the right of the report title area. The control has three drop zones, for Button, Icon, and Values.

2. Click on the newly inserted **Data Button Bar** to select it.

3. Change the name property from **Data Button Bar 1** to **YearButtons**.

4. Right-click on the **YearButtons** button bar and select the **Go To Query** option.

   The query design window for the **YearButtons** button bar is displayed.

5. Change the name of **Query1** to **YearsQuery**.

6. In the **Explorer** bar, mouse over the **Page Explorer** and click on **Page1** to return to the page design.

7. Click on the **Source** tab of the **Insertable Objects** pane and expand the **Inventory** namespace.

8. From the **Time** dimension and **Time** hierarchy within the **Inventory** namespace, drag the **Year** level into the **Button** drop zone of the **YearButtons** button bar.

   Your report header design should look similar to Figure 6.18 at this point.

9. From the **Toolbox** tab of the **Insertable Objects** pane, drag a **Table** object into the report page body.

   The Insert Table dialog box opens.

10. Change the default **Number of columns** to **4** and the default **Number of rows** to **2** in the Insert Table dialog box.

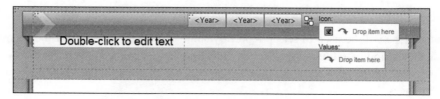

Figure 6.18   Initial active report design

11. Uncheck the **Maximize width** check box and click **OK**.

12. Ctrl-click the bottom four table cells to select them.

13. In the **Toolbar**, click on the **Merge Cells** button.

14. Click on the merged table cell if it is not already selected, and from the Toolbar, click on the **Center** and **Top** buttons.

     Any content added to this cell will be aligned to the center and top of this table cell.

15. From the **Toolbox** tab of the **Insertable Objects** pane, drag a **Data Radio Button Group** object into the first cell of the first row of our newly created table in the page body of the report.

     The Data Radio Button Group control has three drop zones, for Radio Button, Icon, and Values.

16. Click on the newly inserted **Data Radio Button Group** to select it.

17. Change the name property from **Data Radio Button Group1** to **BranchRegion Buttons**.

18. Right-click on the **BranchRegionButtons** region button bar and select the **Go To Query** option.

     The query design window for the **BranchRegionButtons** button bar is displayed.

19. In the **Properties** pane, change the name of **Query1** to **BranchRegionQuery**.

20. In the **Explorer** bar, mouse over the **Page Explorer** and click on **Page1** to return to the page design.

21. Click on the **Source** tab of the **Insertable Objects** pane and expand the **Returned items** namespace.

22. From the **Employee by region** dimension and **Employee by region** hierarchy, drag the **Branch region** level into the **Radio Button** drop zone of the **BranchRegionButtons** radio-button bar.

23. Click on the **BranchRegionButtons** radio-button bar to select it.

24. In the **Properties** pane, change the **Orientation** property from **Horizontal** to **Vertical**.

25. From the **Toolbox** tab of the **Insertable Objects** pane, drag a **Data Deck** object into the second cell of the first row of our newly created table in the page body of the report.

The **Data Deck** control has two drop zones, for **Deck** and **Values**.

The concept of a data deck in active reports is very powerful. Like a deck of cards, a data deck renders a "card" for each of the values that you will populate. The Deck drop zone allows you to determine what you want to render on each card, and the Values drop zone determines how many cards are going to be created. As you might expect, you will increase the size of your HTML file for every value you add.

In this first example, we will create 20 different deck items by creating values for each year (four years) and each region (five regions).

26. Click on the newly inserted **Data Deck** to select it.

27. Change the name property from **Data Deck1** to **RegionYearDeck**.

28. Right-click on the **RegionYearDeck** data deck and select the **Go To Query** option. The query design window for the **RegionYearDeck** data deck is displayed.

29. Change the name of **Query1** to **RegionYearQuery**.

30. In the **Explorer** bar, mouse over the **Page Explorer** and click on **Page1** to return to the page design.

31. Click on the **Source** tab of the **Insertable Objects** pane and expand the **Returned items** namespace.

32. From the **Employee by region** dimension and **Employee by region** hierarchy, drag the **Branch region** level into the **Values** drop zone of the **RegionYearDeck** data deck.

33. Expand the **Time** dimension and the **Time** hierarchy.

34. Drag the **Year** level into the **Values** drop zone of the **RegionYearDeck** data deck below the **Branch region**.

35. From the **Toolbox** tab of the **Insertable Objects** pane, drag a second **Data Deck** object into the third cell of the first row of our newly created table in the page body of the report.

36. Click on the newly inserted **Data Deck** to select it.

37. Change the name property from **Data Deck1** to **ProductLineYearDeck**.

38. Right-click on the **ProductLineYearDeck** data deck and select the **Go To Query** option. The query design window for the **ProductLineYearDeck** data deck is displayed.

39. In the **Properties** pane, change the name of **Query1** to **ProductLineYearQuery**.

40. In the **Explorer** bar, mouse over the **Page Explorer** and click on **Page1** to return to the page design.

41. Click on the **Source** tab of the **Insertable Objects** pane, and expand the **Returned items** namespace.

42. From the **Products** dimension and **Products** hierarchy, drag the **Product line** level into the **Values** drop zone of the **ProductLineYearDeck** data deck.

43. From the **Time** dimension and **Time** hierarchy within the **Returned items** namespace, drag the **Year** level into the **Values** drop zone of the **ProductLineYearDeck** data deck below the **Product line**.

44. From the **Toolbox** tab of the **Insertable Objects** pane, drag a **Data Radio Button Group** object into the fourth cell of the first row of our newly created table in the page body of the report.

45. Click on the newly inserted **Data Radio Button Group** to select it.

46. Change the name property from **Data Radio Button Group1** to **ProductLineButtons**.

47. Right-click on the **ProductLineButtons** button bar and select the **Go To Query** option.

    The query design window for the **ProductLineButtons** radio-button bar is displayed.

48. In the **Properties** pane, change the name of **Query1** to **ProductLineQuery**.

49. In the **Explorer** bar, mouse over the **Page Explorer** and click on **Page1** to return to the page design.

50. Click on the **Source** tab of the **Insertable Objects** pane, and expand the **Returned items** namespace.

51. From the **Products** dimension and **Products** hierarchy, drag the **Product line** level into the **Radio Button** drop zone of the **ProductLineButtons** radio button group.

52. Click on the **ProductLineButtons** radio-button bar to select it.

53. Change the **Orientation** property from **Horizontal** to **Vertical**.

54. From the **Toolbox** tab of the **Insertable Objects** pane, drag a **Data Deck** object into the cell of the second row of our newly created table in the page body of the report.

55. Click on the newly inserted **Data Deck** to select it.

56. Change the name property from **Data Deck1** to **YearDeck**.

    We will reuse the query that was used to populate the button bar control in the page header.

57. Change the **Query** property from **Query1** to **YearsQuery**.

58. Click on the **Data Items** tab of the **Insertable Objects** pane, and locate and expand the **YearsQuery**.

59. Drag the **Year** data item into the **Values** drop zone of the **YearDeck** data deck.

    Your active control layout should look similar to Figure 6.19.

Step 3: Link Active Report Controls

In the following steps, we will link the button and radio-button controls to the data decks. With active reports, we will manage all the interactivity within one dialog.

WARNING   Because the following steps will remain in the Interactive Behavior dialog, if you click on the **Cancel** button to leave the dialog, none of the active report variables is saved.

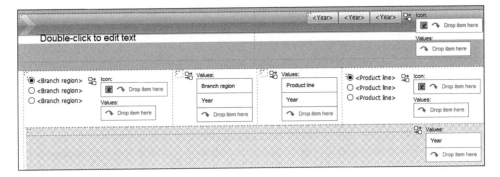

Figure 6.19   Active control layout

1. In the **YearButtons** button bar, click on the **Interactive Behavior** icon.

    The Interactive Behavior dialog box opens.

2. Click on the **Create a New Connection** link in the lower-left corner of the dialog box.

    The Connect dialog box opens.

    In this connection, we will link the year button to display the information for the proper year in the RegionYearDeck.

3. In the middle of the dialog box, change the name of the new variable that will be created from **Year Variable 1** to **vYear**.

4. In the upper-right corner of the dialog box, click on the drop-down menu and select the **RegionYearDeck**.

    Your first Connect dialog box should look similar to Figure 6.20.

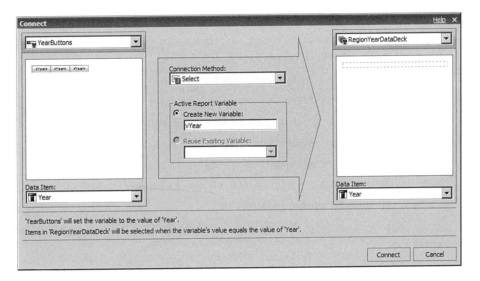

Figure 6.20   First Connect dialog box

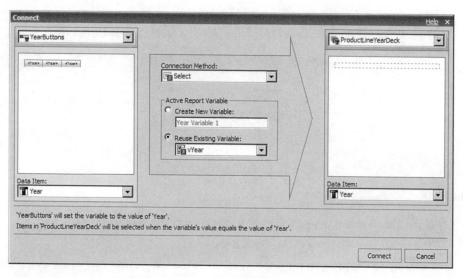

Figure 6.21   Second Connect dialog box

5. Click on the **Connect** button in the lower-right area of the dialog box.

With the first connection created, we will now connect the year buttons to the ProductLineYearDeck.

6. In the Interactive Behavior dialog box, click on the **Create a New Connection** link again.

A new Connect dialog box opens.

7. In the middle of the dialog box, click on the **Reuse Existing Variable** radio button.

Because **vYear** is the only variable created so far, it will be preselected.

8. In the upper-right corner of the dialog box, click on the drop-down menu and select the **ProductLineYearDeck**.

Your second Connect dialog box should look similar to Figure 6.21.

9. Click on the **Connect** button in the lower-right area of the dialog box.

This next connection will link the year buttons to the bottom YearDeck.

10. In the Interactive Behavior dialog box, click on the **Create a New Connection** link again.

Another Connect dialog box opens.

11. In the middle of the dialog box, click on the **Reuse Existing Variable** radio button.

vYear is still the only variable available.

12. In the upper-right corner of the dialog box, click on the drop-down menu and select the **YearDeck**.

Your third Connect dialog box should look similar to Figure 6.22.

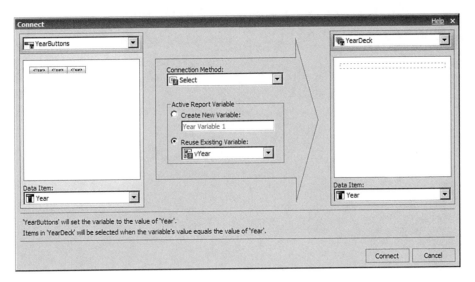

Figure 6.22 Third Connect dialog box

13. Click on the **Connect** button in the lower-right area of the dialog box.

We have completed the connections between the YearButtons button and the three data decks that will contain chart objects. There are two more connections left to complete between the radio-button bars and the data decks.

14. In the Interactive Behavior dialog box, click on the drop-down menu under the **Control** heading at the top of the dialog box and change the selection to **BranchRegionButtons**.

15. Click on the **Create a New Connection** link in the lower-left corner of the dialog box.

A new Connect dialog box opens.

16. In the middle of the dialog box, change the name of the new variable that will be created from **Branch region Variable 1** to **vRegion**.

17. In the upper-right corner of the dialog box, click on the drop-down menu and select the **RegionYearDeck**.

Your fourth Connect dialog box should look similar to Figure 6.23.

18. Click on the **Connect** button in the lower-right area of the dialog box.

For the last connection, we will create the active report variable first and then use it to connect the control and the container.

19. In the Interactive Behavior dialog box, click on the drop-down menu under the **Control** heading at the top of the dialog box and change the selection to **ProductLine Buttons**.

20. Click on the **Manage Active Report Variables** link in the lower-left corner of the dialog box.

The Active Report Variables dialog box is displayed and should look like Figure 6.24.

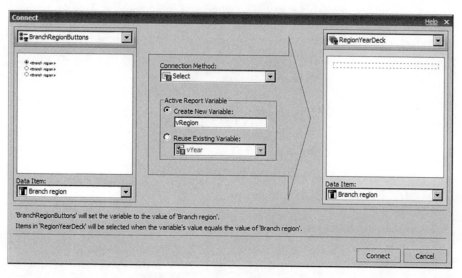

Figure 6.23   Fourth Connect dialog box

Figure 6.24   Active Report Variables dialog box

Notice that for each variable we have created to this point, there is a pane to enter default values, as well as a pane to see where the variables are used.

21. Below the **Active Report Variables** pane, click on the **New** button to display the New Active Report Variables dialog box.

22. Type **vPLine** as the name of the new variable and click **OK** to close the dialog box.

23. Click **OK** to close the Active Report Variables dialog box.

The Interactive Behavior dialog box is displayed and **ProductLineButtons** is the control we are changing.

24. Click on the **Create a New Connection** link again.

Another Connect dialog box opens.

25. In the middle of the dialog box, click on the **Reuse Existing Variable** radio button.

26. Click on the drop-down list for the existing variables and select **vPLine**.

27. In the upper-right corner of the dialog box, click on the drop-down menu and select the **ProductLineYearDeck**.

28. Click on the **Connect** button in the lower-right area of the dialog box.

We have completed the connections between the radio-button bars and the data decks. To complete the interactive behaviors, we will set some default values for the three active report variables we have created so far.

29. Click on the **Manage Active Report Variables** link in the lower-left corner of the dialog box.

30. Click on the **vYear** variable if it is not already selected.

31. Under the **Default Variable Values** box, click on the **New** button.

The New Variable Value dialog box opens.

32. In the **New Variable Value** text box, type **2004** and click **OK**.

33. Click on the **vRegion** variable to select it.

34. Under the **Default Variable Values** box, click on the **New** button.

The New Variable Value dialog box opens.

35. In the **New Variable Value** text box, type **Americas** and click **OK**.

36. Click on the **vPLine** variable to select it.

37. Under the **Default Variable Values** box, click on the **New** button.

The New Variable Value dialog box opens.

38. In the **New Variable Value** text box, type **Camping Equipment** and click **OK**.

With the default values added, the Active Report Variables window should look similar to Figure 6.25.

39. In the **Active Report Variables** window, click **OK** to close it.

40. In the **Interactive Behavior** window, click **OK** to close it.

We have finished setting the default values for the three active report variables, and we have completed the step to link all the Active Report controls.

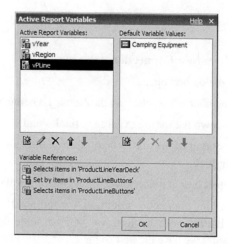

Figure 6.25   Updated Active Report Variables dialog box

Step 4: Insert Charts

In the following steps, we will insert the charts for our dashboard. We will start by adding the three charts into the three data decks that have already been created.

1. From the **Toolbox** tab of the **Insertable Objects** pane, drag a **Chart** object into the **Data Card** area of the **RegionYearDeck** data deck.

   This deck is in the top row and the second cell.

2. In the Insert Chart dialog box, select the **Bar** chart group on the left and select the **Clustered Cylinder Bar with 3-D Effects** chart option.

3. Click **OK** to create the data deck, as shown in Figure 6.26.

4. From the **Toolbox** tab of the **Insertable Objects** pane, drag a **Chart** object into the **Data Card** area of the **ProductLineYearDeck** data deck, which is in the third cell of the top row.

5. In the Insert Chart dialog box, select the **Pie, Donut** chart group on the left and select the **Pie with 3-D Effects and Rounded Bevel** chart option.

6. Click **OK** to create the data deck, as shown in Figure 6.27.

7. From the **Toolbox** tab of the **Insertable Objects** pane, drag a **Chart** object into the **Data Card** area of the **YearDeck** data deck.

8. In the Insert Chart dialog box, select the **Line** chart group on the left and select the **Clustered Line with 3-D Effect** chart option.

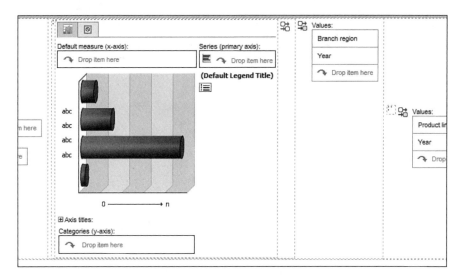

Figure 6.26 Data card area of the RegionYearDeck data deck

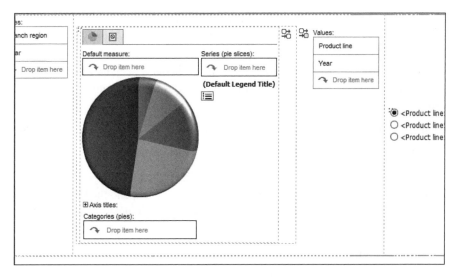

Figure 6.27 Data card area of the ProductLineYearDeck data deck

9. Click **OK** to create the data deck, as shown in Figure 6.28.

    We have completed the insertion of the chart objects.

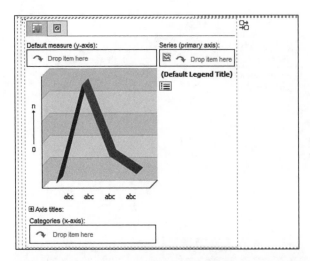

Figure 6.28   Data card area of the YearDeck data deck

Step 5: Set Up the Returned/Shipped Ratio Query

This query will retrieve the quantity sold and quantity returned for each country in order to calculate the ratio of items returned to items sold. This will be displayed in the new type of bar chart in the dashboard.

After we added the three data containers to the dashboard, three new queries were created for each of them. In this step and the following two steps, we will customize the queries associated with each object.

1. In the **Explorer Bar**, mouse over the **Query Explorer** tab and select the **Queries** folder.

2. Rename **Query1** to **Returned/Shipped_Ratio_by_Country**.

3. Double-click on the query to open the query definition.

4. From the **Source** tab of the **Insertable Objects** pane, expand the **Employee by region** dimension and the **Employee by region** hierarchy within the **Sales** namespace.

5. Drag the **Branch region** level into the **Data Items** pane in the work area.

6. Drag the **Country** level into the **Data Items** pane.

7. Expand the **Time** dimension and the **Time** hierarchy.

8. Drag the **Year** level into the **Data Items** pane.

9. Expand the **Sales fact** measure dimension and drag **Quantity** to the **Data Items** pane.

10. Expand the **Returned items** namespace and the **Returned items** measure dimension.

11. Drag **Return quantity** into the **Data Items** pane.

12. From the **Toolbox** tab of the **Insertable Objects** pane, drag a **Data Item** object into the **Data Items** pane.

 The Data Item Expression dialog box is displayed.

13. Using items from the **Data Items** tab on the **Available Components** pane, add the following expression in the **Expression Definition** pane:

 ```
 [Return quantity] / [Quantity]
 ```

14. Validate the expression and click **OK** to close the dialog box.

15. In the **Properties** pane, change the **Name** property to **Return/Ship Ratio**.

16. Change the **Aggregate Function** property to **Calculated**.

17. From the **Run** menu, select **View Tabular Data** to test your query.

 Your results should be similar to those shown in Figure 6.29.

18. Close **IBM Cognos Viewer** to return to your report design.

Branch region	Country	Year	Quantity	Return quantity	Return/Ship Ratio
Americas	United States	2004	2,653,096	61,659	0.0232404
Americas	Canada	2004	979,581	15,364	0.01568426
Americas	Mexico	2004	522,235	12,245	0.0234473
Americas	Brazil	2004	415,979	6,221	0.01495508
Asia Pacific	Japan	2004	1,217,594	26,702	0.02193013
Asia Pacific	Singapore	2004	750,056	18,769	0.02502346
Asia Pacific	Korea	2004	840,150	15,053	0.01791704
Asia Pacific	China	2004	1,128,544	20,614	0.01826601
Asia Pacific	Australia	2004			
Northern Europe	Netherlands	2004	582,440	8,431	0.01447531
Northern Europe	Sweden	2004	403,987	11,245	0.02783505
Northern Europe	Finland	2004	640,898	16,166	0.02522398
Central Europe	France	2004	1,229,528	26,126	0.0212488
Central Europe	Germany	2004	1,003,083	14,935	0.0148891

Figure 6.29 Returned/shipped ratio query results

Step 6: Set Up the Returns by Product Line Query

This query will count the number of items returned by both the product line and the reason that the customer returned the item. This will be displayed in the new type of pie chart on the dashboard.

1. In the **Explorer Bar**, mouse over the **Query Explorer** tab and select the **Queries** folder.

2. Rename **Query2** to **Returns_by_Product_Line**.

3. Double-click on the query to open the query definition.

4. From the **Source** tab of the **Insertable Objects** pane, expand the **Products** dimension and the **Products** hierarchy within the **Returned items** namespace.

5. Drag the **Product line** level into the **Data Items** pane in the work area.

6. Expand the **Time** dimension and the **Time** hierarchy.

7. Drag the **Year** level into the **Data Items** pane in the work area.

8. Expand the **Return reason** dimension and the **Return reason** hierarchy.

9. Drag the **Reason description** level into the **Data Items** pane.

10. Expand the **Returned items** measure dimension.

11. Drag **Return quantity** into the **Data Items** pane.

12. From the **Run** menu, select **View Tabular Data** to test your query.

    Your results should resemble what's shown in Figure 6.30.

13. Close **IBM Cognos Viewer** to return to your report design.

Product line	Year	Reason description	Return quantity
Camping Equipment	2004	Defective product	6,056
Personal Accessories	2004	Defective product	12,399
Outdoor Protection	2004	Defective product	53,932
Golf Equipment	2004	Defective product	891
Camping Equipment	2004	Incomplete product	6,802
Personal Accessories	2004	Incomplete product	5,420
Outdoor Protection	2004	Incomplete product	200
Golf Equipment	2004	Incomplete product	1,604
Camping Equipment	2004	Wrong product ordered	27,149
Personal Accessories	2004	Wrong product ordered	16,762
Outdoor Protection	2004	Wrong product ordered	4,989
Golf Equipment	2004	Wrong product ordered	2,563
Camping Equipment	2004	Wrong product shipped	13,602
Personal Accessories	2004	Wrong product shipped	19,244

Figure 6.30   Returns by product line query results

Step 7: Set Up the Shipping Volume by Month Query

This query will retrieve all the months in the selected year and the expected and actual shipping volumes.

1. In the **Explorer Bar**, mouse over the **Query Explorer** tab and select the **Queries** folder.

2. Rename **Query3** to **Shipping_Volume_by_Month**.

3. Double-click on the query to open the query definition.

4. From the **Source** tab of the **Insertable Objects** pane, expand the **Time** dimension and the **Time** hierarchy in the **Inventory** namespace.

5. Drag the **Year** level into the **Data Items** pane in the work area.

6. Drag the **Month** level into the **Data Items** pane.

7. In the **Insertable Objects** pane, expand the **Inventory fact** measure dimension.

8. Drag **Quantity shipped** into the **Data Items** pane.

9. From the **Source** tab, expand the **Product forecast** namespace and **Product forecast fact** measure dimension.

10. Drag **Expected volume** into the **Data Items** pane.

    We want to ensure that we do not clutter the chart with opening balances or future months that do not have a quantity shipped yet.

11. In the **Data Items** pane of the work area, click **Month** to select it.

12. In the Properties pane, double-click the **Set Definition** property.

    The Set Definition dialog box opens.

13. In the lower-left corner of the dialog box, click **New** and select **Set Filter**.

    The Set Filter Condition dialog box is displayed.

14. In the **Item** pane, click the **Intersection (tuple)** radio button to select it, and click the ellipsis next to it.

    The Members dialog box is displayed.

15. In the **Available members and measures** pane, expand the **Sales and Marketing (analysis)** folder, the **Inventory** folder, and the **Inventory fact** measure dimension.

16. Drag **Quantity shipped** into the **Intersection members and measures** pane.

17. Click **OK** to close the dialog box and return to the **Set Filter Condition** pane.

18. Change the **Operator** property to **is not null**.

19. Click **OK** to close the dialog box.

20. Click **OK** to close the Set Filter dialog box.

21. Click **OK** to close the Set Definition dialog box.

22. Rename the **Month** member set to **Actual Months**.

23. From the **Run** menu, select **View Tabular Data** to test your query.

    Compare your results to those in Figure 6.31.

24. Close **IBM Cognos Viewer** to return to your report design.

Year	Actual Months	Quantity shipped	Expected volume
2004	January 2004	1,575,400	1,224,340
2004	February 2004	1,608,152	1,434,440
2004	March 2004	1,673,653	1,437,240
2004	April 2004	1,507,285	1,294,250
2004	May 2004	1,736,204	1,430,725
2004	June 2004	1,860,657	1,562,440
2004	July 2004	1,735,888	1,500,970
2004	August 2004	1,723,209	1,441,275
2004	September 2004	1,643,052	1,396,265
2004	October 2004	1,529,071	1,314,295
2004	November 2004	1,723,698	1,410,205
2004	December 2004	1,844,284	1,534,885
2005	January 2005	2,016,119	1,508,210
2005	February 2005	2,238,935	1,873,820
2005	March 2005	1,980,088	1,751,235
2005	April 2005	1,893,842	1,632,720
2005	May 2005	1,831,648	1,582,045
2005	June 2005	1,866,577	1,632,885
2005	July 2005	1,641,831	1,535,740

Figure 6.31   Shipping volume by month query results

Step 8: Add Data Items to the Dashboard

With each query created, the data items can be added to the page layout and master-detail relationships can be created between the graphic data containers and the data decks.

1. In the **Explorer Bar**, mouse over the **Page Explorer** tab and select **Page1**.

2. From the **Data Items** tab of the **Insertable Objects** pane, drag **Country** from the **Returned/Shipped_Ratio_by_Country** query into the **Categories (y-axis)** drop zone of the bar/cylinder chart.

3. Drag **Country** again from the **Returned/Shipped_Ratio_by_Country** query into the **Series (primary axis)** drop zone of the bar/cylinder chart.

   This is a quick trick that will ensure that each Country bar will be a different color.

4. Drag **Return/Ship Ratio** into the **Default measure (x-axis)** drop zone.

   Because you are adding a chart within the data deck, you want to filter the results of the chart according to the "card" in the deck, so you will create a master detail relationship between the chart and the deck.

   Before setting the master-detail relationship, make sure that you have selected an object inside the chart.

5. From the **Data** menu, select **Master Detail Relationships**.

   The dialog box to link the data deck and chart queries is displayed.

6. In the top center of the dialog box, click the **New Link** button.

    An arrow defining the link between the two queries is displayed.

7. Ensure that **Branch Region** is selected in both **Master** and **Detail** panes.

8. Click the **New Link** button again.

    It will seem as though nothing happened; however, there are two links now, one on top of the other.

9. Click on the **Year** in the **Master** pane and on the **Year** in the **Detail** pane.

    Your first Master Detail Relationships window should look similar to what's shown in Figure 6.32.

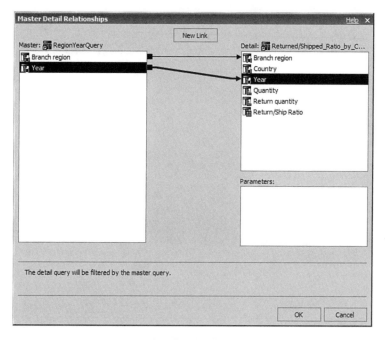

Figure 6.32   First Master Detail Relationships dialog box

10. Click **OK** to close the dialog box.

    Now we will build the pie chart.

11. From the **Data Items** tab, drag **Reason description** from the **Returns_by_Product_ Line** query into the **Series (pie slices)** drop zone of the pie chart.

12. Drag **Return quantity** into the **Default measure** drop zone of the pie chart.

13. Verify that an item inside the pie chart is selected in the work area, and from the **Data** menu select **Master Detail Relationships**.

14. Click **New Link**.

15. Ensure that **Product line** is selected in both **Master** and **Detail** panes.

16. Click the **New Link** button again.

It will seem as though nothing happened; however, there are two links now, one on top of the other.

17. Click on the **Year** in the **Master** pane and on the **Year** in the **Detail** pane.

Your second Master Detail Relationships window should look similar to Figure 6.33.

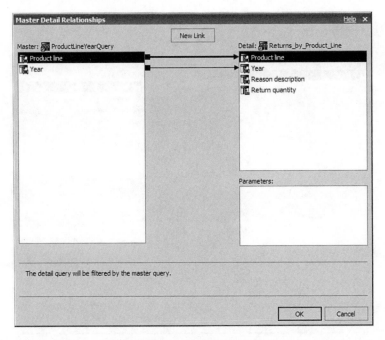

Figure 6.33 Second Master Detail Relationships dialog box

18. Click **OK** to close the dialog box.

Now we can build the third object on the dashboard, the clustered line chart that we will convert to a combination chart.

19. From the **Data Items** tab, drag **Actual Months** from the **Shipping_Volume_by_ Month** query into the **Categories (x-axis)** drop zone of the line chart.

20. Drag **Expected volume** into the **Series (primary axis)** drop zone of the line chart.

21. Click on the chart background to select the whole chart object.

22. In the **Properties** pane, double-click on the **Combinations** property.

The Combinations dialog box opens.

NOTE The new Combinations property gives you more power and flexibility to create complex chart axes. It is quite different from the previous version, in which you had to choose either the Y1 or the Y2 axis.

---

23. In the **Numeric axes** area of the Combinations dialog box, click on the check box next to the **Secondary axis** to select it.

By default, the **Combinations** area shows a **Clustered Bar** option.

Your Combinations dialog box should look similar to Figure 6.34.

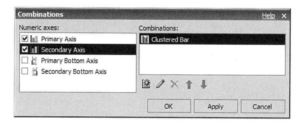

Figure 6.34 Combinations dialog box

24. Click **OK** to close the Combinations dialog box.

The clustered line chart has now become a combination chart. You will notice a new **Series (secondary axis)** drop zone on the chart.

25. From the **Data Items** tab, drag **Quantity shipped** from the **Shipping_Volume_by_Month** query into the **Series (secondary axis)** drop zone of the combination chart.

26. Verify that an item inside the pie chart is selected in the work area, and from the **Data** menu, select **Master Detail Relationships**.

27. Click the **New Link** button.

28. Ensure that **Year** is selected in both **Master** and **Detail** panes.

Your third Master Detail Relationships window should look similar to what's shown in Figure 6.35.

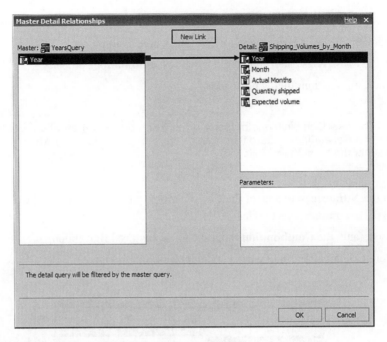

Figure 6.35   Third Master Detail Relationships dialog box

29.   Click **OK** to close the dialog box.

Now we can start formatting the charts.

Step 9: Format the Bar Chart

To improve the chart, we will remove the legend, change the palette for a better contrast, and format the axis and chart titles. Along with that, the chart should also have low and high baselines to better illustrate the returned to shipped ratios.

1.   Click on the bar chart to select it.

2.   Change the **Title** property from **Hide** to **Show**.

3.   Double-click on the chart title text that is now visible inside the chart object and type the following title: **Returned to Shipped Ratio by Country**.

4.   Click on the bar chart to select it again.

5.   Double-click on the **Legend** property.

The Legend dialog box opens.

6.   Uncheck the **Show legend** check box and click **OK**.

7.   Double-click on the **Numeric Baselines** property.

The Baselines dialog box opens.

8. In the lower-left corner of the dialog box, click on the **New** button and select **Numeric Value** from the drop-down menu options.

   A **Numeric Value** baseline will be added to the baselines list on the left. We will add baseline properties for this baseline.

9. Enter the value **0.011** for the value at which to draw the baseline.

10. Change the **Baseline Label** to **1.1 %**.

11. Click on the **Line Styles** button.

   The Line Styles dialog box opens.

12. Set the **Color** to **Green**, **Weight** to **2** pixels, and **Style** to **Solid**.

13. Click **OK** to close the Line Styles dialog box.

14. Click on the **New** button and select **Numeric Value** from the drop-down menu options to add one more numeric baseline.

15. Enter the value **0.015** for the value at which to draw the baseline.

16. Change the **Baseline Label** to **1.5 %**.

17. Click on the **Line Styles** button.

   The Line Styles dialog box opens.

18. Set the **Color** to **Red**, **Weight** to **2** pixels, and **Style** to **Solid**.

19. Click **OK** to close the Line Styles dialog box.

20. Click **OK** to close the Baselines dialog box.

21. Click on the chart's background to select it again.

22. Double-click on the **Padding** property.

   The Padding dialog box opens.

23. Add **20** pixels of padding on the top, on the bottom, and to right of the chart object.

24. Click **OK** to close the Padding dialog box.

25. Double-click on the **Size & Overflow** property.

   The Size & Overflow dialog box opens.

26. Set the **Height** to **225** pixels and the **Width** to **325** pixels.

27. Click **OK** to close the dialog box.

28. Expand the **Axis titles** area within the chart.

29. Click on the first **Axis title** (the y-axis) to select it.

30. In the **Properties** pane, change the **Default Title** property from **Yes** to **No**.

31. Click on the second **Axis title** (the x-axis) to select it.

32. In the **Properties** pane, change the **Default Title** property from **Yes** to **No**.

33. Click on the text item within the x-axis title to select it.

34. Change the **Source Type** property from **Text** to **Data Item Label**.

35. Click inside the **Data Item Label** property that shows up below the **Source Type** property, and from the drop-down menu select the **Return/Ship Ratio** data item.

36. Click on the **Bar** icon in the **Series (primary axis)** area, to the left of the **Country** data item.

37. In the properties of the **Bar** object, double-click the **Palette** property.

The Palette dialog box opens.

38. Click on the **Chart Palette Presets** button in the upper-left corner of the dialog box, and from the drop-down menu select the **Contrast** palette.

39. Click **OK** to close the Palette dialog box.

Your bar chart design should look similar Figure 6.36 at this point.

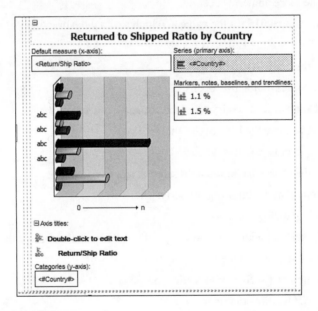

Figure 6.36   Bar chart design

Step 10: Format the Pie Chart

The pie chart should have the legend hidden as we plan to show the pie slice names and values as percentages on the chart. We will adjust the titles and size of the pie chart at this point too.

1. Click on the pie chart to select it.

2. In the **Properties** pane, change the **Axis Title** property from **Show** to **Hide**.

3. Change the **Title** property from **Hide** to **Show**.

4. Double-click on the chart title text that is now visible inside the chart object and type the following title: **Product Line Returns by Reason**.

5. Click on the pie chart to select it again.

6. Under the **Chart Labels** grouping in the **Properties** pane, double-click the **Show Values** property.

   The Show Values dialog box opens.

7. In the dialog box, click on the check box next to the **Slice names** option.

8. In the **Values** drop-down menu, select the **Percentage** option.

9. Click **OK** to close the Show Values dialog box.

10. Double-click on the **Legend** property.

    The Legend dialog box opens.

11. Uncheck the **Show legend** check box and click **OK**.

12. Double-click on the **Padding** property.

    The Padding dialog box opens.

13. Add **20** pixels of padding on the top, on the bottom, and to the left of the chart object.

14. Click **OK** to close the Padding dialog box.

15. Double-click on the **Size & Overflow** property.

    The Size & Overflow dialog box opens.

16. Set the **Height** to **250** pixels and the **Width** to **350** pixels.

17. Click **OK** to close the dialog box.

    Your pie chart design should look similar to Figure 6.37 at this point.

Step 11: Format the Combination Chart

The combination chart should stretch under the two other charts in the dashboard. We will also adjust the palettes of the Series line and bars.

1. Click on the combination chart to select it.

2. In the **Properties** pane, change the **Title** property from **Hide** to **Show**.

3. Double-click on the chart title text that is now visible inside the chart object and type the following title: **Shipping Volumes – Actual vs. Expected**.

4. Click on the combination chart to select it again.

5. Double-click on the **Legend** property.

   The Legend dialog box opens.

6. In the **Preset** area of the Legend dialog box, select the **Align Bottom Center** option.

7. Click **OK** to close the Legend dialog box.

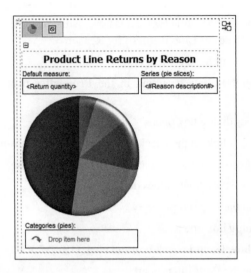

Figure 6.37 Pie chart design

8.   Double-click on the **Padding** property.

     The Padding dialog box opens.

9.   Add **20** pixels of padding on the top.

10. Click **OK** to close the Padding dialog box.

11. Double-click on the **Size & Overflow** property.

     The Size & Overflow dialog box opens.

12. Set the **Height** to **300** pixels and the **Width** to **900** pixels.

13. Click **OK** to close the dialog box.

14. Expand the **Axis titles** area within the chart.

15. Click on the first **Axis title** to select it (this is the x-axis).

16. In the **Properties** pane, change the **Default Title** property from **Yes** to **No**.

17. Click on the second **Axis title** to select it (this is the left y-axis).

18. In the **Properties** pane, change the **Default Title** property from **Yes** to **No**.

19. Double-click on the **Axis title text** that you just enabled.

     The Text box opens.

20. Type the following text: **Expected (000's)**.

21. Click **OK**.

22. Click on the third **Axis title** to select it (this is the right y-axis).

23. In the **Properties** pane, change the **Default Title** property from **Yes** to **No**.

24. Double-click on the **Axis title text** that you just enabled.

The Text box opens.

25. Type the following text: **Actual (000's)**.

26. Click **OK**.

27. Click on the left y-axis **Axis labels** object within the chart.

28. Double-click the **Data Format** property.

The Data Format dialog box opens.

29. Change the **Format** type to **Number** and set the **Scale** property to **-3**.

30. Click **OK** to close the Data Format dialog box.

31. Click on the right y-axis **Axis labels** object within the chart.

32. Double-click the **Data Format** property.

The Data Format dialog box opens.

33. Change the **Format** type to **Number** and set the **Scale** property to **-3**.

34. Click **OK** to close the Data Format dialog box.

35. Click on the **Line** icon in the **Series (primary axis)** area, to the left of the **Expected volume** data item.

36. In the properties of the **Line** object, double-click the **Palette** property.

The Palette dialog box opens.

37. Click on the **Chart Palette Presets** button in the upper-left corner of the dialog box, and from the drop-down menu, select the **Contrast** palette.

38. In the **Style** section of the Palette dialog box, change the **Line weight** property to **2**.

39. Click **OK** to close the Palette dialog box.

40. Change the **Line Shape** property from **Point To Point** to **Smooth**.

41. Click on the **Bar** icon in the **Series (secondary axis)** area, to the left of the **Quantity Shipped** data item.

42. In the properties of the **Bar** object, change the **Bar Shape** property from **Rectangle** to **Box**.

43. Change the **Bar Width** property from **80** to **50**.

44. Double-click the **Palette** property.

The Palette dialog box opens.

45. Change the **Fill type** selection in the drop-down menu from **Linear Gradient** to **Color**.

46. Change the **Transparency** value from **0** to **50%**.

47. Click **OK** to close the Palette dialog box.

Your combination chart design should look similar to what's shown in Figure 6.38 at this point.

The remaining formatting task is to set up the title for the active report.

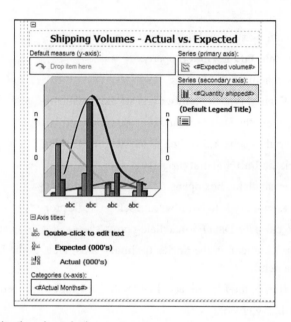

Figure 6.38   Combination chart design

48. Double-click on the **Active Report Title** at the top of the page.

49. Type **Shipping Dashboard** in the text box and click **OK**.

50. From the **Run** menu, select **Run Active Report** to compare the dashboard to Figure 6.39.

Test the report by selecting different Year buttons in the upper-right corner of the report page. Notice how all three charts are changing their displays depending on which year is selected. Furthermore, the two top charts have their own radio-button filter controls.

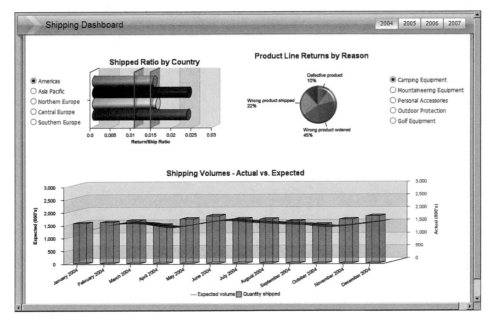

Figure 6.39   Final dashboard view

Statistical Analysis

The sales and marketing team wants to take a look at how the promotions are performing. They want to be able to see the promotional profits against the regular profits for the same period. To do this, we will take advantage of a new add-on to the IBM Cognos Report Studio tool called IBM Cognos Statistics. This is an additional feature that might not be available in your individual environment.

Continuing the evaluation, the staff wants to see how the promotions did statistically. Did the promotions really bring in more profit than would have been made if the promotions did not happen? The staff wants to see a quick comparison of statistic measures, an analysis of the variance between the means, and a chart of exceptional orders for each of the promotions, and see whether the order method affects promotional and regular profits.

The statistics report will prompt the user for different dimensions and a choice of analysis. Figure 6.40 shows the completed prompt page.

One of the statistical analyses should look like Figure 6.41.

Design

The initial report will contain pages for each of the statistics functions using the new Statistics data container. Each page will have code added to the report to open the browser window to a specific size. The page will be displayed only if requested through a prompt.

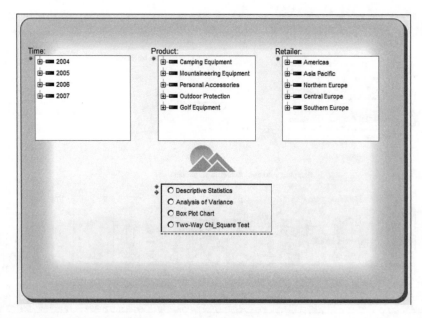

Figure 6.40   Completed prompt page

Analysis of Variance

Gross profit

ANOVA

	Sum of Squares	df	Mean Square	F	Sig.
Between Groups	4374614581.852	4	1093653645.463	15.605	.000
Within Groups	12474758372.164	178	70082912.203		
Total	16849372954.016	182			

Post Hoc Tests

Gross profit

Multiple Comparisons

	(I) Campaigns Only	(J) Campaigns Only	Mean Difference (I-J)	Std. Error	Sig.	95% Confidence Interval	
						Lower Bound	Upper Bound
Bonferroni	TrailChef Campaign	EverGlow Campaign	4,069.309	1,628.846	.134	-560.60	8,699.22
		Hibernator Campaign	-4,670.576	1,788.359	.098	-9,753.90	412.74
		Canyon Mule Campaign	-8,514.457(*)	2,433.860	.006	-15,432.58	-1,596.33
		Rising Star Campaign	-9,390.754(*)	1,986.700	.000	-15,037.85	-3,743.66
	EverGlow Campaign	TrailChef Campaign	-4,069.309	1,628.846	.134	-8,699.22	560.60

Figure 6.41   Completed descriptive statistics report

Step-by-Step

The steps move from the creation of the query used in the statistics data containers. After the queries are built, the layout will be formatted for the first statistics report. After the first report page is complete, this report will be copied and customized for three additional pages and prompting will be added to allow users to pick which statistics report page will be run.

Step 1: Start the Report

1. Launch **Report Studio** and select the **GO Data Warehouse (analysis)** package.
2. Click on the **Create New** option.
3. Select the **Statistics** report template and click **OK**.

   The Select Statistic dialog box is displayed.
4. In the left pane, expand the **Descriptive Statistics** group.
5. Click **Basic Descriptives Statistics** to select it.
6. Click to clear the **Use the wizard** check box at the bottom of the dialog box.

   We will create the query first and then add the data items to the statistics container.
7. Click **OK** to close the dialog box.

   The Create Basic Descriptives Statistics dialog box is displayed.
8. Click the **Descriptive statistics by grouping variable** radio button to select it.
9. Click **OK** to close the dialog box.

   We will be using the **Sales** namespace inside the **Sales and Marketing (analysis)** folder. While there is a **Promotion** namespace, the underlying data model holds the numbers for promotions only. To compare regular sales and promotional sales, we need to use the **Sales** namespace.

Step 2: Create the Query

While we will be doing several statistics reports, we want to use one query so that the prompting will be consistent through all the queries. This query will look at several dimensions, but the query will have several data items based on the Promotions dimension to provide different perspectives.

1. In the **Explorer Bar**, move over the **Query Explorer** tab and select the **Queries** folder.
2. In the work area, click **Query1** to select it.
3. In the **Properties** pane, change the **Name** property to **Statistics_query**.
4. In the work area, double-click **Statistics_query** to open the query definition.
5. From the **Source** tab of the **Insertable Objects** pane, drag **Gross Profit** from the **Sales fact** measures dimension into the **Data Items** pane of the work area.

6.   In the **Source** tab of the **Insertable Objects** pane, expand the **Sales order** dimension and the **Sales order** hierarchy.

7.   Drag the **Order number** level into the **Data Items** pane.

To analyze orders, we will need a variable to tell the statistics engine the "cases" that we want to analyze. We want to see whether the promotions led to more profitable orders, not just orders for promotional items.

The analysis should look at all orders, regular sales only, and promotional sales only.

8.   In the **Source** tab of the **Insertable Objects** pane, expand the **Promotions** dimension and the **Promotions** hierarchy.

9.   Expand the **Members** folder below the hierarchy.

10.   Drag the **Promotions** member into the **Data Items** pane.

11.   In the **Properties** pane, change the **Name** property of the member to **All Sales**.

12.   From the **Source** tab, drag the **Campaign** level into the **Data Items** pane.

13.   Expand the **Campaign** level and the **Members** folder under it.

14.   Drag the **Regular sale** member into the **Data Items** pane.

With all campaigns (including regular sales) and regular sales added to the query, we now will add all campaigns (without regular sales).

15.   From the **Toolbox** tab of the **Insertable Objects** pane, drag a **Query Calculation** into the **Data Items** pane.

The Create Calculation dialog box is displayed.

This process is a new feature in IBM Cognos BI that is a replacement for member function and set functions. You can still continue to create data items and leverage functions like `exclude()`.

16.   Type **Campaigns only** in the **Name** text box.

17.   Click the **Set expression** radio button to select it.

18.   Using the **Hierarchy** drop-down list, select the **Promotions** hierarchy in the **Sales** namespace and the **Promotions** dimension.

19.   Click **OK** to close the dialog box.

20.   In the **Properties** pane, double-click the **Set definition** property to open a dialog box.

21.   Double-click the **Set Expression** icon to open the dialog box.

22.   From the **Data Items** tab in the **Available Components** pane, drag **Campaign** into the **Expression Definition** pane.

23.   Click **OK** to close the Set Expression dialog box.

24.   In the lower-left corner of the Set Definition dialog box, click the **New** button.

25.   Select **Exclude** from the drop-down menu to open the dialog box.

This dialog box allows you to individually select the members that you would want to exclude from the previous set expression.

26. In the **Available Members** pane of the dialog box, expand the **Sales and Marketing (analysis)** and **Sales** folders.

27. Expand the **Promotions** hierarchy.

28. Drag the **Regular sale** member into the **Members** pane.

29. Click **OK** to close the dialog box.

The Set Definition dialog box should look like Figure 6.42.

Figure 6.42   Completed exclude set definition

30. Click **OK** to close the Set Definition dialog box and return to the work area.

Step 3: Create the Descriptive Statistics

With most of the query built, we will look at the analysis of the gross profit for orders grouped by the different campaigns.

1. In the **Explorer Bar**, mouse over the **Page Explorer** tab and select the **Report Pages** folder.

2. In the **Report Pages** pane of the work area, click **Page1** to select it.

3. In the **Properties** pane, change the **Name** property to **Descriptive Statistics**.

4. In the work area, double-click the **Descriptive Statistics** page to open it.

5. From the **Data Items** tab of the **Insertable Objects** pane, drag the following items into the statistics container:

   - **Gross profit** into **Analysis variable**
   - **Campaign** into **Grouping variables**
   - **Order number** into **Cases variable**

6. From the **Run** menu, select **Run Report – HTML** to compare the report to what's shown in Figure 6.43.

Descriptive Statistics

	Regular sale	TrailChef Campaign	EverGlow Campaign	Course Pro Campaign	Hibernator Campaign	Canyon Mule Campaign	Rising Star Campaign	Seeker Campaign	Outdoor Protectio
Mean	34,599.58	9,881.22	6,745.40	26,884.95	13,710.84	21,068.40	15,430.11	7,370.86	
Std. Deviation	48,785.431	6,380.565	4,121.616	36,465.004	13,869.243	19,564.779	14,187.011	5,244.521	
N	52997	1016	576	1164	730	854	689	182	
Median	18,387.88	8,457.56	6,297.16	13,133.64	9,648.22	16,741.42	10,742.76	6,668.22	
Minimum	26	849	493	-186	400	780	1,252	819	
Maximum	779,701	44,179	28,124	334,142	106,634	148,669	73,006	28,452	

Figure 6.43   Initial analysis results

7. Close **IBM Cognos Viewer** to return to your report design.

Step 4: Add Parameters to the Query

This query should also filter the profit totals by time, product, and retailer information.

1. In the **Explorer Bar**, mouse over the **Query Explorer** tab and select **Statistics_query**.

2. From the **Toolbox** tab of the **Insertable Objects** pane, drag **Slicer Member Set** into the **Slicer** pane in the work area.

   The Slicer Member Expression dialog box is displayed.

3. In the **Sales** namespace, expand the **Time** dimension.

4. Drag the **Time** hierarchy into the **Expression Definition** pane.

5. Add **->?Selected Time?** after the hierarchy in the **Expression Definition** pane.

   The expression should resemble the following:

   ```
   [Sales].[Time].[Time]->?Selected Time?
   ```

6. Click **OK** to close the dialog box.

7. From the **Toolbox** tab of the **Insertable Objects** pane, drag another **Slicer Member Set** into the **Slicer** pane in the work area.

   The Slicer Member Expression dialog box is displayed.

8. In the **Sales** namespace, expand the **Products** dimension.

9. Drag the **Products** hierarchy into the **Expression Definition** pane.

10. Add **->?Selected Product?** after the hierarchy in the **Expression Definition** pane.

    The expression should resemble the following:

    ```
    [Sales].[Products].[Products]->?Selected Product?
    ```

11. Click **OK** to close the dialog box.

12. From the **Toolbox** tab of the **Insertable Objects** pane, drag another **Slicer Member Set** into the **Slicer** pane in the work area.

    The Slicer Member Expression dialog box is displayed.

13. In the **Sales** namespace, expand the **Retailers** dimension.

14. Drag the **Retailers** hierarchy into the **Expression Definition** pane.

15. Add **->?Selected Retailer?** after the hierarchy in the **Expression Definition** pane.

    The expression should resemble the following:

    ```
    [Sales].[Retailers].[Retailers]->?Selected Retailer?
    ```

16. Click **OK** to close the dialog box.

17. From the **Run** menu, select **Run Report – HTML** to compare the dashboard to that shown in Figure 6.44. When prompted, select the root members from all three dimensions.

Descriptive Statistics

	Regular sale	TrailChef Campaign	EverGlow Campaign	Course Pro Campaign	Hibernator Campaign	Canyon Mule Campaign	Rising Star Campaign	Seeker Campaign	Outdoor Prote
Mean	34,599.58	9,881.22	6,745.40	26,884.95	13,710.84	21,068.40	15,430.11	7,370.86	
Std. Deviation	48,785,431	6,380.565	4,121.616	36,465.004	13,869.243	19,564.779	14,187.011	5,244.521	
N	52997	1016	576	1164	730	854	689	182	
Median	18,387.88	8,457.56	6,297.16	13,133.64	9,648.22	16,741.42	10,742.76	6,668.22	
Minimum	26	849	493	-186	400	780	1,252	819	
Maximum	779,701	44,179	28,124	334,142	106,634	148,869	73,006	28,452	

Figure 6.44   Updated descriptive statistics

The results should not change because we chose the root members of all dimensions.

18. Close **IBM Cognos Viewer** to return to your query design.

Step 5: Format the Report Page

With the creation of the report page, we will now look at some formatting options to change the presentation.

1. In the **Explorer Bar**, mouse over the **Page Explorer** tab and select the **Descriptive Statistics** page.

2. To change the name of the report to the page name, click the sample title text to select it.

3. Change the **Source Type** property from **Text** to **Report Expression**.

4. Double-click the **Report Expression** property to open the dialog box.

5. In the **Expression Definition** pane, type **PageName()** to use the assigned name of the report page as the title.

6. Validate the expression and click **OK**.

7. With title text in the work area still selected, click the **Select Ancestors** button and select **Page**.

8. In the **Properties** pane, double-click the **Gradient** property to open the dialog box.

9. Click the check box next to **Gradient** to select it.

10. Click the drop-down list for **From color**.

11. In the drop-down window, change the custom color properties for **Red**, **Green**, and **Blue** to **FF**, **FF**, and **CC**, respectively.

12. Click the **Apply** link in the lower-right corner of the window to close it.

13. Click the drop-down list for **To color**.

14. In the drop-down window, change the custom color properties for **Red**, **Green**, and **Blue** to **33**, **FF**, and **FF**, respectively.

15. Click the **Apply** link in the lower-right corner of the window to close it.

16. Click **OK** to close the dialog box.

17. From the **Run** menu, select **Run Report – HTML** to compare the dashboard to that shown in Figure 6.45. When prompted, select the root members from all three dimensions.

Descriptive Statistics

Descriptive Statistics

	Regular sale	TrailChef Campaign	EverGlow Campaign	Course Pro Campaign	Hibernator Campaign	Canyon Mule Campaign	Rising Star Campaign	Seeker Campaign	Outdoor Prote
Mean	34,599.58	9,881.22	6,745.40	26,884.95	13,710.84	21,068.40	15,430.11	7,370.86	
Std. Deviation	48,785.431	6,380.565	4,121.616	36,465.004	13,869.243	19,564.779	14,187.011	5,244.521	
N	52997	1016	576	1164	730	854	689	182	
Median	18,387.88	8,457.56	6,297.16	13,133.64	9,648.22	16,741.42	10,742.76	6,668.22	
Minimum	26	849	493	-186	400	780	1,252	819	
Maximum	779,701	44,179	28,124	334,142	106,634	148,669	73,006	28,452	

Figure 6.45   Formatted descriptive statistics

When looking at the descriptive statistics, regular sales have some quite different numbers for the mean and the median. This would say that there are a large number of very large orders, which raises the mean value when it comes to regular sales. Other promotions have means and medians that are much closer together. This could lead to further analysis on specific promotion performance.

18. Close **IBM Cognos Viewer** to return to your query design.

Step 6: Build the Prompt Page Background

Now we will build the prompt page to create a report that allows for dynamic analysis of the promotional data. To improve the presentation, we will add a custom background for the page body of the prompt page.

1. In the **Explorer Bar**, mouse over the **Page Explorer** tab and select the **Prompt Pages** folder.

2. From the **Toolbox** tab of the **Insertable Objects** pane, drag a **Page** object into the **Prompt Pages** pane in the work area.

3. In the work area, double-click **Prompt Page1** to open the page.

4. From the **Toolbox** tab of the **Insertable Objects** pane, drag a **Block** object into the **Page Body** in the work area.

5. In the work area, click the **Block** object to select it.

6. In the **Properties** pane, double-click the **Padding** property to open the Padding dialog box.

7. Change each of the padding fields to have **15 px** spacing along all sides.

8. Click **OK** to close the dialog box.

9. In the **Properties** pane, double-click the **Background Effects** property to open the Background Effects dialog box.

10. On the left side of the dialog box, click the **Border** check box to select it.

11. Set the **Corner radius** to **15 pt**.

    Leave the remaining options at their default values.

12. On the left side, click the **Fill** check box to select it.

13. Click the drop-down list for **Fill type** and select **Radial Rectangle Gradient**.

14. Click the **Color** link in the middle pane.

    The Color dialog box is displayed.

15. Click the **Custom Color** tab.

16. Change the color properties for **Red**, **Green**, and **Blue** to **FF**, **FF**, and **CC**, respectively.

17. Click **OK** to close the dialog box.

18. Below the **Colors** pane, click the **New** button to add another gradient color.

19. With the new color selected, click the **Color** link to open the dialog box.

20. Click the **Custom Color** tab.

21. Change the properties for **Red**, **Green**, and **Blue** to **33**, **FF**, and **FF**, respectively.

22. Click **OK** to close the dialog box.

23. Change the **Focus size** to **75%**.

24. On the left side, click the **Drop Shadow** check box to select it.

     With it selected, we will accept the default values.

25. Click the **Images** check box to select it.

26. At the bottom of the dialog box, click **New** to add an image in the background.

27. Click the **Browse** button to open the dialog to select the image.

     The logo we will select is stored in the sample data in the images directory.

28. Click **logo_great_outdoors.gif** to select it.

29. Click **OK** to close the dialog box.

30. Set the **Transparency** property to **75%**.

31. Under the **Position** drop-down list, click the **Align Middle Center** button.

     The Background Effects dialog box should look like Figure 6.46.

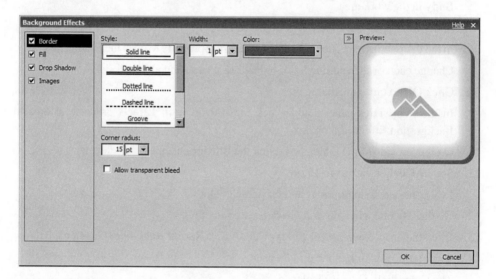

Figure 6.46   Formatted block background

32. Click **OK** to close the dialog box.

NOTE   In the information pane below the **Properties** pane, notice that it says that objects using background effects must have a fixed height and width. Along with the alignment of objects, we will also be creating a fixed-size block.

---

33. In the **Properties** pane, change the **Horizontal Alignment** to **Center**.

34. Double-click the **Size & Overflow** property to open the dialog box.

35. Change the **Height** to **500 px** and the **Width** to **700 px**.

36. Click **OK** to close the dialog box.

   Now that the prompt page has a nice background, we will add the prompts for the report within the block.

Step 7: Build Prompts on the Page

The prompts will change the three dimension parameters as well as an option to run a specific type of analysis.

1. From the **Toolbox** tab of the **Insertable Objects** pane, drag a **Table** object into the **Block** in the work area.

   The Insert Table dialog box is displayed.

2. Change the **Number of columns** to **3** and the **Number of rows** to **2**.

3. Click **OK** to close the dialog box.

4. Click the **Select Table** dots in the upper-left corner of the table.

5. In the **Properties** pane for the **Table**, double-click the **Margin** property to open the Margins dialog box.

6. Set the top margin to **50 px** and the bottom margin to **75 px**.

7. Click **OK** to close the dialog box.

8. From the **Insertable Objects** pane, drag a **Text Item** object into the first table cell.

   The Text dialog box is displayed.

9. Type **Time:** and click **OK** to close the dialog box.

10. Drag a second **Text Item** object into the second table cell.

11. Type **Product:** and click **OK** to close the Text dialog box.

12. Drag a third **Text Item** object into the third table cell.

13. Type **Retailer:** and click **OK** to close the Text dialog box.

14. From the **Toolbox** tab, drag a **Tree Prompt** object into the first cell of the second table row.

   The Prompt Wizard dialog box is displayed.

15. Click the radio button for **Use existing parameter** to select it.

16. Click the drop-down list for the parameters and choose **Selected Time**.

17. Click **Next** to go to the Populate Control dialog box.

18. Click the ellipsis next to **Values to use** to open the Choose Package Item dialog box.

   We want to see only the available years in the initial tree prompt view.

19. Expand the **Sales and Marketing (analysis)** folder, the **Sales** namespace, the **Time** dimension, and the **Time** hierarchy.

20. Click on the **Year** level to select it and click **OK** to close the dialog box.

21. Click **Finish** to create a query for the prompt and complete the wizard.

22. In the work area, click the newly added prompt to select it.

23. In the **Properties** pane, double-click the **Size & Overflow** property to open the dialog box.

24. Change the **Height** to **150 px** and the **Width** to **175 px**.

25. Click **OK** to close the dialog box.

26. From the **Insertable Objects** pane, drag a second **Tree Prompt** object into the second cell.

27. Click the radio button for **Use existing parameter** to select it.

28. Click the drop-down list for the parameters and choose **Selected Product**.

29. Click **Next** to go to the Populate Control dialog box.

30. Click the ellipsis next to **Values to use** to open the Choose Package Item dialog box.

    We want to see only the available product lines in the initial tree prompt view.

31. Expand the **Sales and Marketing (analysis)** folder, the **Sales** namespace, the **Products** dimension, and the **Products** hierarchy.

32. Click on the **Product line** level to select it, and click **OK** to close the dialog box.

33. Click **Finish** to create a query for the prompt and complete the wizard.

34. In the work area, click the newly added prompt to select it.

35. In the **Properties** pane, double-click the **Size & Overflow** property to open the dialog box.

36. Change the **Height** to **150 px** and the **Width** to **175 px**.

37. Click **OK** to close the dialog box.

38. From the **Toolbox** tab, drag a third **Tree Prompt** object into the third cell.

39. Click the radio button for **Use existing parameter** to select it.

40. Click the drop-down list for the parameters and choose **Selected Retailer**.

41. Click **Next** to go to the Populate Control dialog box.

42. Click the ellipsis next to **Values to use** to open the Choose Package Item dialog box.

    We want to see only the retailer regions in the initial tree prompt view.

43. Expand the **Sales and Marketing (analysis)** folder, the **Sales** namespace, the **Retailers** dimension, and the **Retailers** hierarchy.

44. Click on the **Region** level to select it, and click **OK** to close the dialog box.

45. Click **Finish** to create a query for the prompt and complete the wizard.

46. In the work area, click the newly added prompt to select it.

47. In the **Properties** pane, double-click the **Size & Overflow** property to open the dialog box.

48. Change the **Height** to **150 px** and the **Width** to **175 px**.

49. Click **OK** to close the dialog box.

50. From the **Toolbox** tab, drag a **Value Prompt** below the table in the work area.

51. From the **Prompt Wizard**, change the name of the new parameter to **Select Statistic** and click **Finish** to close the dialog box.

52. In the work area, click the **Value Prompt** to select it.

53. In the **Properties** pane, double-click the **Static Choices** property to open the Static Choices dialog box.

54. In the lower-left corner of the dialog box, click the **Add** button to display the Edit dialog box.

55. In the **Use** text box, type **1**.

56. In the **Display** text box, type **Descriptive Statistics**.

57. Click **OK** to close the dialog box.

58. Click the **Add** button again.

59. Type **2** in the **Use** text box.

60. Type **Analysis of Variance** in the **Display** text box.

61. Click **OK** to close the Edit dialog box.

62. Click the **Add** button again.

63. Type **3** in the **Use** text box.

64. Type **Box Plot Chart** in the **Display** text box.

65. Click **OK** to close the Edit dialog box.

66. Click the **Add** button one more time.

67. Type **4** in the **Use** text box.

68. Type **Two-Way Chi-Square Test** in the **Display** text box.

69. Click **OK** to close the Edit dialog box.

70. Click **OK** to close the Static Choices dialog box.

71. In the **Properties** pane, change the **Select UI** property to **Radio button group**.

Your prompt page should look like Figure 6.47.

With the prompt page built, we can now add conditional rendering on each page to display only the descriptive statistics page if it is selected in the prompt.

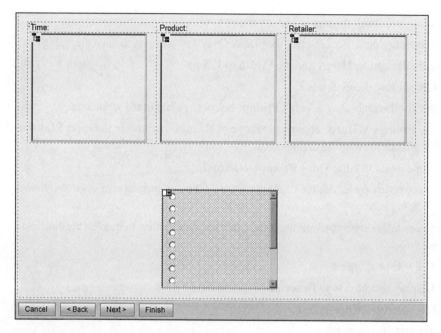

Figure 6.47   Completed prompt page

Step 8: Add a Conditional Variable to the Report

We will add a variable for the report that will use the parameter use value and attach it to the page and render the appropriate page.

1. In the **Explorer Bar**, mouse over the **Condition Explorer** tab and select the **Variables** folder.

2. From the **Insertable Objects** pane, drag a **String Variable** object into the **Variable** pane in the work area.

    The Report Expression dialog box is displayed.

3. From the **Parameters** tab in the **Available Components** pane, drag the **Select Statistic** parameter into the **Expression Definition** pane.

    Since the default function is `ParamDisplayValue()`, we need to change the function to leverage the use value.

4. In the Expression Definition pane, change the function to the following:

    ```
    ParamValue('Select Statistic')
    ```

5. Click **OK** to close the dialog box.

6. With the variable **String1** selected, change the **Name** property in the **Properties** pane to **ChosenPage**.

7. In the work area and below the **Values** pane, click the **Add** button to display the Add dialog box.

8. Type **1** and click **OK** to close the dialog.

9. Click the **Add** button again.

10. Type **2** in the dialog box and click **OK**.

11. Click the **Add** button.

12. Type **3** in the dialog box and click **OK**.

13. Click the **Add** button one more time.

14. Type **4** in the dialog box and click **OK**.

Your Condition Explorer work area should look like Figure 6.48.

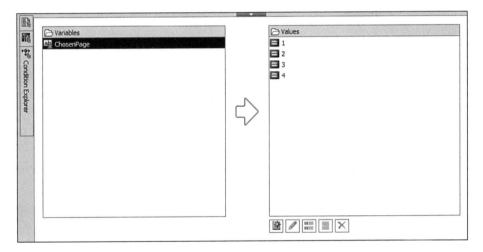

Figure 6.48   Completed conditional variable

With the prompt page built, we can now add conditional rendering on each page to display the descriptive statistics page only if it is selected in the prompt.

Step 9: Add the Variable to Render the Page

With the addition of the variable, now we can use it for conditional rendering of the page.

1. In the **Explorer Bar**, mouse over the **Page Explorer** tab and select the **Descriptive Statistics** page.

2. In the work area, click any object within the page to select it.

3. In the **Properties** pane, click the **Select Ancestor** button and choose the **Page** object.

4. With the **Properties–Page** pane displayed, double-click the **Render Variable** property. The Render Variable dialog box is displayed.

5. From the **Variable** drop-down list, select **ChosenPage** to display the possible render values.

6. Remove the check boxes for **2**, **3**, and **4**.

7. Click **OK** to close the dialog box.

8. From the **Run** menu, select **Run Report – HTML**. When prompted, select **2004**, **Camping Equipment**, **Americas**, and **Descriptive Statistics**.

    The Descriptive Statistics page should be displayed.

9. Close **IBM Cognos Viewer** to return to your query design.

   Now that the first statistics report page has been built, the other pages can be created from this template and customized.

Step 10: Create an Analysis of the Variance Report

As the next type of statistical analysis, we want to compare the means of the gross profit and see whether there is a significant difference between the different promotions.

1. In the **Explorer Bar**, mouse over the **Page Explorer** tab and select the **Report Pages** folder.

2. In the work area, copy and paste the **Descriptive Statistics** page.

3. With the **Descriptive Statistics1** page selected, double-click the **Render Variable** property in the **Properties** pane.

    The Render Variable dialog box is displayed.

4. In the **Render for** pane, remove the check for option **1**.

5. Add a check for option **2**.

6. Click **OK** to close the dialog box.

7. In the **Properties** pane, change the **Name** property to **Analysis of Variance**.

8. In the **Report Pages** pane of the work area, double-click the **Analysis of Variance** page to open the page design.

9. In the page body, click the **Descriptive Statistics** object to select it.

10. From the toolbar, click the **Cut** button to remove the data container.

11. From the **Toolbox** tab of the **Insertable Objects** pane, drag a **Statistics** object into the page body.

    The Select Statistic dialog box is displayed.

12. In the left pane of the dialog box, expand **Means Comparison**.

13. Click **One-Way ANOVA** to select it.

In the information pane, you have a fairly detailed description of how to use this test.

14. Click **OK** to close the dialog box.

15. In the work area, click the **One-Way ANOVA** container to select it.

16. In the **Properties** pane, change the **Query** property to **Statistics_query**.

17. Change the **Bonferroni** property to **Yes**.

The Bonferroni range test compares the different campaigns in an attempt to find which campaigns have means that are significantly different from each other.

18. From the **Data Items** tab of the **Insertable Objects** pane, drag the following items into the statistics container:

- **Gross profit** into **Dependent variable**
- **Campaigns Only** into **Independent variable**
- **Order number** into **Cases variable**

19. From the **Run** menu, select **Run Report – HTML** to compare the dashboard to what's shown in Figure 6.49. When prompted, select members **2004**, **Camping Equipment**, and **Asia Pacific**, along with the Analysis of Variance.

With a significance of .000, the ANOVA shows that there are significant differences between the means of orders for all promotions. The Bonferroni post hoc range test shows which campaigns performed significantly better than others. For example, the TrailChef Campaign did significantly worse than the Rising Star Campaign when it comes to generating a higher gross profit.

20. Close **IBM Cognos Viewer** to return to your query design.

Step 11: Create the Box Plot Chart

For the next type of statistical analysis, we want to show individual orders whose gross profit significantly exceeds others within each campaign.

1. In the **Explorer Bar**, mouse over the **Page Explorer** tab and select the **Report Pages** folder.

2. In the work area, copy and paste the **Analysis of Variance** page.

3. With the **Analysis of Variance1** page selected, double-click the **Render Variable** property in the **Properties** pane.

The Render Variable dialog box is displayed.

4. In the **Render for** pane, remove the check for option **2**.

5. Add a check for option **3**.

Analysis of Variance

Gross profit

ANOVA

	Sum of Squares	df	Mean Square	F	Sig.
Between Groups	4374614581.852	4	1093653645.463	15.605	.000
Within Groups	12474758372.164	178	70082912.203		
Total	16849372954.016	182			

Post Hoc Tests

Gross profit

Multiple Comparisons

	(I) Campaigns Only	(J) Campaigns Only	Mean Difference (I-J)	Std. Error	Sig.	95% Confidence Interval	
						Lower Bound	Upper Bound
Bonferroni	TrailChef Campaign	EverGlow Campaign	4,069.309	1,628.846	.134	-560.60	8,699.22
		Hibernator Campaign	-4,670.576	1,788.359	.098	-9,753.90	412.74
		Canyon Mule Campaign	-8,514.457(*)	2,433.860	.006	-15,432.58	-1,596.33
		Rising Star Campaign	-9,390.754(*)	1,986.700	.000	-15,037.85	-3,743.66
	EverGlow Campaign	TrailChef Campaign	4,069.309	1,628.846	.134	8,699.22	560.60

Figure 6.49   Completed Analysis of Variance report page

6. Click **OK** to close the dialog box.

7. In the **Properties** pane, change the **Name** property to **Box Plot Chart**.

8. In the **Report Pages** pane of the work area, double-click the **Box Plot Chart** page to open the page design.

9. In the page body, click the **One-Way ANOVA** object to select it.

10. From the toolbar, click the **Cut** button to remove the data container.

11. From the **Toolbox** tab of the **Insertable Objects** pane, drag a **Statistics** object into the page body.

    The Select Statistic dialog box is displayed.

12. In the left pane of the dialog box, expand **Descriptive Statistics**.

13. Click **Boxplot** to select it.

14. Click **OK** to close the dialog box.

15. In the work area, click the **Boxplot** container to select it.

16. In the **Properties** pane, change the **Query** property to **Statistics_query**.

17. From the **Data Items** tab of the **Insertable Objects** pane, drag the following items into the statistics container:

- **Gross profit** into **Analysis variable**
- **Campaigns Only** into **Grouping variable**
- **Order number** into **Cases variable**

18. From the **Run** menu, select **Run Report – HTML** to compare the dashboard to what's shown in Figure 6.50. When prompted, select members **2004**, **Camping Equipment**, and **Asia Pacific**, along with the Box Plot Chart.

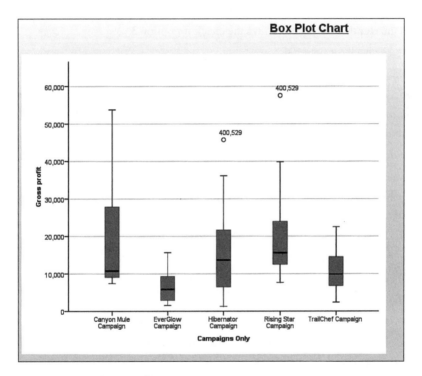

Figure 6.50   Completed Box Plot Chart report page

This report shows that order number 400529 was a significantly large order in which the retailer used items from two different campaigns in the order.

19. Close **IBM Cognos Viewer** to return to your query design.

Step 12: Create the Two-Way Chi-Square Test

For the next type of statistical analysis, we want to show whether different order methods generate more promotional participation by retailers.

1. In the **Explorer Bar**, mouse over the **Page Explorer** tab and select the **Report Pages** folder.

2. In the work area, copy and paste the **Box Plot Chart** page.

3. With the **Box Plot Chart1** page selected, double-click the **Render Variable** property in the **Properties** pane.

   The Render Variable dialog box is displayed.

4. In the **Render for** pane, remove the check for option **3**.

5. Add a check for option **4**.

6. Click **OK** to close the dialog box.

7. In the **Properties** pane, change the **Name** property to **Two-Way Chi-Square Analysis**.

8. In the **Report Pages** pane of the work area, double-click the **Two-Way Chi-Square Analysis** page to open the page design.

9. In the page body, click the **Boxplot** object to select it.

10. From the toolbar, click the **Cut** button to remove the data container.

11. From the **Toolbox** tab of the **Insertable Objects** pane, drag a **Statistics** object into the page body.

    The Select Statistic dialog box is displayed.

12. In the left pane of the dialog box, expand **Nonparametric Tests**.

13. Click **Two-Way Chi-Square Test** to select it.

14. Click **OK** to close the dialog box.

    A Create Two-Way Chi-Square Test dialog box is displayed.

15. Select the **Two-Way Chi-Square with counts measure** radio button.

16. Click **OK** to close the dialog box.

17. In the work area, click the **Two-Way Chi-Square Test** container to select it.

18. In the **Properties** pane, change the **Query** property to **Statistics_query**.

19. Change the **Show observed count** property to **No**.

20. Change the **Show percent of row** property to **Yes**.

    This will allow the crosstab to show the percentage that each order method contributes to the number of orders for a campaign.

21. From the **Data Items** tab of the **Insertable Objects** pane, drag the following items into the statistics container:

- **Campaign** into **Analysis variable 1**
- **Order number** into **Cases variable**

The chi-square test involves a second variable to compare the frequency of the orders as well as tracking the count of the order transactions.

22. From the **Source** tab in the **Insertable Objects** pane, expand the **Order method** dimension and the **Order method** hierarchy within the **Sales** namespace.

23. Drag the **Order method type** level into the **Analysis variable 2** in the work area.

For the last variable, we want to count the number of orders (with a gross profit) as our measure.

24. From the **Toolbox** tab of the **Insertable Objects** pane, drag a **Query Calculation** into the **Counts variable** in the work area.

The Create Calculation dialog box is displayed.

25. Type **Order count** in the **Name** text box.

26. Select the **Calculated measure** radio button.

27. Click the drop-down list for **Measure Dimension** and select **Sales fact** below the **Sales** namespace.

28. Click **OK** to close the dialog box.

The Calculated Measure Expression dialog box is displayed.

29. Create the following expression in the **Expression Definition** pane:

```
count( [Gross profit] )
```

30. Click **OK** to close the dialog box.

31. From the **Run** menu, select **Run Report – HTML** to compare the dashboard to that shown in Figure 6.51. When prompted, select members **2004**, **Camping Equipment**, and **Asia Pacific**, along with the Two-Way Chi-Square Test.

The first piece, the crosstabulation, shows the relative percentage of the order method sales for each campaign. The Canyon Mule campaign seemed to have an exceptional number of web and fax orders. The chi-square test results are looking for a pattern of exceptional order methods for a promotion. The chi-square test shows that the numbers in the crosstabulation are not significantly different. If the company wants to continue the Canyon Mule campaign, marketers may want to focus on these order methods to increase orders.

32. Close **IBM Cognos Viewer** to return to your query design.

In addition to looking at different statistics reports, we created reports with new background formatting and used conditional rendering to display only the selected report pages.

% within Campaign

Campaign * Order method type Crosstabulation

		Order method type							Total
		Web	Special	Telephone	Sales visit	E-mail	Mail	Fax	
Campaign	Regular sale	35.0%	2.1%	23.9%	19.6%	13.5%	2.3%	3.5%	100.0%
	TrailChef Campaign	23.3%	6.7%	31.7%	18.3%	13.3%	3.3%	3.3%	100.0%
	EverGlow Campaign	33.3%		26.7%	20.0%	20.0%			100.0%
	Hibernator Campaign	38.0%		30.0%	18.0%	12.0%		2.0%	100.0%
	Canyon Mule Campaign	53.3%		6.7%	6.7%	20.0%		13.3%	100.0%
	Rising Star Campaign	26.9%		38.5%	23.1%	11.5%			100.0%
Total		34.7%	2.0%	24.5%	19.5%	13.7%	2.2%	3.4%	100.0%

Chi-Square Tests

	Value	df	Asymp. Sig. (2-sided)
Pearson Chi-Square	40.511[1]	30	.095
Likelihood Ratio	47.809	30	.021
Linear-by-Linear Association	.175	1	.676
N of Valid Cases	2512		

[1] 18 cells (42.9%) have expected count less than 5. The minimum expected count is .30.

Figure 6.51   Completed Chi-Square Test page

Summary

In this chapter, we showed examples that contained the key enhancements in IBM Cognos 10 Report Studio: active reports, enhanced charts, external data sources, and statistics.

The first example in the chapter replicated a report that had HTML programming and replaced the tabbing functionality in an active report.

The second example showed how you could create an external data source and maintain a separate list of items to select from a report. This can be a replacement for some prompting examples.

The third example showcased many of the features of active reports along with some new chart types to enhance the overall appearance of a dashboard.

The last example allowed report consumers to pick a style of analysis of gross profit numbers in a cube.

By working on some more formatting and customization examples, we showed additional properties that have changed in this latest release, as well as some techniques that would work in the previous version. Some techniques that you may want to integrate into other reports include these:

- Using repeater tables to enhance page breaks
- Using the three red dots in the upper-left corner of containers to quickly select them
- Using the new query calculation dialog to create advanced set calculations
- Using the Set Definition property as an alternative to building complex dimensional data items
- Adding color to your pages using background effects on your fixed-size objects
- Building complex reports using conditional rendering of objects, including pages

Index

This could be the best advice you get all day

The IBM® International Technical Support Organization (ITSO) develops and delivers high-quality technical materials and education for IT and business professionals.

These value-add deliverables are IBM Redbooks® publications, Redpapers™ and workshops that can help you implement and use IBM products and solutions on today's leading platforms and operating environments.

See a sample of what we have to offer

Get free downloads

See how easy it is ...

ibm.com/redbooks

- ➢ Select from hundreds of technical deliverables
- ➢ Purchase bound hardcopy Redbooks publications
- ➢ Sign up for our workshops
- ➢ Keep informed by subscribing to our weekly newsletter
- ➢ See how you can become a published author

We can also develop deliverables for your business. To find out how we can work together, send a note today to: redbooks@us.ibm.com

IBM® Cognos® 10:
Intelligence Unleashed
Smarter Decisions. Better Results.

Business Analytics Software Services & Education
Your Next Smart Decision

Who Are We?

We provide expert services and training focused exclusively on the IBM Business Analytics product portfolio. Our depth of experience and extensive proven practices help customers maximize their software investment and mitigate risks.

How Can We Help?

We are committed to seeing each client through to success, offering proven technical expertise on IBM Business Analytics products. Our offerings are flexible and adaptable to each client's unique needs, and will take you from solution planning and technical architecture through implementation and training, guiding you to business analytics excellence.

Benefits

Companies who choose IBM BA Services and Education find that they:

- Lower risk in implementing Business Analytics solutions
- Build Business Analytics skills for long term success
- Raise the quality of their Business Analytics solutions

For more details on the quality education options available to you, visit:

ibm.com/cognos/training

"Organizations that take a measured, well-managed approach to their IBM Business Analytics implementations, with the right skills, guidance and practices, are more likely to succeed."
Paul Green, Global Business Unit Executive, Business Analytics Software Services